Painting of the chancel at St Michael & All Angels Parish Church, Marwood.
With kind permission of the artist, Kathryn Greenslade.

St Michael & All Angels (September 29th)

Lord, give Thine Angels every day
Command to guide us on our way,
And bid they every evening keep
Their watch around us while we sleep

So shall no wicked thing draw near
To do us harm or cause us fear,
And we shall dwell, when life is past,
With Angels round Thy throne at last.

J.M. Neale
The Church Monthly, 1896.

Marwood

A fond encounter with a rural Devon parish

Anna-Louise Bowman

Published by Merewode Books.

ISBN 978-0-9570598-0-1

Printed & Bound by CPI Antony Rowe Ltd
Bumper's Farm Industrial Estate
Chippenham
Wiltshire
SN14 6LH

The information contained in this volume has been obtained through extensive research, including interviews and transcription of archived materials. Content is based on interpretation of the various sources of information, with every effort made to ensure accuracy. The author therefore accepts no responsibility for any content that may subsequently be shown to be erroneous.

Preface

Have you ever paused to contemplate what life would have been like for our ancestors? For as long as I can remember, I have held a deep rooted fascination for learning how lifestyles have evolved over the centuries in Britain, whether it be during Roman occupation, Saxon, Medieval or later centuries, particularly the Victorian era.

When my family and I moved to the parish of Marwood almost two years ago, we received an incredibly warm welcome from the local community, and within a short space of time we felt like we belonged here. This may be a dash of romanticism, but I really sensed that I had come home.

As I walked our dog around the parish, I often found myself stepping back in time, as I kept discovering lovely dwellings that had clearly stood here for centuries. Wandering down the quiet lanes, I stood and pictured the labourers working in the fields, hearing the clip clop of hooves as a horse and coach passed by, taking the Rector of the parish to visit the infirm. I imagined a time when there was no traffic racing through the winding roads, no aircraft powering through the sky and the only discernable sound being birds singing and cattle lowing.

My curiosity grew and after initially scouring the numerous census records for information and locating a few old photographs, I started to ask my new neighbours about the history of the parish. Many people suggested I spoke with Harold Hopkins, and I was fortunate to have been invited to meet Harold and his wife Yvonne.

Harold was born in the *The Old Inn*, in the hamlet of Guineaford, Marwood, in December 1921. He has lived the majority of his life in the parish, only in later years residing in the neighbouring parish of Braunton. Eager for some first-hand experience of Marwood over the twentieth century, I subjected poor Harold to a good couple of hours of questioning. Fortunately for me, Harold was happy to oblige and so began a number of fascinating tales of life in Marwood. This time with Harold and Yvonne was the beginning of a number of get-togethers where I was rewarded with more stories, photographs and other materials, which really inspired me to proceed with this book.

As I began my research in earnest, I discovered that information on the parish was not easily obtainable. References to Marwood were scarce in other published accounts of North Devon history, so this meant I would need to spend many hours in the North Devon Record Office. Here I was able to access some parish treasures, including *Marwood Church Monthly* newsletters dating from 1895 to 1905; minutes of Parish Council meetings, from 1894; accounts of Parish Vestry meetings, as well as search through reels and reels of back copies of the North Devon Journal on microfilm.

To enrich my findings, I requested local newsletter 'Marwood Matters' to publish a plea to invite people to share memories, stories or photographs to help bring the story of the parish to life. This led to some encounters with lifelong residents whose predecessors settled here over the last two hundred years. It soon became evident that their stories gave the most unique and heart-warming insight into Marwood's history that I could have hoped for. A similar notice in the North Devon Journal also generated a number of new acquaintances with stories to share and without all these riches, I could not have hoped to produce the book you read today.

I am focusing primarily on Marwood from 1837, the beginning of the Victorian era, through to the 1950s, and I have endeavoured to make it an interesting read whether you already have connections with the parish, or if you're someone like me who simply has a fondness for learning about days gone by.

Anna-Louise Bowman
October 2011

Acknowledgements

There are so many people that I must acknowledge, who have helped bring this story to life.

I dedicate this book to Harold and Yvonne Hopkins, without whom, I am not sure I would have developed the inspiration and commitment to writing this, my first book. I offer my heartfelt thanks for all your support and your time.

Special thanks to all those who have kindly met with me and given hours of their time, sharing many stories, memories and photographs:

Brian Barrow	Peter Gammon	Pauline & Raymond Stentiford
Beatrice Brooks	Kathleen Harris	Gordon & June Tamlyn
Norman Brooks	Stella Money	Neil Thurlow
Pam Chapple	Pearl J Powell	Christine Watts
Maureen Chugg	David Pugsley	Hilda Watts
Vivien Chugg	Jean Ridd	Sue Watts
David Fairchild	Edie Spear	Beryl Yeo
	Lou Spear	

And to the many people who have lent their treasured photographs, books, documents, deeds and maps, most of whom but not all are local to the parish:

Rebecca Bartlett	Margaret Greenslade	Desmond Painter
Tom & Hilary Bigge	Kathryn Greenslade	Graham & Evelyn Pell
Brian & Julia Chugg	Ian Huxtable	Margaret & Sam Pover
Jo Clinton	Julia Coats	Peter Spencer
Gill Cragg	Brian Kettle	Tony van der Spiegel
Mike & Sheelagh Darling	Helen Knight	Simon & Tracey Wallis
Graham & Carol Edwards	Kate Moore	Maureen White
Norman & Doreen Facey	Kim & Liz Neville	Priscilla White
Brian & Jean Gibbins	Yvonne & Tony Liddon	Pauline & Graham Williamson

I am also extremely grateful for the help and support I received from:

Steve Knight, on behalf of RL Knight, Photographer
The team at the North Devon Record Office and Athenaeum
Braunton Library
Jane Rattue & Marwood Primary School
Kathryn McKee (St John's College, Cambridge – Library)
Malcolm Underwood (St John's College, Cambridge – Archives)
The *Marwood Matters* Newsletter Team
Patricia Stout & Marwood Hill Gardens

Some friends who helped me with the book are sadly no longer with us, though they all inspired and assisted me in their own special ways – in tribute to the late Gill Spencer, Linda Law, Gill Cragg and David Pugsley.

Finally, last but not least, a huge thank you to Richard and Madeleine, who have put up with many months of me either being firmly lodged behind my laptop or squirreled away in the Record Office for hours on end. Richard has been an amazing help, poring over reels of microfilm, scanning photographs and spending countless hours proof-reading. I am deeply grateful to you both for your ongoing support and encouragement, as it is true to say that I could not have done it without you.

With much love,
Anna

Contents

Chapter One
Marwood Matters

The parish of Marwood is extensive and beautiful, situated approximately three miles to the north west of Barnstaple, in the predominantly rural county of North Devon. Small hamlets are dispersed over five thousand acres, connected by winding lanes and bordered by tall earth banks. The many fields are framed by thick hedgerows which are often studded with seasonal wild flowers and fruits.

Steeped in history with associations as far back as the Saxons, many of the farmsteads and hamlets that still exist today, have their origins in the early medieval period. The Domesday Book refers to Marwood as *Mereuda* or *Meroda*, and records the existence of three manors, and farms including Metcombe *Metcoma*, Whitefield *Whitefella*, Whiddon *Willeden* and Varley *Fallei*. By the late sixteenth century the parish had become known as *Merewood*, before finally evolving to Marwood; said to mean 'boundary wood'.

A brief description of the origins of each hamlet or smaller enclosures is suggested in the book *Place Names of Devon* (Gover et al, 1931):

Location Name	Previously Known As	Earliest Origins
Blakewell	Blachewilla, Blakewill(e)	From 1086 Domesday Book, meaning 'black stream or spring'
Guineaford	Giniver, Ginnever, Guinnevere, Guinneford	From c.1800, 'hart hill' in old English
Honeywell	Huniwell, Honiwell	From c.1249 probably denoted a spring with sweet water
Kings Heanton	Hagintona, Hamtona, Kyngesheighamton, Kyngs Heaunton	From 1086 Domesday Book, 'Home Farm' in old English
Lee House	Legh	From c.1438
Marwood (parish)	Meroda, Merehoda, Mereuda, Merewode, Merwode	From 1086 Domesday Book, meaning 'boundary wood', being on the boundary between Braunton and Shirwell Hundreds

Location Name	Previously Known As	Earliest Origins
Marwood (hamlet)	Cherchemerewode	Church Marwood estate
Metcombe	Metcoma, Medcome, Medcumbe, Medecoumb, Meddecomb	From 1086 Domesday Book meaning 'meadow valley' or 'hay land' in old English
Middle Marwood	Middelmorwude, Middelmerwode, Myddel Marwode	From c.1234
Milltown	Miltoune	From c.1609
Muddiford	Modeworthi, Modworthy, Madeford, Mudford, Mudworthy	From c.1303, probably meaning 'Moda's worpig' – farm enclosure
Patsford	Pattesford, Patchole	From c.1330 'Paetti's ford'
Prixford	Pirkewurth, Pirkisworthe, Pyrkesworthy, Prikesworthy, Prixworthy	From c.1238, probably derives from a person's name, i.e. Piroc's farmstead
Swindon Down	Swyndon, Swinham	From c.1660 meaning 'Swine hill'
Townridden	Marwood Barton	From c.1830 probably means 'village clearing'
Varley	Fallei, Falleia, Fernlegh	From c.1086 Domesday Book, meaning 'bracken clearing' or 'Fern covered lea'
Westcott	Westecoth, Westecotedoune	From c.1242
Whiddon	Willeden, Willedenna, Wyddene, Wydedon, Wytedon, Witdedene, Weeding, Whidden	From 1086 Domesday Book, meaning 'wild valley' in old English
Whitefield	Witefella, Whytefeud, Whytefeld, Whitefelle, Whitefella	From 1086 Domesday Book, meaning 'White open country', dry open pasture ground

Source: Gover et al, 1931.

Such is the heritage and charm of the parish that in 1977, certain areas of Marwood were designated as sites of special architectural and historic interest, as a means of ensuring the preservation and enhancement of their character. These were specified as follows:

> 1. Marwood-Guineaford-Kings Heanton Conservation Area.
> The area comprises 68.8 acres or thereabouts centred on the settlements of Marwood, Guineaford and Kings Heanton in the Parish of Marwood in the County of Devon embracing, inter alia St. Michael's Church, Hill Farm, Marwood Rectory, Rock Cottage, Highfield, Herders' Tenement, Thorns and Huish as is more particularly delineated on the said map.
>
> 2. Middle Marwood Conservation Area.
> The area comprises 6.35 acres or thereabouts centred on the settlement of Middle Marwood in the Parish of Marwood in the County of Devon embracing inter alia Primrose Cottage, Alderhurst, Hordens, The Mission Church, Holly Cottage, Pettswood, Stepps Farm and Bowen Farm as is more particularly delineated on the said map.

Source: *The London Gazette*, 20 December 1977.

The Domesday Book intimates that there has been a church in Marwood since at least the eleventh century. The existing parish church, St Michael & All Angels, has thirteenth century origins and a wealth of interesting monuments, carvings and items of great historical importance. It has maintained a pivotal role in the lives of many Marwood parishioners for centuries and in January 1937, the North Devon Journal suggested:

> Tribute should, perhaps, be paid to the fact that the great cause of religion has always been most worthily upheld in the Parish, being indeed, a widespread family tradition in many cases.

Source: North Devon Journal, 28 January 1937.

There are two other churches in the parish. The Marwood Methodist Church in Prixford was first built in 1829, although due to the growth of the congregation it soon became necessary to build a larger chapel close by in 1873 and Muddiford United Reformed Church first opened its heavy oak door in 1846. There were further places of worship, including small chapels at Westcott, Whitefield and Patsford that are no longer standing, and others no longer in use and now converted to living accommodation in Middle Marwood and Whitehall.

A more detailed exploration of the ecclesiastical aspects of life in Marwood over the years is found in Chapter Four.

In 1937, the North Devon Journal described Marwood as 'a strictly agricultural parish', indeed, working the land has been central to parishioners' existence here for centuries. As farming practices have evolved, they have brought visible changes to the way people have lived and worked in Marwood.

Enclosure Acts in Britain
For hundreds of years before the first Enclosure Acts were passed, parishioners had the historic right to keep their animals on common land owned by the lords of the manor. The land was divided into furlongs and strips and allocated to each tenant, who would use the land to graze a cow or maybe a pig, plant some vegetables and gather fuel for their fires. Pieces of land owned by one smallholder could often be scattered over a fairly large area, making it difficult to manage and cultivate.

With the advancement in agricultural practices and land management, the major landowners began to realise that merging these small plots of land would create larger, more workable areas of arable and pasture, which in turn would improve the yield and achieve economies of scale.

Enclosure Acts allowed the big landowners to consolidate and enclose areas of land, ejecting smallholders from their strips, in exchange for one parcel of land that roughly equated to the total area previously held. The smallholder then had to meet the cost of fencing or planting hedgerows and to dig ditches to define the new boundaries. That cost was unfeasible for many who found they had little choice other than to sell their land and livestock, often for little compensation.

As a result, life in rural agricultural parishes such as Marwood became very difficult for those who could no longer subsist by farming their own strips of land. They were left with little choice other than to become employees of the larger landowners, yet due to the meagre wages they received, many struggled to make ends meet and standards of living were poor.

> See the transcription of the 1850 Whiddon Enclosure Agreement in the appendices (with kind permission of Desmond Painter).

By the 1870s, a combination of rapid advances in farming technology, increased competition from imported grain bringing down prices and some poor harvests, meant that farmers across Britain experienced severe financial problems particularly those specialising in arable and sheep farming. The subsequent fall in crop prices and land values led to this period of British history becoming known as the great agricultural depression, which was to last until the outbreak of the First World War. Vast areas of arable land were laid to grass and Hoskins (1954) notes that by 1889, the acreage of grass 'exceeded that under the plough for the first time'. Inevitably, working conditions for labourers became even more difficult. Although North Devon was probably less seriously impacted than some other parts of the country, wages were already amongst the lowest in the country and conditions were extremely tough. Many workers had to be laid off, facing serious poverty and the prospect of life in the workhouse.

Dwindling Population

After Marwood's population peaked in 1851 at 1,054, a steady decline followed until the late twentieth century. This decline can be explained by the migration of farm labourers who were left with no alternative than to look beyond the parish for alternative employment. Some headed for urban areas, such as Barnstaple in the hope of finding a living. In many cases farm work was the only skill they possessed, which influenced some labourers and their families to make the long journey overseas to Australia, New Zealand or Canada, where their skills were in demand.

In the Marwood census of 1851, there were over 330 parishioners directly employed in farm work. By 1911, this had fallen to approximately 150.

Population of Marwood 1801-1931		Both areas show a huge leap in population between 1801 and 1851. From 1851 onwards, the number of parishioners living in Marwood shows a significant and steady decline.	Population of Barnstaple 1801-1931	
1801	632		1801	3748
1851	1054		1851	8667
1871	995		1871	11636
1891	787		1891	11411
1911	654		1911	12231
1931	612		1931	12191

Source: www.visionofbritain.org.uk.

The evolution of farming had a knock on effect on local craftsmen, whose livelihoods largely depended on farm work and gradually, the variety of trades existing in these small communities began to diminish. In a parish like Marwood, hamlets had once been vibrant and buzzing places that were largely self-sufficient. Imagine the small hamlet of Guineaford in the 1850s, with John Geen, the blacksmith hammering at his forge by the bridge. The familiar smell of sawdust emerges from workshops just a few yards up the road towards Prixford; where his brother William is busy with the saw and the plane. Francis Fairchild stands outside his inn, surveying the busy scene as he puffs on his pipe. John Marshall has opened up the post office for business, and Mrs Slocombe, the grocer, is selling her wares from the comfort of her own home. Local children hurry by, on their way to the Church school, passing the women chatting, as they fill their pails with water from the spring, ready for the day's chores. Over the coming years, this scene was to change beyond recognition.

The decline in the number of tradesmen who relied on farming to make their living, such as blacksmiths, carpenters and farriers, is evidenced in the census returns for Marwood. In 1851 there were twenty-one carpenters recorded, however by 1911 this number had reduced to six. At the same time, other small trades began to disappear from the parish, notably the self-employed dressmakers, tailors and shoemakers, who struggled to compete with mass production in the emerging urban factories nation wide. In 1851 there were twenty-four tailors and dressmakers residing in the parish, but by 1911, there were just six. Similarly, there were fourteen boot and shoemakers in 1851 and by 1911 there were two.

By the mid twentieth century and ever since, very few parishioners have been able to take advantage of living and working within the parish, with most forced to travel to Barnstaple and beyond for employment.

The challenges of farm labouring and other occupations in the nineteenth and early twentieth centuries will be explored further in Chapter Three.

Above: Marwood Sheep-Shearing Competition, c.1920.

Researching Our Past

In recent years there has been an explosion of interest in genealogy and there are more tools available than ever before to help researchers uncover their ancestral roots. The online publication of the population censuses covering the period from 1841 to 1911 has been a revelation, making it far easier for us to learn about the occupations, residences and families of our ancestors. Other online databases enable us to trace important records such as indexes of births, marriages and deaths, military service and immigration.

Equipped with these tools and ample time to dedicate to hands-on research, i.e. through interviewing relatives, friends and visiting archive offices, it is possible to gain a real insight into the lives of our ancestors.

The chapters that follow provide facts, figures, photographs and fables of life in Marwood, spanning the last two hundred years and with a little imagination, will allow the reader to temporarily trade places with the characters of the parish in days gone by.

Guineaford Bridge, c.1920s.

With Kind Permission of Mr S Knight,
RL Knight Photographers.

Chapter Two
Dwellings Built to Last

Living conditions

Until the early 1900s, many labourers in rural areas lived in 'tied' farm cottages built of cob and roofed with thatch or reeds. It was not uncommon for families to have as many as six or more children as well as care for elderly parents, creating extremely cramped living conditions. Hygiene and cleanliness were little understood then and there were sporadic outbreaks of contagious diseases, such as scarlet fever and diphtheria.

There was no piped water and for the housewife, this created a huge amount of effort. In Valerie Porter's excellent book, *Yesterday's Countryside* (2006) there is a useful reflection on the challenge:

> '...every drop of water for drinking, cooking, house cleaning, bathing, brewing and laundering had to be drawn manually and often laboriously – caught from springs, dipped from streams and ponds, drawn from rainwater tanks and butts, hand-pumped or wound up from garden wells'.
>
> Source: Valerie Porter (2006).

These days we have the luxury of turning on a tap for an instant supply of hot or cold water, so it is perhaps hard to imagine the arduous task of having to fetch it manually. Having to traipse out in all weathers to the local spring, then struggle back home with the heavy pail(s) full of water is almost beyond belief today. Some of those who do still remember having to obtain their water in this way however, speak fondly of the frequent visit to the nearest well or spring. Often a friend or relative would be filling up, allowing an opportunity for a quick chat while they were waiting. As young boys, David Fairchild and Lou Spear remember having to fetch water from the well near Prixford Barton, where they would race to try to empty it before it could refill.

David Pugsley lived in Guineaford as a child in *The Cottage*, the last dwelling in the hamlet on the lane leading to Kings Heanton. David could remember his parents Archie and Mildred taking an old tin bath and two buckets down to fetch water from the spring opposite *Byeways* every Sunday evening in readiness for Monday, traditionally washday. Maureen Chugg grew up at *Hillsview* in Muddiford and still has the old 'copper' which her mother May Pugsley had once used to heat water for washing and bathing.

Imagine having to face the long and drawn out task of doing the laundry under these circumstances. To begin with, the fire had to be lit beneath the copper to heat the water. Once it was boiling the clothes would be immersed in the water with a 'dolly', scrubbed and rinsed. Then came the mangle for those who could afford it, followed by drying either outside on a line or suspended in front of the fire or range in wet and wintry conditions. Finally the task of heating the old flat iron on the range to just the right temperature, to smooth the crumpled clothing and sheets. With the arrival of the washing machine, tumble dryer and electric steam iron, many hours of hard toil can now be avoided. Today we may still grumble about doing the laundry, but surely we can only be thankful for the advances in technology that make the task far less daunting.

Complaints about sanitary conditions and cleanliness of the water supply in Marwood often appeared on the agenda at parish council meetings. In April 1895, Mr George Delve commented that concerns had been raised about the water supply in Guineaford and Kings Heanton, and Mr Charles Pugsley reported the same issue at Milltown Hill, Crockers and Muddiford. In August 1895 it was recommended that new water pipes should be laid to improve the supply in Guineaford, and further works continued across the rest of the parish. In January 1935, the council continued to propose improvements to local water supplies in response to public demand. These included building up the spring in Lower Prixford lane to prevent pollution and to have the well in Higher Muddiford cleaned out and deepened.

In the absence of running tap water or flushing toilets in cottages, earth closets or 'privy' facilities were found outdoors in a small shed or stone building at the end of the garden. Inside, a wooden 'box' with a small hole (or two) would allow any deposits to fall either directly into a hole dug into the ground, or into a bucket. If there were an urgent need to go in the night, most would have used a chamber pot indoors, which would be emptied in the morning. Locals remember that it was usually father's unpleasant job to empty the deposits, digging them into the ground nearby, mixing in ash as a disinfectant and smell neutraliser. Many cottage vegetable gardens thrived in these conditions!

Today, the thought of needing to use the old privy in cold and wintry conditions is particularly unappealing, not to mention the threat of spiders which might be lurking inside. This obviously did not deter the Kelly sisters of Guineaford, who were still using their outdoor privy until the early 1990s, long after it had become possible to install an indoor lavatory.

Mains water was not widely available in many parts of Marwood until the early 1950s, with Prixford, Guineaford and Kings Heanton connected in 1952 (ceremonially switched on by Blanche Conibear) although Middle Marwood was not connected until 1958. Despite the risk of infection and disease from the more traditional water sources, some residents did not trust the new mains water, including Richard Tamlyn (1878-1960) of *Rose Cottage*, Muddiford. In August 1959, the parish council reported that Richard had refused to connect to the mains water, despite being informed that analysis of the water in the well had proved to be unsatisfactory. He was adamant that he would drink only from his own supply and would not be convinced by anyone, not even his son Reuben that the water was unfit to drink. As far as Richard was concerned, he had been drinking from the well for fifty years without having to see a doctor for any ailment, so why change now? Lizzie and Elsie Kelly of Guineaford were also wary of mains water and were still seen filling their pails at the local spring until it was eventually blocked up in the 1980s due to hygiene concerns.

In Marwood, as in many rural areas, cottagers would rely on candles for their lighting until paraffin-fuelled oil lamps became available from the 1850s for those who could afford them. Both options were potentially hazardous and accidents were not uncommon. Some locals remember a man named Jim Brown who arrived with his horse and wagon every Tuesday, selling paraffin as well as ironmongery, soap, candles, china, saucepans, clothes pegs and many other household necessities. Lou Spear remembers using 'tilley' lamps in his house and one particular occasion sprung to mind of a time he was playing monopoly with his brothers and sisters by its light. They were busy arguing when their father awoke abruptly from his nap in the armchair and jumped up to remonstrate with his children, managing to knock the lamp onto the floor. All the children knew this would mean trouble, so they immediately ran off to escape the wrath of their father! Denzil went to his Nan's at *Prixford Cottages* and Lou ran next door to the Fairchilds', but poor Garfield was caught! The children were wise not to return until they knew father was asleep in bed He went to bed early because he got up at 5am to work as a newspaper wholesaler.

Electricity was eventually connected in some of the hamlets of Marwood in 1951, evidenced by the Kelly sisters who wrote about the occasion in their late father's journal. They specifically noted that the house was being wired up for electric lighting and that it worked for the first time on Friday March 30 1951. Christine Watts distinctly remembers electricity being installed at her parents' cottage in Varley because she trapped the electrician in the loft by removing his ladder! Electricity did not reach Marwood school or the hamlets of Whitehall and Middle Marwood until the 1960s.

Shortly after electricity was connected, David Fairchild remembers that Reginald Main of *Byeways* in Guineaford purchased what was possibly one of the first television sets in the parish. During the coronation of Queen Elizabeth in 1953, many locals crowded into Reginald's house to watch the official broadcast of the occasion!

Waste Not Want Not
There were no rubbish collections in rural areas until the 1950s and in the past, people would dig a pit in their garden to dispose of any rubbish that couldn't be burnt on the fire. There was far less refuse than we turn out today, partly because people would repair or reuse whatever they could, and any food scraps would be fed to chickens or pigs. Broken pottery would be dug into the soil as it assisted drainage and is now often found when digging our gardens, along with clay pipes and other non-degradable objects such as glass bottles, which would also have been dug into waste pits. Before the introduction of plastics in the 1950s, there was little or no packaging to dispose of

other than paper which would be burnt on the fire or reused in the privy, before the advent of the soft toilet paper we rely on today!

In 1937, local farmer Frederick Parkhouse of Prixford Barton complained about the amount of litter that was appearing in the parish such as tins and bottles discarded in hedges and on waste ground. The recent Public Health Act of 1936 had stated that the accumulation of any waste that might be prejudicial to health or simply a nuisance was illegal, therefore Frederick, formerly of Townridden, proposed that the district council should commence regular refuse collections and it was left to the parish council to debate the matter. After a vote which saw seven in favour and nine against, the motion was defeated because it would generate an increase in household rates. Subsequently, it was proposed that each hamlet would have its own 'waste store' and in April 1946, the parish accepted the district council's offer to collect refuse from each hamlet, once every three months at an approximate cost of twenty-five pounds per annum.

Getting from A to B
Until the mid-twentieth century, most people in rural areas walked or cycled to reach their destinations. This was no different in Marwood where some would walk miles each day. Ernest Harding walked from Guineaford to Milltown every day for his work as blacksmith and Hilda Watts (nee Carter) walked three miles into Barnstaple and back each day for the majority of her working life. Beatrice Brooks (nee Holland) remembers gathering with friends, Pat Sadd, Christine Jenkins and Tony Watts at Guineaford Bridge, before walking to Barnstaple to go dancing at the Queen's Hall on a Friday night. When they returned in the small hours, they would take off their shoes as they walked through Prixford so they wouldn't be heard!

Many parishioners recall having no option other than to walk to school each day. Being located in Whiddon, this meant it was a long walk for some, especially those who lived in Varley and Longpiece. From the age of ten, Alan Harris would ride his Royal Enfield motorcycle to school from his home in Varley. He was stopped by a policeman one day who told him he couldn't ride the motorcycle on the roads with an engine, so every Monday he would remove the engine and use the bike to coast down the long hills to school, even though he would often have to push it up the other side! On Friday afternoons, Alan would replace the engine so he could go off scrambling around the green lanes and fields of the parish - such was his determination.

No matter the weather, snow, hail, rain or shine, many children would walk over a mile to school each day. These days only very few are able to walk safely due to dangers from road traffic, although given the option most would probably stick to the luxury of being chauffeur driven to the gate by their parents!

Before the widespread use of the motor car during the mid to late twentieth century, most parishioners did not have the luxury of owning their own horse. If they had to make an especially long journey, they could pay a local carter to transport them.

In the early 1900s, local farmer Fred Kelly provided a service carting people and goods, and some of his journeys are meticulously recorded in his journal, shown below. These give interesting insights, particularly regarding the work carried out for Mr Arthur, who was resident at *Marwood Hill House* at the time:

Extracts from Fred Kelly's Journal:

3 Oct 1903	*Carting two load of brick and gravel to Longpiece cottage*	*5s 6d*
3 Nov 1904	*Carting two load of board from Shapland & Petters for George Worth*	*6s*
25 May 1904	*Carting roller to tennis court for Mr Arthur, Marwood Hill House*	*2s 6d*
1 Aug 1904	*Carting Mr Main and family to Saunton*	*7s*
23 Aug 1904	*Carting Miss E Skinner to Great Western station*	*3s*
29 Oct 1904	*Carting 2 load of pipes and furnace for Greenhouse, Mr Arthur*	*6s*
14 Feb 1905	*Carting platform to school for concert committee*	*1s*
24 Mar 1905	*Carting Larch poles from Spencers Wood, Mr Arthur*	*4s*
01 Apr 1905	*Carting 10 ½ loads of dung for Mr J Cutcliffe*	*2s 6d*
30 Jul 1905	*Taking a party to Instow via Westward Ho!*	*7s*
07 Aug 1905	*Mrs Skinner and Edith Arthur to Ilfracombe*	*7s*
13 Jul 1906	*Carting case of mineral waters from station for Mr Arthur*	*9d*
13 Jul 1906	*Carting luggage to station for Miss Thomas (the weight of which was 7.3.17 costing 36s 5d in carriage to Norfolk)*	*4s*
28 Jun 1907	*Carting 100 of wood from Oakpiece wood - Rev A Johnson*	*7s*
16 Oct 1907	*Carting luggage from London & South Western station*	*2s*
21 Jan 1908	*Fetching servants' boxes from station – Rev A Johnson*	*2s 6d*
20 May 1908	*Taking pig to Blatchford for Noah Passmore*	*6d*
25 Jul 1908	*Taking gravestone to Mr Bryant's for Mrs Gould*	*gratis*
20 Aug 1908	*Bringing Mrs Gould's headstone back*	*gratis*
4 Aug 1909	*Carting 3 boxes of silver plate to Fox & Fowlers Bank, Barnstaple for Mr Arthur*	*2s 6d*

Source: FJ Kelly Journal: 1903 - 1921.

In the late nineteenth century, only the more wealthy parishioners such as the local squire or rector may have owned a coach and horses, although Reverend Pryke of Marwood (1893-1900), was unfortunate to be involved in two carriage accidents, as reported in the *Marwood Church Monthly* newsletter of May 1899:

"It never rains but it pours!" The Rector was in two carriage accidents, both collisions on two successive days, April 13 and 14th. In one, a heavy waggon on the wrong side of the road ran into and broke off his wheel near Upcott - the youthful driver of the waggon was behind and out of sight, talking with a friend, "a most dangerous and blameworthy thing to do". The second and more serious, a dog cart, driven rapidly down the High Street, Barnstaple, struck an open landau, broadside, in which Mr Hockin, second master of Lancaster School, Mr Knowles and the Rector, were being driven from the town station to Marwood. The carriage was overturned, the near hind wheel broken to pieces, and the driver thrown to the ground and seriously hurt. Such accidents as the above might be prevented if farmers would warn young inexperienced drivers not to leave their teams of horses; and if a policeman were stationed at least on market days, at the Pilton end of Barnstaple High Street, to regulate the traffic.

Source: *Marwood Church Monthly*, May 1899.

Milltown farmer, Mr Charles Pugsley suffered a similar experience while travelling in a horse and trap, as reported in the North Devon Journal in June 1919:

An accident happened on Friday last to Mr Charles Pugsley of Milltown. He was driving to Barnstaple with his wife, when at Littabourne the horse was frightened by a passing motor. It bolted down the hill, both Mr and Mrs Pugsley being thrown out of the trap, as well as a large number of eggs intended for sale. Mr Pugsley was conveyed to the surgery of Dr Manning, where his injuries were attended to, after which he was able to proceed to his home. Mrs Pugsley was badly shaken. We are glad to learn that under medical treatment they are making good progress towards recovery.

Source: North Devon Journal, 19 June 1919.

Above: Charles Pugsley, c.1936.

Hat-astrophe!

Charles Pugsley had another unfortunate experience with a motor car in August 1933. This time he was walking home after attending a fete at Prixford chapel and had got as far as No Man's Land cross, when a car pulled up alongside. The driver asked for directions to West Down, and while Charles was advising him, one of the occupants of the car reached over, snatched his felt hat, and the car quickly sped off before he could take its number. The next day, the driver of the car was identified as a young man from Landkey (Mr Dinneman), and when police visited his friend's residence (Mr Stoneman), they found the said hat.

Mr Stoneman was charged with theft and the case went to court at Barnstaple, as reported in the North Devon Journal on August 17 1933. When questioned about his actions, the defendant argued that he had only taken the hat as a joke and fully intended to return it; however the police inspector challenged him, replying that it was not much of a joke and that he couldn't have planned to return it as he hadn't the faintest idea who it belonged to. Charles was asked to appear as witness, and he stated that as he had been unable to recover the hat before the car pulled away, he had phoned the police hoping that the men might be apprehended at West Down. Charles told the bench that he had valued the felt hat at 7s 6d and that it was a good job he had another; otherwise he would have had to buy a new one! The Bench ordered Stoneman to return the hat, giving him a stern warning and a fine of eleven shillings.

Charabancs

In the late nineteenth century the charabanc was a popular form of transport, particularly for day trips. Originally horse drawn, with a large folding hood in case of bad weather, it was often used for short journeys such as the annual day out to the seaside.

Above: Gubb's charabanc, Ilfracombe . August 1906.

Charabancs were used on Tuesday 9 July 1895, when seventy schoolchildren from the Marwood Church school were taken to Woolacombe Sands for their annual treat. All were thankful for 'the splendid weather, the exhilarating air, the donkeys, the races, the salt water - to say nothing of the excellent things provided to eat and drink at dinner and tea' (*Marwood Church Monthly*, August 1895).

By the early 1900s, the first motorised charabancs were introduced to North Devon and a budding entrepreneur from Marwood capitalised on these advancements. William Herbert Gubb (b.1862), son of mason, John Gubb, was born and raised in Muddiford. He later moved to Ilfracombe to take up an apprenticeship with a baker and confectioner in the High Street, and by 1891 he was running the bakery. At the turn of the twentieth century, a change of career led to William making a living as the proprietor of a charabanc business – initially horse drawn and later motorised *(pictured below)*. His company, Lucky Violet Cars provided day trips for holidaymakers to popular destinations such as Clovelly, Bray Valley and Saunton.

Above: Lucky Violet Cars, Ilfracombe.

Above: It may well have been a Lucky Violet charabanc that transported Marwood folk for their annual treat at Woolacombe on August 13 1924.

Motor Cars

In March 1905, Fred Kelly recorded the exciting event of the first motor car being driven through Kings Heanton by Dr Ware. William Lynch (1905-1996) recalled seeing his first car in Muddiford in 1910, driven by his uncle Jim Scott. It belonged to Major-General Charles Sheppey Sturt, who was residing at *Muddiford House,* and he recalled it would struggle to make it up the hill at times!

It was a rare occurrence for cars to be seen in the area until after the First World War, when some wealthier families and landowners acquired their first vehicles. Such was the increase in the use of motor cars after the war that in April 1922, Marwood Parish Council received letters expressing concern about the 'excessive speed of many of the motorists through this village', who were believed to be driving at 25-30mph 'which as you may well know is exceedingly dangerous'. If only motorists were still driving at this speed through Marwood today! In March 1927, Mr Percival Brailey, clerk to the council, raised the urgent need for 'School - Danger' signs to be affixed nearby in Milltown. The potential menace of road traffic was already in evidence.

Kathleen Harris (nee Braunton) remembers one of her first experiences of a car ride, was when she was taken out for the day to Woolacombe with Olive Parkin and other friends from Marwood school. The James sisters of *Marwood Hill House* had kindly arranged this outing as a treat for the girls, and had lined up their brother Captain Edward H. James to provide the transport.

Above: Kathleen and friends in a Lea Francis 12-14 hp tourer, c.1928.

Kathleen learned to drive in the 1930s, which was a rare accomplishment for young women in those days. She remembers driving up the lane from Longpiece towards Prixford on one occasion, following behind Mr Baker in his car. As he approached

Varley, he started waving his right arm out of the window, as one would do before the introduction of indicators to signal turning off the road. Kathleen continued to drive forward, believing that Mr Baker was about to turn off towards Varley Farm, when she was suddenly forced to slam the brakes on hard to avoid driving into the back of his car. Both hopped out of their vehicles and Kathleen hurriedly explained to Mr Baker that she thought he was waving his arm to indicate turning right. He just laughed and said 'It's alright me dear, I was just banging out my pipe!'.

Mr and Mrs Fred Yeo of Guineaford suffered a terrible tragedy in May 1929, as a consequence of motorised transport. Their twenty-year old daughter Alice was killed when her bicycle was involved in a collision with a motorcyclist, a young mason from Milltown. The North Devon Journal-Herald reported that Alice had been visiting her parents in Guineaford, and was on her way back to Heanton Court where she was in service. The accident occurred at West Ashford Cross on the main road from Barnstaple to Braunton, less than a mile from Alice's workplace. The motorcyclist was found guilty of negligence and given a stern warning by the coroner, Mr George WF Brown, who told him he was lucky to have survived the collision. Mr Brown hoped that the incident 'would burn itself into his [the motorcyclist's] memory and that when he was on the road he would ride properly, and if he could not ride his motorcycle without travelling at a fast rate, then he should get rid of it'.

Unlike today, when there is an average of two cars per household, only a small number of people had cars in the parish, even by the mid twentieth century. Lou Spear recalls his family were fortunate to have had a car by the 1940s – seen outside *Prixford Cottages* in this photograph. Petrol was rationed at this time and would have been difficult to obtain.

Left: *Prixford Cottages*, c.1940. Jack Spear is pictured outside with his car.

Many locals remember Ern Lethaby who used to provide a taxi service, charging six pence for a ride to Barnstaple. In order to alert Ern of the need for a taxi, people would display a Union Jack flag in the window as a signal. Ern used to have two cars, both Austins and if one was in need of repair, he would switch the number plate and use the other!

The Kelly sisters of Guineaford had a little car that was driven by Elsie, and Harold Hopkins recalls it was a Standard 8. Elsie had failed her driving test on many occasions and it was never known whether she eventually passed or just drove without a licence. She was a nervous driver and on market days when the sisters would sell produce at the Barnstaple pannier market, Elsie refused to drive any further than Pilton Bridge and they would walk to the market from there! Kings Heanton farmer, Richard Dobbs also had a car *(pictured below, with his daughter Ida)*. When Ida passed away in 1982, her many properties in Kings Heanton were put up for sale and to the surprise of the executors, this car was found abandoned in an old barn.

Above: Richard and Ida Dobbs with their Wolseley, c.1930s.

Above: Mildred Pugsley (nee Hunt) in her Austin 12/4
Clifton saloon at Kings Heanton c.1930.

Food

Before the days of supermarkets and the mass food production we know today, families had to be as self-sufficient as possible. Most would grow vegetables and some fruit in their gardens. Fred Kelly kept detailed records of the varieties he planted in his garden at *Kellys' Cottage* in Guineaford. Some examples of his notes are below:

Planted 1908:   *Lower corner:*
            2 short rows Royal Kidney [potato]
            Remainder: Carters Snowballs [turnip]
            Tilled a few kidney beans also some peas.

Planted 1909:   *West side of big garden:*
            5 rows of white hebrons [potato]
            ½ row of peas

Planted 1910:   *Sowed onion seeds (white Spanish)*
            4 rows of Sir J Llewellyn [potato]
            6 rows of Scotch Triumphs [potato]
            ½ row of peas

Planted 1911:   *Put some old broad beans in cabbage bed*
            Tilled the Eschalots in lower garden
            Tilled seed onions
            2 ¾ rows of Suttons Abundance [potato]

Apple trees planted 1912: *Outside kitchen window - Gladstone*
            SW corner - Ecklenfield
            Next adjoining - Blenheim Orange
            Next to closet - Sandringham

In Fred's journals, he made frequent reference to rows of vegetables that he grew on behalf of local households who purchased the produce later in the season. Vivien Chugg remembers that Fred's daughter Elsie continued his good work, often working late into the evening to keep the splendid vegetable garden in order.

Most households kept a few chickens and often a pig to supplement their diets. Once slaughtered, it was common for pigs to be scraped out on the roadside and hung out to dry in sheds. Harold Hopkins remembers that George Welch of Middle Marwood was the local pig slaughterer, who, for a payment of half a crown would slay the animal and return the next day to prepare the cuts of meat. The joints were then submersed in one of Brannam's clay salters, a traditional form of preservation, prior to the invention of refrigerators, preventing the growth of bacteria and fungi. People would often sell some joints to their neighbours to help raise enough money to buy another small pig to fatten up.

In Kings Heanton, Norman Brooks remembers that like many locals, his mother Maud kept pigs, especially during wartime. After slaughter, the carcass would be rinsed out in the stream over the road near *Heanton Mill* and hung out to dry. Maud often made 'hogs pudding' which was a resourceful way of using the less appealing remains of the pig, such as the blood, heart and liver. The offal would be blended with a mix of suet, pepper and other spices, then stuffed into a skin and cooked, not unlike a sausage but much larger.

Above: Maud Brooks feeding one of her pigs c.1940.

Acquiring meat is easy prey for today's households. Rarely do we have to trap, slaughter, pluck, skin or dismember before we prepare our meals; instead we simply have to untangle the shrink-wrap and the polystyrene trays that in most cases surround the meats we purchase. There are probably precious few people today who would feel confident to deal with freshly slaughtered livestock.

Meals have never been easier to prepare. Today we take for granted that at the flick of a button we can choose to fry, bake, boil, grill, microwave, roast, steam, (and the list goes on...). In the past, people were limited to cooking their meals in large pots over open fires until technology advanced. The only enclosed means of 'baking' was in the stone bread ovens, which worked on the basis that the fire was built up inside the oven until it had absorbed enough heat. Then the fire was raked out, the base of the oven cleaned and then the bread could be placed inside to bake. At *Highfield* in Guineaford, there are remains of an old bread oven engraved with the name 'E. Fishley', a nineteenth century clay oven manufacturer of Fremington.

One of the first cooking ranges to become affordable for households was the 'Bodley'. In 1802, George Bodley of Exeter patented a new cast iron range, officially known as a 'Kitchener'. It had a cast-iron hotplate over the fire with removable boiling rings and was one of the first ranges to enclose the fire within either a single or double oven. This was an improvement on the earlier open range, which could result in the food closest to the fire burning before the rest was cooked. Each morning the 'Bodley' had to be cleaned, black-leaded, polished and re-lit before any cooking could be done. Maureen Chugg can remember her mother polishing the range each day until it shined, which always seemed a terribly arduous task.

Amongst Fred Kelly's journal entries in the early 1900s, there are frequent references to carting coal for the 'Bodley' to his customers and in June 1907 he recorded the installation of the same oven in his own cottage in Kings Heanton, at a cost of £2 18s 6d. Fred listed the costs of materials and work involved:

Bodley and fittings £2 1s 3d	Fire brick 1s	Cartage of material 2s 6d
Iron bars for valve 10s	Red brick 7d	Slate 6d
Tin Brunswick Black 6d	Gravel & lime 3s	3 pint kettle 1s 2d

Masonry work carried out by Arthur Skinner 4s 6d

Not every family could afford a range, so some managed with an open hearth until well into the twentieth century.

Tithing

The practice of 'tithing' began in medieval times, and involved the taking of one tenth of all agricultural produce of a parish, including crops, livestock and profits from activities such as milling, to enable the upkeep of the parish church and clergy. In the 1780s, Samuel Weston Ryder, then rector of Marwood opted to replace the produce tithe with a cash equivalent sum, known as commutation, probably because produce was difficult to collect and largely inaccurate. Unfortunately the Reverend and the parishioners failed to agree the amount that should be paid and in the Vestry records it is noted that 'in lieu of tithes, the parishioners paid to Mr Weston £300 per annum. He asked for £350 and because they refused, he declared that he could not afford to reside. He was non-resident many years'.

When Reverend Richard Riley arrived in Marwood in 1804, there was further disagreement over the value of the tithes. Accepting that the parishioners would not pay the sum demanded, the Reverend reverted to the method of tithing one tenth of all produce, much to the annoyance of the Marwood folk.

Author, Emma Augusta Bridges (1881) wrote about the ill feeling within the parish arising from Reverend Riley's actions. She wrote 'He was to have the tenth day's milk, the tenth lamb, the tenth haycock, the tenth bag of apples and potatoes; in fact the tenth of everything except the babies!' She recalled how the rector's assistant would always appear just at the right time to ensure that Reverend Riley received all that he was due.

On one occasion when the apples from the orchards at *Marwood Hill House* were due to be picked, Emma's father offered to send the bags directly to the rector. Riley obviously had so little trust in his parishioners that he responded 'the rector meant to see that he had his rights, and so his man should come in and keep watch while the apples were being picked'. Another time when the Bridges family had a dinner party, Emma describes how the gardener dug up some early potatoes and within the hour a message was received from the rectory, demanding 'the portion due to them of the potatoes taken up that morning'.

A Case of Clergy vs. Squire

During the course of his duties the Reverend regularly travelled from the rectory, down the lane to Townridden, as a shortcut to the hamlet of Middle Marwood. At the time, this land belonged to George Ley Esq of *Lee House*, and he wrote to the rector, requesting a nominal fee of one penny a year for the use of the lane. Riley replied that he had every right to use the lane and would continue to do so at his own pleasure.

A gate had stood at the top of the lane near the church for many years. Irritated by Riley's response, Squire Ley chained it up, but being quite old and worn it was easily forced by Riley who continued to use the lane. Squire Ley then erected a stronger six-bar gate to deny access, but the feisty Reverend chained a couple of carthorses to the gate and tore it down! Amidst much local interest, the case went to court and it was ruled that it was indeed a private road, with right of way only to the miller of Whitehall and the farmer at Westcott Barton. The remains of the gateposts at the top of Townridden lane are still just visible underneath some prolific ivy.

In a dramatic conclusion to the court case, the damages and costs amounted to a sum that was impossible for Reverend Riley to pay. He was bankrupted and as was custom in those days, he was imprisoned for debt at His Majesty's Gaol of St Thomas the Apostle in Exeter. *The London Gazette* reported on May 24 1814, that Riley was charged in custody on 6 November 1813, for the non-payment of debts:

> By order of the court for the Relief of Insolvent Debtors; Richard Riley, formerly of Little Gransden, in the county of Cambridge, and late of Marwood, near Barnstaple, in the county of Devon, Clerk, now a prisoner in His Majesty's Gaol of St Thomas the Apostle, in the said county of Devon, for debt, will be examined before his Majesty's Justices of the Peace for the said county, either at a General Session of the Peace, or an Adjournment of a General Session of the Peace..
>
> Source: *The London Gazette*, May 24 1814.

Reverend Riley's list of creditors was also published in the gazette, and these included Thomas Hill of Prixford Blacksmith; James Pearse, shoemaker; Elizabeth Pearse, shopkeeper; John Radford, stonemason; Henry Hill, stonemason; Thomas Berry, stonemason; John Robins, carpenter; Edward Mules, Clerk and the executors of the late William Westacott of Marwood.

Whilst Riley was imprisoned, the parishioners showed goodwill and frequent gifts of flour, game and vegetables were delivered to the rectory in support of his wife and young family. In spite of his bankruptcy and subsequent imprisonment, Riley remained Rector of Marwood when he returned from prison two years later, and he continued in post until his death in 1853, aged ninety.

Tithe Apportionments and Maps

To avoid the conflict arising from the tithing of produce across the country and well exemplified in Marwood, it was eventually ruled that tithes must be converted to a cash payment chargeable against land and dwellings. In 1836, Tithe Commissioners were invited to survey all parishes in England to calculate the acreages of every field, woodland, waterway, road and building and from this, the payment due from each parishioner. A Tithe Map was drawn for each parish, with each individual plot being numbered which could then be cross-referenced against the list of tithe apportionments.

The information collected in the tithe apportionment records included:

a)   Name of the landowner(s)

b)   Name of the occupier(s)

c)   Reference number allocated to the plot of land/building (corresponding to number on map)

d)   Name or description of the plot of land or building

e)   Category of land, whether arable, meadow etc.

f)   The area of land, measured in acres, roods, and perches[1]

g)   Amount of tithe rent charge to be paid

In Marwood, the commutation of tithes to cash was eventually reinstated in 1844 at which time the amount paid by the parish was £635 14s 2d per annum.

> A copy of the Marwood Tithe Map is stored at the North Devon Record Office in Barnstaple and can be viewed with the assistance of a staff member.

Who lived in my house?

Tithe maps are invaluable to historians as they give detailed information of the owners and occupiers of properties. Until the early twentieth century, the majority of Marwood parishioners were tenants, with only the clergy and local gentry owning their own properties. As mentioned earlier, many labourers lived in 'tied' accommodation owned by the landowner or farmer who employed them, and then let to the labourer for as long as they remained in service (weekly rent usually one shilling). This gave families little security, as labourers would often be hired on short-term contracts.

---

[1] Equivalent measures: 1 perch = 25 sq m; 1 rood = 40 sq perches (1011 sq m); 1 acre = 4 roods (0.4 hectares – or half an average football pitch)

Guineaford

In the earliest maps of the parish, the area now known as Guineaford was once characterised by the existence of a large pond opposite *The Old Inn* and *Poole Cottage* on the lane leading to Kings Heanton. In Benjamin Donn's 1765 map and in the property deeds of *The Old Inn, Byeways, Thynnes* and *Highfield*, the surrounding area is referred as 'Ginniver Pool' or 'Guinevere Pool'. In the tithe map of 1840, the same area was labelled 'Guinneford' and in the census taken one year later the hamlet name had evolved to Guineaford. The old English translation given for the name is 'hart hill', presumably from a stag deer, however one wonders whether there might be some remote link to the queen of Arthurian legend, Guinevere, since Tintagel is only fifty miles down the coast? Perhaps stretching the imagination a little too far!

At a parish council meeting in July 1895, it was agreed that the pond should be cleaned out and a channel cut through, with the 'stuff taken from this channel used to fill up the pits and then the water would have a free course, and no silling up of the mud would recur'. It seems that once the pond was filled in, the water was redirected to form the narrow stream that still runs along the lane today.

The position of the Guineaford dwellings have been transferred onto the basic map below, using the names that we use today as a reference, e.g. *Rock Cottage*. In most cases, there were no property names listed in the census or apportionments, and the census enumerator would not necessarily visit houses in the order they appear on the road. To make matters even more difficult, a few properties do not feature on the tithe map because they were classed as 'non-tithable'. Therefore today, a 'best guess' approach has to be taken where there is doubt as to the identity of the occupiers.

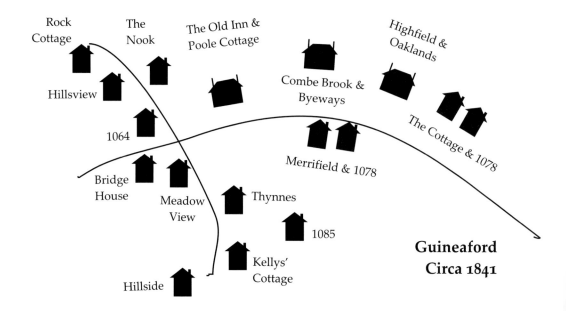

The names of those individuals who were believed to have owned and/or occupied the properties are listed below, obtained by cross-referencing the 1841 census, tithe records and property deeds, where available.

Property	Owner	Occupiers	Occupation & Age
Rock Cottage	John Dendle	John Daniel	60 - Mason
Rose Cottage, Hillsview	Miss Cutcliffe	William Tucker	65 - Farm Labourer
		Elizabeth Tucker	60
		James Tucker	20 - Shoemaker
1085 (property no longer standing)	Thomas Chugg	Thomas Chugg	50 – Publican
		Ann Chugg	45
		Charlotte Chugg	15
		James Chugg	10
		John Chugg	7
		Eliza Chugg	5
Bridge House	Thomas Chugg	John Marshall	40 - Tailor
		Susanna Marshall	40
		Henry Marshall	9
		Harriet Marshall	6
		Maria Marshall	4
		William Parson	15 - Apprentice
		Henry Phillips	15 - Apprentice
Meadow View	Richard Crang	Robert Skinner	35 - Mason
		Mary Ann Skinner	35
		John Skinner	10
		Thomas Skinner	7
		Eliza Skinner	5
		Rachel Skinner	1
Hillside	Zachariah Hammett Drake	John Adams	25 - Tailor
		Prudence Adams	25
		Susanna Adams	4
		Mary Adams	3
		John Adams	1
		John Balment	15 - Apprentice
		George Taylor	15 - Apprentice
Kellys' Cottage	James Laramy	John Geen	25 - Blacksmith
		Mary Geen	25
		John Geen	3
		John Wybron	20 - Apprentice
1085 (property no longer standing)	James Laramy	John Yeo	40 - Farm Labourer
		Sarah Yeo	45
		William Yeo	10
		Sarah Yeo	10
		Mary Yeo	8
		Samuel Yeo	5

Property	Owner	Occupiers	Occupation & Age
Thynnes	John Geen	John Geen	60 - Carpenter
		Elizabeth Geen	55
		William Geen	25
		Elizabeth Geen	20
		Jane Geen	15
		Richard Geen	15
		Ann Geen	12
1085 *(converted, now forms part of Merrifield)*	Margaret Woolacott	Samuel Beer	40 - Farm Labourer
		Samuel Beer	7
		Sarah Beer	11
		George Bament	40 - Pauper
		Sarah Bament	75 - Pauper
Merrifield	Margaret Woolacott	John Main	50 - Thatcher
		Elizabeth Main	45
		Mary Main	15
The Nook	Henry Hill	Henry Hill	60 - Mason
		Ann Hill	60
		Ann Hill	20
		Richard Hill	15
		Henry Hill	5
		Mary Fooke	65 - Pauper
The Old Inn	Henry Hill	Henry Hill	30 - Mason
		Mary Hill	40
Poole Cottage	Henry Hill	Charles Hill	25 - Mason
		Mary Hill	25
		Elizabeth Hill	2
Combe Brook	William Warren	William Warren	35 - Thatcher
		Sarah Warren	30
Byeways	William Warren	William Knill	35 - Farm Labourer
		Grace Knill	30
		Thomas Knill	5
		Elizabeth Knill	2
		William Knill	1 month
Highfield (1)	William Warren	John Gore	40 - Blacksmith
		Jane Gore	40
		John Gore	3
		Mary Huxtable	10 - Servant
Highfield (2)	William Warren	Richard Reed	25 - Shoemaker
		Jane Reed	20
		Mary Reed	1
Oaklands	Thomas Wrey Harding Esq.	Grace Warren	45 - Schoolmistress
		Grace Warren	20
		Mary Warren	15
		John Warren	12

Property	Owner	Occupiers	Occupation & Age
The Cottage	Richard Thorne (of Thornes Tenement, Kings Heanton)	William Smyth	25 - Farm Labourer
		Mary Smyth	35
		Thomas Smyth	1
		William Tucker	9
1085 (property no longer standing)	Richard Thorne (of Thornes Tenement, Kings Heanton)	Robert Corney	35 - Farm Labourer
		Maria Corney	25
		William Corney	6
		Walter Corney	4
		Thomas Corney	2

The Nook, The Old Inn & Poole Cottage

In the early 1800s, local mason and parish clerk, Henry Hill (b.1781, Marwood) leased a plot of land opposite the pond in Guineaford, for the annual rent of four shillings or 'a fat goose in lieu thereof'. There he built *The Old Inn* and *Poole Cottage* and the deeds show that by 1817 Henry had a mortgage on the properties, described as:

> Two cottages and gardens, Marwood, bounded on the north and north east by a field called New Park, on the south by the road leading to Kings Heanton, and on the west by the road from Barnstaple to Ilfracombe.

> Source: North Devon Inn Deeds, NDRO B522/1-21.

At first, Henry and his family lived in one of the cottages and the Furse family lived in the other. In 1831, Henry's daughter Elizabeth married William Furse, and following his appointment as gardener to Thomas Wrey Harding Esq. of Upcott House, they were given a tied cottage called Upcott Lodge. Meanwhile Henry's sons Henry junior and Charles had also married in the early 1830s, so Henry built *The Nook* next door, where he lived with his wife Ann and younger children, while Henry junior occupied *The Old Inn* and Charles was given *Poole Cottage*. Henry's daughter Ann married William, son of Whitehall millers Henry and Jane Gammon, and after the death of Henry's wife in 1850, he lived with Ann and her family at *The Nook* for several years.

In 1845, Henry Hill borrowed three hundred pounds from George Balsdon, maltster of Barnstaple, using the three cottages and some land nearby as security, increasing this sum by fifty pounds in 1849. There are no formal records to suggest that an inn had been established before this period, therefore it seems that a license may have been granted between 1845 and 1849, because the first official reference to the *North Devon Inn* appears to have been made in White's 1850 trade directory. At this time, sixty-six year old farmer Francis Fairchild and his wife Mary were recorded as innkeepers, which is also confirmed in the 1851 census. Although it was officially called the *North Devon Inn*, it was also known locally as *Fairchild's Hotel*, as evidenced by an advertisement in the North Devon Journal, announcing the sale of corn and hay from the premises.

Meanwhile, property *1064* which once stood opposite *The Nook*, was occupied by Thomas Chugg (b.1790, Combe Martin) and his family, who also owned *Bridge House* just across the lane. Interestingly, in the 1841 census Thomas was listed as a publican, and in White's 1850 trade directory, as a beer seller, suggesting that he had established an alehouse – licensed only to sell beer, not spirits. The 1851 census also records Thomas' occupation as innkeeper, so it is interesting that he was running his alehouse, less than fifty yards away from the newly established *North Devon Inn*, run by Francis Fairchild.

Francis Fairchild died in 1853 and two years later the inn was put up for sale. A notice was placed on May 31 1855 in the North Devon Journal, announcing the sale by auction of the 'first rate business premises' the *North Devon Inn* and two cottages adjoining, all property of Henry Hill. William Tamlyn (1803-1877), maltster of East Down became the proud new owner and let the inn to tenant landlords. In another interesting twist, there are two records which reveal that Thomas Chugg became William's first tenant landlord. The first is an article in the North Devon Journal dated May 29 1856, which describes an event held in the parish to celebrate the end of the Crimean war, followed by a dinner provided by Thomas Chugg at the *North Devon Inn*. The second is an entry in the Billings trade directory of 1857, which also confirms Thomas as 'victualler, North Devon Inn'. In September 1857, Thomas' wife Ann died, which seems to have prompted his decision to retire, evidenced by the 1861 census which lists his residence in Lower Muddiford and occupation 'retired innkeeper'. His property *1064* in Guineaford was either demolished or more likely, left to fall down, since it does not appear on later ordnance survey maps.

John Fairchild (only son of the late Francis Fairchild) and his wife Selina took over the running of the inn until 1865, when John chose to return to his main occupation of farming. William Tamlyn then leased the inn to William and Ann Gammon, Henry Hill's daughter and son in law. Property deeds show that they were charged twelve pounds per year in rent and six pounds per year for use of the brewing casks and utensils, and the agreement specifically stated that the Gammons were to purchase all their malt and hops for brewing from the proprietor. When William Tamlyn died in July 1877, he bequeathed the inn to his son in law, Ebenezer Jones, who immediately sold it to Charles Bastin, maltster of East Down, for the sum of three hundred and sixty pounds. He allowed the Gammons to continue in their tenancy until they eventually took their well earned retirement in 1883. They were succeeded by Henry Yeo, followed by John Skinner of Shirwell, who agreed a short term tenancy with Charles Bastin in 1893. As before, the agreement stipulated that John was to purchase all malts and hop from the proprietor, and if he ceased to brew, he was also obliged to purchase the beer from Charles.

Above: Guineaford c.1900.
Reproduced with kind permission of Mr S Knight, RL Photographers.

The *North Devon Inn* can just be seen to the rear of the photo, with the sign above the door. Adjacent to the Inn, on the right, is *Poole Cottage*. The Smithy is the small building to the right and *Meadow View* is opposite.

After tenancies by William Taylor who later purchased the freehold, followed by James Dennis, the last recorded publican was Ralston Watts, who had managed a public house in Bideford prior to taking on the *North Devon Inn*.

In the autumn of 1916 following almost eighty years of trading, Ralston put the inn up for sale after finding that his application to renew the licence was refused. A notice in the North Devon Journal in November 1916 revealed the new owner as Robert Hopkins (b.1865), a farmer from Middle Marwood, and the article described the property as being sold for £140 as a private dwelling, having a carriage house, stable and garden, previously known as the *North Devon Inn*, Guineaford. Just five years later, his grandson, Harold Hopkins was born there in December 1921.

More information about the many Marwood inns can be found in the next chapter.

Now known as *The Old Inn*, the property remained in the occupation of members of the Hopkins family until the 1970s, by which time the old stables and clubroom had been converted into a new dwelling known today as *Friendship*.

Above: The old stables and clubroom c.1940, prior to its conversion to *Friendship*.
Harold's father in law, Sidney H Gubb is in the foreground with his horse.

In the late 1940s *Poole Cottage* became home to Ernie and Hilda Watts. Hilda, one of five daughters, and originally from High Bickington, had been in the Wrens during the Second World War, and whilst she was away, her parents John and Ellen Carter moved to *Rose Cottage, Hillsview* in the mid 1940s.

Ernie was a native of Marwood and his widowed mother Ellen, was living in *Thatch Cottage*. Hilda and Ernie happened to meet while they were both on service leave, and were married after the war in 1947. They made their first home in *Rose Cottage*, Kings Heanton and their landlady was Maud Brooks, mother of Norman and Bernard. Hilda remembers much of Kings Heanton was derelict at this time, with many dilapidated farm buildings and many cottages owned by Ida Dobbs. After a short time, they moved on to rent one of *Prixford Cottages,* but their ultimate aim was to buy their own house. Fortunately, *Poole Cottage* came up for sale because its former elderly occupant Mr Manning, who was blind, decided to relocate. The couple were delighted to settle in Guineaford, just a stone's throw from their mothers, who were both widowed by that time.

Merrifield
In the late 1890s, the dwelling known today, as *Merrifield* was originally the site of two cottages, one of which became home to young widow, Hannah Down (b.1863, nee Beard). She had been brought up at *Bowen Farm*, Middle Marwood and in 1884, she married William H Down of Filleigh, who had moved with his parents to *Stepps Farm* next door. William and Hannah had five children Lucy (b.1885), William (b.1886), Walter (b.1888), Ethel (b.1890) and Gilbert (b.1893). Tragically, in February 1895, whilst William senior was harvesting at *Stepps*, a freak accident occurred. He had been loading sheaths onto the back of a cart when the horse suddenly kicked up, forcing the handle

of the pitchfork hard into William's stomach. The next day he was still suffering significant pain yet somehow he managed to walk to the North Devon Infirmary unaided, where a day or two later he died at the age of thirty-three years.

Widowed with five children, Hannah moved to Guineaford along with three of her young children Walter, Ethel and Gilbert. Her older son William remained in Middle Marwood working at *Stepps Farm* as a cattle boy for new owners, the Isaacs and her older daughter Lucy went into service at Litchdon Terrace, Barnstaple.

Hannah's parents, William[1] and Selina Beard retired from farming and moved to Guineaford to be nearer to Hannah, who worked long hours to support her family, either picking cabbages or potatoes for local farmers or taking in laundry. She is also recorded as being in receipt of the annual Poor Lands' money 'Aclands Gift', in the late 1890s in recognition of her hardship and raising her family alone. By 1917 Hannah had left the parish, and settled in Vicarage Street, Barnstaple.

Left: William Henry Down (b.1861) in Devonshire Yeomanry uniform, c.1880.

After leaving school at fourteen in 1902, Hannah's son Walter went to work for Richard Dobbs at *Herders'* farm in Kings Heanton along with his older brother William. By 1912 the pair had left to begin work at Rock quarry, supplying stone for the new roads. Walter later married Martha Chugg in July 1911 and settled in *Kingsheanton Cottage*. Martha worked for the Montagues of *Lee House*, partly as nursery maid to the two youngest daughters, Joan and Nancy, and also as a seamstress.

Neil Thurlow, Walter Down's grandson recalls a story that has been passed down through his family. Evidently Walter and his brothers were good friends with George Worth (b.1887) of *Colam House*, Muddiford, and they would get up to all sorts of mischief. On one occasion they had been playing cricket and afterwards noticed that a travelling preacher had parked his caravan up the hill. They went to investigate and after fiddling with it, managed to accidentally dislodge the caravan, which rolled away down the hill! On another occasion they went to chapel at Prixford and were messing about in the back row – George was pretending to swallow the chain of his watch and was dangling it over his mouth when he starting to choke, making all the boys giggle. The minister was so annoyed at their behaviour that he visited Walter's mother Hannah, to make his

Above:
Hannah Down
c.1910

---

[1] William Beard fought in the Crimean war and although he was blinded, he was still able to manage his farm later in life and would astound people by his knowledge of each and every hedge, field and lane.

complaints known. Hannah was not so much interested in their misbehaviour, replying 'Chapel? They should have been at church!' Apparently the young scamps had gone to chapel instead of church just for a change, although it is likely that Walter and his brothers learnt their lesson that time!

By 1917 Hannah had moved to Barnstaple and *Merrifield* became home to retired farmer, William John Wensley (b.1860) and his wife Agnes (nee Nicholls). William was an eccentric fellow, having lived with his parents until his marriage in 1913 at the age of fifty-three years, and was renowned for being a difficult character. Similarly, Agnes and her brother, Walter Fry Nicholls, had both lived and worked with their parents until late in life, farming at Martinhoe Mill. After their father's death in 1899, Agnes and her brother lived in Lynton, until Agnes married William Wensley and moved to Guineaford.

To the amusement of the locals, William Wensley had an ongoing dispute with one of his neighbours, Henry Baker of *Highfield*, just across the road from *Merrifield*. Harold Hopkins remembers observing one particular disagreement between the two in approximately 1930 which led to both ending up in the local court, where Harold was required to give evidence.

Merrifield used to have a thatched roof until Mr Wensley decided to remove it, and replace it with tiles. As the roof was replaced, he brushed the loose bits of thatch out into the lane and lit a bonfire. Mr Baker had been fetching two pitchers of water from the spring just down the lane and on his way back to *Highfield* he noticed the blaze. Furiously he confronted Mr Wensley, loudly protesting that he had no right to light a fire in the highway. As Mr Baker bent over to set his pitchers down to continue the conversation, Mr Wensley saw his opportunity, grabbed his pitchfork and struck Mr Baker across the shoulders! Harold had also been fetching water from the spring and witnessed the whole scene. Mr Wensley was later summonsed to appear in court to explain his actions. Chuckling at the memory, Harold recalls the Judge asked, 'Did you hit him Wensley?' to which the candid reply was 'yes sir, and I'd hit him again'. Mr Wensley received a significant fine for his actions.

Shortly afterwards, both Harold and Kathleen Harris (nee Braunton) recall that Mr Wensley erected a large galvanised iron fence across the front of his property, to prevent his neighbours from being able to see Agnes using the privy. Unfortunately the fence also blocked the view of the village, much to his neighbours' annoyance! Mr Baker wrote to the parish council in 1935 to complain about the obstruction, but was later informed the council were unable to take action. Harold remembers that the local boys would gather at Guineaford Bridge on Sunday evenings, once they had attended church or chapel. They would collect pockets full of stones and throw them at the fence to annoy Mr Wensley, who would run after them swinging a long horsewhip. Fortunately, the boys were always too quick for him or else he could have inflicted a nasty lash on them!

Homeleigh Cottage

Hannah Down's eldest son William began courting Mary Elizabeth Manning, daughter of William and Sarah Manning, of *Bridge House*, Guineaford. They married in September 1911 and initially lived in *Rock Cottage*.

They had five children, with Alec (b.1912) the first to arrive, followed by Olive (b.1915). In 1917, William went off to fight in the First World War in the road construction corps, but thankfully returned safely from the devastation in France, enabling the family to grow with new arrivals, Eva (b.1921) and in 1927, twins Jean and Raymond. By then the family was living at *Homeleigh Cottage* near Guineaford Bridge, where Mary ran a small shop, and they later moved to *Bell Cottage*, Prixford.

William H Down, c.1910.

Mary E Manning, c.1910.

Locals can remember one occasion when the twins decided to go for a walk on their own, aged about five years. When she realised they had gone missing, Mary panicked and immediately a search party was organised to track down the pair. They were eventually found safe and sound in Muddiford!

Left: Mary, with Jean and Raymond, c.1928.

Bridge House

Mary could look to her parents, William and Sarah Manning (nee Yeo) for guidance in running a store. For many years, they had been the proprietors of a general store at *Bridge House*, which remained in business from around 1889 until the 1940s, when it was taken over by the Jenkins family. The store supplied a variety of goods including maize and meal for pigs and poultry. The Mannings also kept bees and made their own honey. Other items such as sweets and tobacco could be purchased.

Sarah was known as Granny Manning to the locals, and was known to be quite a domineering lady. One night, a crowd had gathered by the bridge at Guineaford, possibly to listen to a preacher or a politician. Evidently Sarah marched outside, spotted her husband William amongst the numbers and hauled him back inside the house, loudly proclaiming that he should know that Saturday night was bath night!

Above: William and Sarah Manning, outside *Bridge House*, c.1925.

Sarah and William had married in April 1879, and were blessed with nine children; Henry (b.1881), John (b.1883), Fred (b.1885), George & Evon (b.1887), Annie (b.1888), William (b.1889), Mary (b.1892) and Albert (b.1895). There are many creditable mentions of the children during their time at the Church school and in many ploughing matches. Amongst all the achievements of their many children and grandchildren, perhaps their saddest moment came in April 1916, when the news arrived of the death of their youngest son Albert who was fighting with the Grenadier Guards in the First World War.

When William died in July 1931 aged seventy-three, the funeral service took place at the Methodist Church at Prixford with Reverend Fuller officiating. His coffin bearers were his lifelong friends and neighbours Noah Passmore, George Cutcliffe, Robert Hopkins, Fred Kelly, Ernest Harding and Arthur Lean. Sarah passed on the following year in August 1932, aged seventy-nine years. Reverend Balman led her funeral, and the men who had carried her husband's coffin just one year earlier, repeated the honour for Sarah.

The *Bridge House* store was later taken over by George and Rose Jenkins. George (b.1872) an Engine Driver, was the son of Robert and Jane Jenkins, who had lived in *The Cottage*, Guineaford since the mid 1880s. Rose (b.1873) was born and raised in Guineaford, along with her sisters Charity and Emily, daughters of the late John and Elizabeth Carpenter, who were former teachers of the nearby Church school.

Rose initially went into service in Exeter and Georgeham, and later returned to Marwood as cook for Reverend Pryke between 1893 and 1900.

In the summer of 1905, George and Rose were married and went on to have three children, Violet, Leonard and Horace. Following in their father's footsteps, both sons went to work for the County Council as Engine Drivers. Harold Hopkins remembers that they both had motorbikes that he would clean on Saturday afternoons for one shilling each. Their daughter Violet became firm friends with Reverend Mattinson's daughter Eva, and together with Rose, she became greatly involved in the Marwood Women's Institute, with meetings often held at *Bridge House.*

Kellys' Cottage

Kellys' Cottage is situated on the Ilfracombe Road, halfway up the hill towards Prixford. It is named after its previous occupants the Kelly family, who lived in the property from November 1912 until 1995. The move in 1912 had felt like a momentous occasion for the head of the household, Fred Kelly, who noted in his journal that after forty-two years of residing in Kings Heanton it was his first house move, albeit less than a mile down the road!

Fred's father, Thomas Kelly, married Sarah Laramy of Blakewell in December 1846, and they had two sons, George (b.1849) and Thomas junior (b.1851). The family lived in Varley until Sarah died suddenly in May 1855, after which Thomas and his sons moved to a farm of eight-two acres near Pippacott. In 1860, he met and married Elizabeth Clarke, however the family was beset by further tragedy when oldest son George Kelly tragically died aged just seventeen years in March 1865, only a few months before Fred was born. By 1871, the family had returned to Marwood and settled in Kings Heanton.

Thomas junior became a grocer's apprentice in Barnstaple High Street, before emigrating to Canada, where he settled and married in the late 1870s. He died in February 1888 in Hamilton, aged thirty-seven years.

In 1906 Fred married his cousin Eliza Kelly, daughter of his Uncle Robert. Eliza was born in Clifton, near Bristol and brought up in Henbury, Gloucestershire. By 1891 she had moved to Barnstaple to live with her aunts Elizabeth and Mary German, who were landlords of the Commercial Inn, Boutport Street and she remained with them for the next ten years. Fred and Eliza married in 1906 and had three daughters, Elizabeth (b.1906), Elsie (b.1907) and Amy (b.1910).

Hilda Watts remembers Amy being the life and soul of the party, but sadly she died of cancer in 1955. Elsie worked as housekeeper for many years at *Lee House* and Lizzie looked after matters at home, often seen wandering the lanes searching for kindling wood. The sisters also grew their own produce which they would sell at the Barnstaple Pannier Market each week.

In later years, Vivien Chugg spent much time looking after Lizzie and Elsie, who had been her long term next door neighbours. She would go in each day to clean out the range and light it for them, and help with other jobs around the house, often perplexed by their primitive way of life. They had no bathroom or kitchen, just a solitary tap which was only installed after considerable persuasion, and as mentioned earlier in the chapter, they still used an outside privy at the top of the garden. Vivien recalls that they were quite determined ladies, who knew what they wanted!

Fred followed in his father's footsteps becoming a farmer. He was a meticulous diarist, and two of his journals covering dates between 1903 and 1948 still exist. These fascinating books contain details of tasks he carried out on a day-by-day basis and the amount charged for his work. But in a charming twist, the books are also interlaced with personal memoirs and observations that provide a real insight into his life in the early twentieth century.

Above: Lizzie (left), Elsie (right) and Amy Kelly (centre) c.1915.

As referenced earlier in this chapter, the first of Fred's journals kept record of the many carting trips that he undertook around the parish, but also observations such as the date the first swallows arrived in Marwood each year and the date he heard the first cuckoo. In January 1905 he records picking the first primroses of the year in Beara Charter Lane, and in May the same year he notes that a very severe frost had damaged the potato crop very badly, Noah Passmore's in particular.

The second journal contains more detailed information about Fred's farming work, particularly sheep and poultry. It also makes touching references to his daughters growing up, such as their first steps, first shoes and first day at school.

Hillside

The first official Postmaster in Guineaford was a tailor by trade, named John Marshall (b.1801, Bishops Nympton). He and his family had previously lived in *Bridge House*, Guineaford and in November 1851 they moved a short distance up the hill towards Prixford, to an existing cottage known today as *Hillside*, where they established the village post office. The very early photograph below shows his wife Susannah with youngest daughter Maria outside the post office in the 1860s. It is just possible to see the words *Post Office* painted on the porch over the door.

Above: Susannah and Maria Marshall pictured in front of the post office, c.1860s.
Photograph reproduced with kind permission of Desmond Painter.

In 1859 Maria Marshall married Thomas Carder (b.1818), who was twenty years her senior, at Barnstaple Methodist Church. Previously widowed twice, Thomas was a prominent Marwood farmer, initially at Whiddon, where he succeeded his father, farming 120 acres and later at Milltown, where he farmed a respectable 197 acres, employing two labourers.

Thomas and Maria had six sons and three daughters, and they were photographed together in 1893.

Above: Thomas and Maria Carder with Emily, William, John, Henry,
Marion, Thomas, Edith, Ernest and Sydney (1893).

Thomas Carder was active in the public life of Marwood, serving on the School Board, Parish Council and as a trustee of the Methodist Church at Prixford, where he was eventually laid to rest. He died of pneumonia brought on by influenza on June 20 1900 and his obituary in the North Devon Journal described him as 'a man of strong character [who] had the kindliest of dispositions, and was never happier than when he was able to do a good turn to anybody'. Thomas's son John (known as Jack) took over the farm upon his father's death.

The Worth family were the next inhabitants of Guineaford post office in 1871. William (b.1821) was a carpenter by trade and his wife Elizabeth (nee Bament) became postmistress. They had seven children, John (b.1850), George (b.1852), William (b.1855), Elizabeth (b.1862), Henry (b.1863), Robert (b.1865) and Alice (b.1869). Youngest daughter Alice eventually took over the role of Postmistress, which she retained until her marriage to Thomas Pugsley in May 1916. Horatio and Lucy Lean (*pictured right*) succeeded the Worth family as tenants of the post office.

The Leans, c.1940.

In the 1920s, youngest son Robert Worth sold the land attached to the post office to Richard Dobbs, and the property to Winifred F Bourne who lived at *The Nook*. Thirty years later in 1956, she sold to carpenter Douglas Hamley whose family ran the post office until its eventual closure in the early 1980s.

Rock Cottage

In September 1900, *Marwood Church Monthly* reported that at the age of ninety-four years, Miss Elizabeth Gower Riley had passed away peacefully at home in *Rock Cottage, Guineaford*. She was the last surviving daughter of Reverend Richard Riley and it was mournfully noted that 'Miss Riley was the last link of connections with a period of Marwood history which few can now remember'. She had donated the marble plaques dedicated to her father and brother, which can be seen on the south wall of the parish church.

By the 1940s, James (b.1871) and Jane Kimber (b.1872) were residing at *Rock Cottage*. They had previously lived in London, where James had worked as a foreman at a fancy soap stamper & finisher in London, as did his father before him. James used to keep a pretty pony and trap and would take Harold Hopkins for a ride with him on Sunday afternoons. The cottage, with all its fixtures and fittings was later sold 'lock stock & barrel' to Harold for one hundred and fifty pounds.

Meadow View

The Skinner family who were masons by trade, occupied *Meadow View* for many years as evidenced by the census and tithe information. In the 1930s Noah and Mary Jane Passmore, who previously lived at *Combe Brook*, moved a hundred yards down the lane to make it their home. Incidentally, Mary Jane's mother Rachel Gore, nee Skinner, had previously lived at the same cottage as a child.

Noah (b.1874, Winkleigh) had been living with his parents in Shirwell and Mary Jane (b.1869) was born and raised in Guineaford. Her father, John Gore was a much-loved farrier, popular amongst local farmers for his discretion and good nature, but sadly died of a stroke just six months before Noah and Mary Jane were married.

The *Marwood Church Monthly* reported, 'We earnestly hope and confidently believe that the marriage between Mr Noah Passmore and Miss Mary Jane Gore on Saturday November 13, laid the foundation of a happy and a Christian home'. Among the presents given to the bride, were a teapot from the choir and bell ringers, and a clock from the Reverend and Mrs Pryke. Mr John Skinner, Mary's uncle, gave her away, and Frederick J Kelly was best man. Miss Annie Gore, Mary's younger sister who worked as a housemaid at the rectory, was bridesmaid.

Both Noah and Mary Jane were devoted churchgoers and active participants in secular duties. At a garden fete for the church lighting fund in 1947, Reverend Rickett made a presentation on behalf of the congregation to Noah, 'who for over half a century has given loyal devoted service to the church, being for many years church warden and captain of the ringers'. Noah was presented with an armchair and an illuminated address[1]. Vivien Chugg (nee Hopkins) is one of many locals who have fond memories of Noah and Mary Jane, who would always give her two shillings on her birthday.

---

[1] Illuminated addresses were a popular way to mark special occasions or outstanding service.

When Beatrice Brooks worked at *Marwood Hill House* in the 1950s, she could remember seeing Noah at work in the old tithe barn, with his Old English sheepdog that would often stick its head out of the door to watch the world go by!

In their wills the couple bequeathed a significant sum to the parish church and a plaque was erected in honour of their generosity.

There is an old legend described in a manuscript written by the Reverend Collison, rector of Marwood 1853-1886. Upon investigation, the author has discovered that it relates to Mary's father John Gore.

> *This woman afterwards married a blacksmith, who, being a seventh son, was thought to have the gift of healing certain diseases. The operator and the patient had to meet fasting on seven successive Sundays, or whatever had been the day of the week on which the blacksmith had been born. The operation was called "Striking" and seems to have resembled mesmeric passes, and the operator was said to be sometimes such exhausted by the process. No money could be taken for the cure but the patient gave a present.*
>
> *An old woman who was suffering from a bad leg was one of his patients. She set out on a winter's morning when the steep lane was covered with a sheet of ice. Poor Nancy got a fall in which her lantern went out and her arm was broken, but she had the spirit to go on to her destination, and she assured me that she had received great benefit from the "striking". We have had other gifted men who had learned words by which they could stop bleeding. Their help has been offered to me to stop bleeding of the nose, but as I could not make a satisfactory declaration of faith, the experiment has not been tried in my case.*
>
> Source: NDRO 3398A/PV1.

John Gore (b.1838) was in fact the seventh born son of John and Jane Gore of Guineaford, and both father and son are listed in the census as farrier/blacksmith. Despite being the only child, parish records show their six previous sons died at very young ages, making him the seventh son. It is therefore likely that it was John who possessed this gift of healing, as described by Reverend Collison. John married Rachel Skinner, daughter of Robert and Mary Jane Skinner of *Meadow View*. They had two daughters, Mary Jane who married Noah Passmore, and Annie who married blacksmith, Ernest Harding.

Highfield & Oaklands

The dwelling known today as *Highfield* is one of the oldest in Guineaford, evidenced by the year of 1647 which was etched on the lintel over one of the inglenook fireplaces. It was formerly two cottages, later extended towards *Byeways* to form a third property, creating a significant challenge in determining the occupiers of each cottage. Today, the eastern end of the property is known as *Oaklands*, which was once a sweet shop run by Mary Jane Summerfield.

One of the earliest references in the property deeds is of William Warren, a yeoman farmer, who is recorded in the tithe apportionments as the owner of two cottages. In 1852, William sold the cottages to local shoemaker Richard Reed, who in 1864 sold them to another shoemaker, John Cutcliffe of Ashford for £160. At that time the plot included 'all those two cottages or dwelling houses, formerly one cottage, with the field, garden and orchard of approximately one acre, in Ginneyford Pool'. John lived there with his six children, John junior (b.1866), Mary Jane (b.1868), William (b.1870), Charles (b.1872), George (b.1874) and Edward (b.1877). In 1888, John purchased *Oaklands*, formerly owned by the Harding family, making him the owner of all three cottages.

John Cutcliffe lived at *Highfield* with three of his sons, John junior, George and Edward, until his eventual death in May 1908. John junior was a boot maker and he owned the workshop outside *Poole Cottage* where he carried out his craft. Edward was a farm labourer, who later moved to Braunton and worked as a machinist. George was a market gardener, known to be quite a character, remembered for his peculiar ways but friendly disposition. Lou Spear remembers he was a lively fellow who would offer the children threepence if they could recite the alphabet backwards! Hilda Watts recalled that George would till and work his land growing garden vegetables which he sold at the market, and every night he would be seen walking up to the *Ring O' Bells* with a bundle of sticks on his shoulder.

In 1910 George purchased the two *Highfield* cottages for £140 and the 1911 census shows that he continued to reside there together with John junior and Edward. Second eldest brother William, became the new owner of *Oaklands*, though he let the cottage to the Summerfield family before selling to Reginald Main in 1938, who also allowed the Summerfields to remain as tenants. At the same time, George sold a large piece of land to Reginald for ten pounds, enabling him to extend his garden at *Byeways* where he lived with his wife Edna.

When George died in 1950, his younger brother Edward sold *Highfield* to Reginald Main, giving him ownership of all three cottages, as well as *Byeways* next door. By then, the property had become quite run down, so Reginald was able to purchase it at the price of seventy-five pounds.

Reginald's parents Wilfred and Emily Main and their children, had originally lived in *Byeways* since the late 1880s, and Reginald himself was born there in 1890.

Reginald returned to live at the cottage with his wife Edna in 1930, having retired from his position of music teacher at Worksop College in Nottinghamshire.

Above: Parts of *Highfield* had grown to become derelict over the years with one part even used as a fowl house, requiring significant restoration work.

Thynnes

In March 1818, an agreement was made between the right honourable Lord George Thynne of Baycliff, Wiltshire, William Lord Courtenay of Powderham Castle and a 'poor labouring person' named John Geen of Kings Heanton. The terms of the agreement stated that tenancy of a plot of wasteland near 'Ginneford Pool' in Marwood would be granted to John Geen on payment of five shillings for a term of ninety-nine years.

The lease was granted on condition that within the space of two years at his own cost, thirty-five year old John would *'erect, build, finish and complete in good substantial and workmanlike manner on the said premises, a convenient dwelling house'*.

Rent of two shillings was due to be paid on the four feasts:
- ✢ The birth of our Lord God.
- ✢ The annunciation of the Blessed Virgin Mary.
- ✢ The Nativity of St John the Baptist.
- ✢ St Michael the Archangel.

John Geen was a carpenter, married to Elizabeth (nee Gore) with two children, John (b.1811) and William (b.1816). As per the terms of the agreement he built the dwelling house as required with several outhouses, and his family grew with the addition of Elizabeth (b.1821), Jane (b.1826), Richard (b.1826) and Ann (b.1829).

It would seem that John and his son William went on to build additional accommodation on their land, namely *Thatch Cottage* and *Rose End Cottage*. His eldest son, also named John, became a blacksmith and appears to have been living at *Thatch Cottage*. This suggests that the 'smithy' next to Guineaford Bridge was built around the same time. In February 1847, the family were fortunate to have been granted the opportunity to purchase the entire freehold for the sum of thirteen pounds, because the terms of Lord Courtenay's will had enabled the disposal of his estate via sealed deeds.

Harold Hopkins is one of only a few locals who remember William (b.1863), the last member of the Geen family to have lived at *Thynnes*. Unlike his ancestors who were carpenters, William was a farmer and used to keep a cow in the building now used as a garage, where Harold and other neighbours could buy milk. At the age of seventy-three, after sadly witnessing the untimely deaths of his wife Elizabeth and only daughter Gladys, William began to sell off his land and properties including the former 'smithy' to Reginald Main in April 1935, which is also now used as a garage.

Kings Heanton

Norman Brooks was born in *Rose Cottage*, Kings Heanton in May 1930, the first-born son of Richard and Maud Brooks (nee Latham). Norman's father Richard Brooks was born in Bittadon in 1898, one of eleven children. Initially a farm worker, he then joined up to fight in the First World War and on the first day of the Battle of the Somme he received a gun shot wound to his shoulder, which led to him being invalided out of the army and sent home. He married Maud in 1927 and they bought *Rose Cottage* in Kings Heanton, next-door but one to *Little Foxbury* where Maud had previously lived with her parents.

Above: *Rose Cottage*, c.1930.

Above: Richard, Maud & Norman, c.1930.

Above: Richard & Maud, c.1950s.

44

Norman's mother Maud was born in Arlington Beccott in 1900, the youngest of nine children. Her family moved on to Berrydown and from there, Maud trained as a dressmaker, later running a small shop where she first met her future husband Richard. In the 1920s, her parents William and Mary-Jane Latham moved to Kings Heanton, along with their youngest daughters Nell and Maud, and lived in *Little Foxbury*.

Above: *Little Foxbury*, Kings Heanton, c.1935.

Above: Norman Brooks, c.1940.

Norman and his younger brother Bernard both attended Marwood school until the age of thirteen and a half. In 1943, Norman gained a place at the Barnstaple School of Science & Art for a pre-apprentice course in building construction, much to the delight of his teacher, Mr Price. He spent two years learning his trade, following which he was offered a five year apprenticeship with Wilfred Loosemore, House and Church Decorator. This involved some interesting assignments and the one which still sticks in Norman's memory was the time he was asked to do some painting at the old Barnstaple Workhouse on Alexandra Road, which he recalled as a most eery building.

Norman was later called up for National Service, along with his friends Arthur Leverton and Garfield Spear. The trio are captured in the photograph below representing the proud young men of Marwood in the army, air force and navy.

Above: Left to right - Arthur Leverton, Norman Brooks
and Garfield Spear c.1950.

After his two years of service, Norman returned to North Devon and in November 1952, made the decision to join the Devon Constabulary where he served thirty years. Norman and his wife Betty are now happily retired and living in Yelland.

Left: Norman Brooks, ready to embark on his thirty year career with the police force.

This photograph of Kings Heanton circa 1928, holds a secret story of its own which Norman learnt from his mother.

Above: Kings Heanton c.1928.
Reproduced with kind permission of Mr S Knight,
RL Knight Photographers.

The lady pictured in the foreground to the right, is in fact his mother Maud, anxiously looking for Mary Delve on her way home from school. Maud is keeping watch because one of the local farmers owned a bull that had a habit of escaping and there were also geese by the pond that occasionally terrorised the children by chasing them down the lane!

In a magnified version of the same photograph it is just possible to see the geese wandering freely in the background. Norman believes that the three little girls on the left of the lane were Gwendoline Webber, Winnie Cook and Mary Delve.

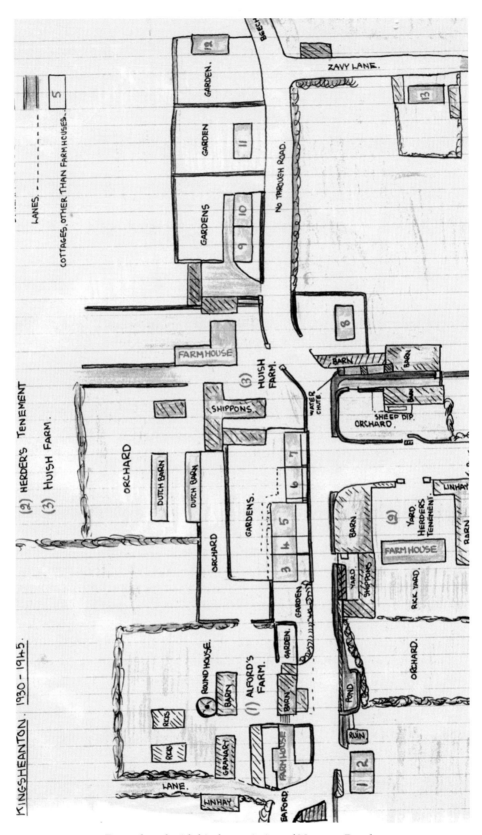

Reproduced with kind permission of Norman Brooks.

Norman has a keen interest in local history and drew the map on the opposite page to illustrate Kings Heanton as he remembers it between 1930 and 1945. He has also suggested the names of occupants of each property in the list below:

List of Properties and some of their occupants between 1930 and 1945
(Today's property names are shown in italics)

Farm (1) *Ibis House* - Alfords' Farm (Mrs Emily Alford)
Farm (2) *Herders'* Tenement (Richard Dobbs & daughter Ida)
Farm (3) *Huish Farm* (Hugh and Agnes Westcott)

Cottage 1 *Brookside* (Family of evacuees)
Cottage 2 *Brookside* (Leverton family)
Cottage 3 *South Cottage* (Miss Ashton)
Cottage 4 *Fern Cottage* (Mildred & Archie Pugsley)
Cottage 5 *Rose Cottage* (Richard & Maud Brooks and family)
Cottage 6 *The Folly* (Russell family)
Cottage 7 *Little Foxbury* (William, Mary Jane and Nell Latham)
Cottage 8 *Smith's Heanton* (Harry & Florence Manning)
Cottage 9 *Huish Cottage* (Webber family)
Cottage 10 *Rosebarn Cottage* (various)
Cottage 11 *Kingsheanton Cottage* (Winifred & Alfred Cook)
Cottage 12 *Fritham Cottage* (John & Frances Manning)
Cottage 13 *Sleepy Hollow* on Zavy Lane (Fitton family)

It is interesting to observe the amount of development that has occurred in the last seventy years in this hamlet. Although some were demolished, most of the barns, shippens and linhays have now been converted into dwellings, particularly since the late 1980s, with several now in use as holiday accommodation.

Herders' Tenement

Herders' was occupied by farmer John Fairchild for over thirty years between 1865 and 1897. John (b.1824) was married to Selina (nee Hodder) in 1856 and they were blessed with three children, Rosa (b.1859), William (b.1863) and Annie (b.1866).

An interesting court case involving Selina was heard at the Barnstaple County Court, as reported by the North Devon Journal on July 25 1895:

A MARWOOD LITIGATION CASE
At Barnstaple County Court on Tuesday, Selina Fairchild, wife of a farmer residing at Marwood, sued John Yeo, an old man of the same place, for the sum of £33; whilst John Yeo proceeded against Selina Fairchild for the recovery of a bank book of the value of £90. Mr A F Seldon appeared for Mrs Fairchild, Yeo being represented by Mr G W F Brown.

Source: North Devon Journal, July 25 1895.

A précis of the case is as follows. John Fairchild's older sister, Ann (b.1816) married Thomas Yeo in 1841, and they spent all of their married life in Kings Heanton, in a cottage close to the Fairchilds' farmhouse (*Herders'*). When Ann died in July 1894 Thomas was aged eighty-one, quite infirm and in need of care. He asked Selina to look after him and she agreed, providing him with all his meals and necessities for the first four weeks while he remained in his cottage. This was carried out with the aid of a servant and neighbour, Mrs Susan Tucker, who cooked and cleaned for Thomas.

Thomas was dissatisfied with this and requested to be in the personal care of Selina, who then arranged additional pay for a servant in her own household to undertake additional duties, enabling her to tend to Thomas's needs. In gratitude for her support, Thomas bequeathed ninety pounds in his will to Selina's disabled daughter Annie. Unfortunately the will was only witnessed by one person, which made it null and void upon his death.

Thomas boarded with the Fairchilds up until his death in March 1895. At his funeral, some of Thomas's relatives asked if he had left a will and John Fairchild replied that he had. It was reported that the relatives were very anxious at his death, but never came to see him when he was alive. John Yeo of Guineaford, the deceased's brother, claimed that he had seen his brother regularly up until his wife's death in 1894, but had not seen him since and had not known he was ill. He claimed he was never asked to look after his brother nor pay the costs of the funeral.

In summing up, Judge Beresford reflected that this was one of those unfortunate, but sadly frequent cases, where upon realising their relative to be worth something, the family suddenly showed interest. However during Thomas Yeo's lifetime, the same people were not prepared to look after him in the way that Selina Fairchild had done. Realising that Thomas had intended to leave his money to Selina's daughter, but the will being inoperable, Judge Beresford awarded thirty-three pounds costs to the Fairchilds and ordered the bank book to be returned to John Yeo.

Whilst the Fairchilds were in residence at *Herders'*, artist W.E.P Jones painted a picture of the farmhouse, an important piece of history that immortalises the scene in the nineteenth century. This precious heirloom is now in the possession of Francis Fairchild's great great grandson, David Fairchild, who was born and raised just up the road in Prixford.

Herders' Tenement, 1884 - With kind permission of David Fairchild.

The next occupants of *Herders'* were the Dobbs family, who moved into the farmhouse in around 1903.

Richard Dobbs was born in Instow in 1865, the third son of John and Eliza Dobbs. Richard began his working life as a farm labourer but on June 30 1888 he boarded the *S. S. Taroba* which had docked in London. Seven weeks later in August 1888 he arrived in Brisbane, Queensland and from there he made his way to the gold mining town of Charters Towers.

Charters Towers was founded in the early 1870s after a young aboriginal boy discovered gold, and between 1871 and 1917, over two hundred tonnes of gold were mined there. The population more than tripled as optimistic fortune hunters arrived in their thousands, to what were described as rich and productive fields. The numbers of miners in Queensland grew steadily, but it was a very dangerous occupation, with frequent reports of severe injuries or death caused by falling into the mineshaft or explosions.

Above: Charters Towers mining settlement circa 1890.
Source: http://en.wikipedia.org/wiki/Charters_Towers.

It was at Charters Towers that Richard Dobbs met his future wife Kate Hancock. Kate (b.1864) was born in Redruth, Cornwall, one of five children. In 1888, at the age of twenty-four, Kate and two of her sisters (Susan and Eliza) boarded the *S. S. Merkara*, arriving in Brisbane on February 5 1889.

It is unknown where the pair first met, but they were married by April 1890 and their first child Ida was born in August 1891. Three years later, they welcomed a son, Ernest, who was born in August 1894. Presumably Richard made a small fortune while the family remained in Queensland, yet they decided their future was in England. Richard, Kate, Ida and Ernest boarded the *S. S. Orizaba* arriving in London in June 1897, and from there they headed back to Instow.

Richard clearly had a plan in mind because within just two months of their arrival in the England, he had purchased a large farm in Marwood. On Friday, August 20 1897, an auction was held, listing the sale of three farms, known as *Kennacott*, Kings Heanton and *Herders'* Tenement.

Marwood Church Monthly reported in September 1897, that Herders' Tenement, of 122 acres, in the occupation of Mr Fairchild, was sold to Mr Dobbs, of Instow, for £2860. Heanton Farm, of 152 acres, occupied by Mr WJ Gear, was withdrawn at £2900, and *Kennacott* Farm, of 157 acres, occupied by Mr R Rudd, was withdrawn at £3950. Mr Dobbs also purchased three cottages, and the other small lots were withdrawn'.

This was an enormous amount of money at that time, supporting the theory that Richard, the son of a farm labourer, had earned substantial money in the gold mines of Queensland.

Richard, Kate, Ida, Ernest and Kate's younger sister Lilie lived together at *Herders'* for many years, but the commencement of the First World War was to bring change for the Dobbs' household. Ernest by this time was twenty years old and had been working on the farm with his father, as well as taking on small jobs for other local farmers. Fred Kelly recorded Ernest cutting grass for him at Wigley field at the rate of three shillings per acre in 1912. Like many farmers' sons, being an accomplished horse rider, Ernest joined the Imperial Yeomanry Guards. He was required to undertake regular military training and in May 1913 he sent a postcard to Ida from Larkhill Camp in Wiltshire, where he was on exercise, describing things there as 'A1'.

When the war broke out, Ernest was transferred to the Royal North Devon Hussars, Household Cavalry and Cavalry of the Line, and being a territorial regiment it was mobilised immediately. At first they were sent to the east coast of England to defend against an expected invasion. When it became evident that the threat of invasion was diminished, in September 1915 Ernest was among the many Hussars who travelled on the *S. S. Olympic* to Gallipoli and it was here that so many soldiers lost their lives, not from a bullet or explosive shell but from the deadly diseases of typhoid, dysentery, enteric fever and pneumonia. Tragically Lance-Corporal Ernest Dobbs died from dysentery on November 10 1915, aged twenty-one.

Ida attended the Devon County Travelling Dairy School which occasionally visited Marwood, where she took lessons in butter and cream making. She became renowned for her dairy skills and won many prizes at Young Farmer and County Dairy Competitions and was given responsibility for managing all the dairy work at Herders'.

Later in life when Ida lived alone, few who knew the conditions in which her cream was made would still be prepared to eat it. In her old age Ida had become increasingly eccentric and her attention to hygiene was limited to say the least. She would nurse sick farm animals including sheep in the comfort of her own home, particularly around lambing time, and chickens would be allowed to roam around the kitchen – perhaps giving a new definition to the term 'free range'!

Stella Money (nee Balment) can recall going to *Herders'* with her father Tommy Balment, to use the sheep dip as it was the nearest one in the area (now *Heanton Mill*). Ida came out with a chicken in her arms, explaining that she was nursing it back to health. Tommy could clearly see the poor bird was riddled with foul pest and its time on this earth was limited, but Ida took the infectious chicken back to the warmth of her kitchen.

Many locals remember Ida for being a real character, but as she grew older she became increasingly stubborn. She was literally a thorn in the side of the parish council for many years due to her blunt refusal to cut back the hedges bordering her land. The minutes of council meetings are punctuated with references to the ongoing problems during the 1950s and 1960s.

Ida owned almost all of the land and property in Kings Heanton, much of it derelict. In March 1963 the council voiced concern about six of her cottages being unoccupied, at a time when there was a real shortage of housing in the area. It was later concluded that the district council were unable to take any action, because two of the cottages were 'quite uninhabitable' and another two would 'require significant work'.

When Ida died in 1982 it was the end of an era, prompting the sale of acres of land and many properties. Kings Heanton soon became a project for local developers and the sympathetic restoration works have done much to preserve the historic character of the hamlet.

Above: Ida Dobbs, c.1960.

Prixford

In the 1940s, David Fairchild and Lou Spear were next-door neighbours at the newly built *South View* in Prixford.

David lived at no. 2 with his older brother Tony and parents Charlie and Vera Fairchild. David has fond memories of his early years in the hamlet, when he would 'wander aimlessly' around the countryside with the other local children. Looking back he now realises how fortunate they were to have had the freedom to roam in those days, when they knew every field, hedge and stream in Prixford, Varley, Milltown, Muddiford, Patsford, Middle Marwood and Lee Woods.

Above:
Tony Fairchild and
Lou Spear, c.1940.

Today, David and Lou chuckle at their antics as young boys, especially climbing trees and making dens in the copse at Prixford Barton and Lee Woods. Other adventures included climbing into the old round corn bins on the back of the horse and cart and riding around the parish or trying to empty the well down at Prixford Barton but finding it filled up just as soon as they had finished and driving six inch nails into tree trunks to enable them to climb higher . Both now shudder at the thought of the injuries they could have received! David remembers one particular fir tree in Prixford Barton that he virtually lived in, spending hours up there.

Lou recalls David's brother Tony climbed the drain pipe at *South View* one night, falling off as it came away from the wall and another occasion when Tony tied one of his shoes to the end of a rope to try and loop it over the branch of a tree. Unfortunately the rope came down but the shoe came off and got stuck up the tree. They had to get a ladder to fetch it before his parents found out!

David's father Charlie was born in 1905, the son of William H Fairchild (b.1863) and Jane Kelly (b.1868). Descending from a long line of successful farmers, including great-grandfathers Francis Fairchild and Richard Kelly; grandfathers John Fairchild and Charles Kelly, followed by his father William, it was perhaps inevitable that Charlie would follow in their footsteps.

Charlie had approximately fifty acres of land including pasture in No Man's Land, Lee and

Above: William and Charlie Fairchild
c.1930.

Ashford, as well as a barn at Prixford Barton. David can remember helping his father and other local farmers, as was customary, with the harvest each year. A horse-drawn reaper was used to cut the oats and bind them into sheaths. David and his brother Tony would follow behind, propping up small batches of sheaths to form 'stooks', which helped the drying process, and finally the sheaths were thatched into a rick for storage. One of the highlights of the harvest for local children was the arrival of the steam powered threshing machine, which came from Umberleigh – so noisy that they could hear it on the way up from Bradiford! Sheaths were thrown into the top of the thresher, separating the corn or oats from the straw in seconds, and once the job was completed the machine would then be transported on from farm to farm. This was work that would have taken a team of men weeks to do in earlier centuries, and just one example of how mechanisation of farming reduced the need for manpower.

David's mother Vera (nee Gilbert) was born in 1903 and raised in Pilton, just a couple of miles away from Marwood. Along with her sister Olive, Vera worked for the renowned local photographer, RL Knight. She was an active member of the Marwood Women's Institute from the early 1940s through to the 1980s and during this time was elected president for a number of years. Vera was also a talented singer, often performing in concerts locally. Harold Hopkins remembers that she would often sing 'Cherry Ripe', an old English folk song:

Cherry ripe, cherry ripe,
Ripe I cry,
Full and fair ones
Come and buy
Cherry ripe, cherry ripe,
Ripe I cry,
Full and fair ones
Come and buy

Above: Vera Fairchild selling her wares at a Marwood Fete c.1950s.

As a boy, David remembers attending the parish church every Sunday without fail when Reverend Rickett was the incumbent. The church was well attended and David was a member of a large choir that filled the stalls on both sides of the chancel.

There was a great social network amongst the churchgoers and parties were often held at the church hall with lovely food and games. In particular, the New Year's Eve gatherings were considered exceptional and not to be missed. David does have one sore memory linked to those parties however, arising from the occasion Vera made him stand up and sing 'Bless This House' in front of everyone, at the age of ten!

Both David and his brother Tony left the parish where they'd grown up in search of adventure. After completing his national service in the Royal Navy, Tony pursued a career in journalism. His first position was with the North Devon Journal-Herald and after a position as deputy editor of Yachting and Boating Weekly, he found himself freelancing on Fleet Street. Tony signed up as a sports journalist with the Daily Telegraph in 1966, where he remained until his retirement in 1988 as a hugely successful specialist yachting correspondent. Sadly Tony died from cancer in 1994 when he was living in the United States.

David began his career as an apprentice engineer at Frandor Works, now Hobarts, later serving as an officer in the Merchant Navy. In September 1964 David's motor vessel the *Trentbank* was in a serious collision with a Portuguese tanker almost three times its gross weight. All but one of the crew and passengers of the *Trentbank* were rescued before it finally sank, just off the coast of Egypt. David was lucky to escape uninjured, much to the relief of his parents Charlie and Vera. He later spent some years living in Bahrain but is now happily settled in Barnstaple.

Above: In 1947, the Fairchild family moved just a few houses along the road to *Wayside*, known today as *Chedlee*. This was the former home of Josiah Sanders, local Marwood constable for many years.

Lou Spear's father Jack (b.1898) was born at *Hartnoll Cottages* and spent his school years in Milltown and Shirwell. He married Jessie Tamlyn (b.1902) in 1923 and they went on to have five children, Barbara, Garfield, Louis, Denzil and Brenda. They lived at no.1 *South View* where Lou would happily entertain himself playing cricket or racing hoops down the lane, without the fear of traffic speeding past as it does today.

One of Lou's first paid jobs as a child was as a 'Telegram boy', receiving one shilling each time he delivered a telegram anywhere in the parish, either on foot or by bicycle.

On Friday evenings, Lou used to attend a youth club run by Reverend Rickett at the back of the Marwood rectory and later at the church hall, which provided the opportunity for activities such as boxing, snooker and table tennis. Norman Brooks also remembers attending the club with his Kings Heanton friends. On Saturday nights, Commander Martin of *Marwood Hill House* provided an exciting new form of entertainment for local children. He generously opened up his billiard room and set up a projector to make it possible for local children to watch Charlie Chaplin and Buster Keaton films. Lou remembers that it was such a treat that all the local children would go! He also attended Marwood Parish Church every Sunday as a choirboy and member of the bell-ringing team with Noah Passmore and Jack Watts.

Above (L-R): Lou Spear, John Watts, Brenda & Denzil Spear, at Tunnels Beach, Ilfracombe c.1940s.

Every June there would be a parish-wide collection to raise funds for the Marwood Sports day, which was held in Chapel Field between Prixford and Guineaford. There were the usual running races for the children, followed by a tea in the old chapel school room. In the evenings it was the adults' turn including cycle races, skittles and a football match between Prixford and Muddiford which always a very competitive affair!

Left: Lou and his older brother Garfield, outside *Prixford Cottages* with their father, Jack Spear c.1939.

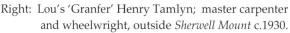

Right: Lou's 'Granfer' Henry Tamlyn; master carpenter and wheelwright, outside *Sherwell Mount* c.1930.

Another of Lou's hobbies included skittles and he is pictured below with the *Ring O' Bells* skittles team in the 1950s, which included his brother in law and landlord Gordon Lock, Henry Coats, also of *South View*, Jack Sadd of Prixford Barton, Dennis Spear and Bruce Ashton.

Right: The *Ring O' Bells* Skittles team, c.1950s.

Gordon Lock and Lou's sister Barbara were landlords of the *Ring O' Bells* at the time of the disastrous Lynmouth floods of August 1952. The rain was so heavy that it poured through the walls of the beer cellars and flowed like a river through the garden of no. 1 *Prixford Cottages*, down the lane to Prixford Barton.

Gordon's father Bill was a popular butcher, with a shop on Butchers' Row in Barnstaple. He lived at *Homeside,* opposite *Bell Cottage* and the *Ring O' Bells*. His daughter Margaret married Raymond Down in 1954.

Pictured at a fete in the rectory garden, c.1955:

Standing L-R, Fred Smith, Josiah Sanders.

Seated L-R, Bill Lock, Lou Spear, Charlie Fairchild, Frank Quick, Mr Robinson.

Lou remembers spending many hours larking about at the cider press at *Prixford House*. The apples were delivered onto the first floor on Saturdays, pulped on the Monday and pressed over the following few days. By Friday, the cider had been transferred into barrels, ready for delivery and as the farmers would be out all day at the market, the boys used to sneak back and pour themselves a glass or two. It was strong stuff apparently and made them fairly giddy!

Harold Hopkins also recalls that for the want of something to do, he and his friends would go to the press after school, busying themselves making gallons of cider. Then they would set to work to drink the entire lot, only to wake up the next morning with such awful stomach upsets they couldn't go to school!

Above: The cider house at Prixford – left to right: Fred Parkhouse, Jack Watts and Philip Goss late 1930s.

Prixford Cottages

Some of the earlier occupants of *Prixford Cottages* included George Coats (1890-1971), who joined the Royal Marines as a young man. The 1911 census lists him on board the dreadnought battleship *HMS Vanguard*[1] which was docked in Portland harbour. He went on to serve in the First World War receiving the 1914-1915 Star, Victory and British War medals.

---

[1] *HMS Vanguard* was involved in the Battle of Jutland but it is not known whether George was on board.

George was born in *Dingles Cottage*, East Down, the first of twelve children of John and Annie Coats. By 1897, the family had moved to Marwood and for many years they lived at *Collacott*. He married Emily Parkin, whose sister Ivy married Stanley Gammon of Muddiford, and they had three sons. Later in life, George made a living as a rabbit trapper, just as his father had before him. Harold Hopkins remembered that sometimes George would go out on Exmoor in the summer and wouldn't be seen again until December.

Lou's father Jack Spear owned no. 5, one of the middle cottages, which housed his mother Martha and later his mother in law Emily Tamlyn. He bought the cottage for £50 and sold it a few years later in 1948 for £250 to Mr Goss, a fair return on investment!

Above: George is pictured later in life, receiving a special award for his military service.

Above: *Prixford Cottages*, c.1930s.

Front Left: Charlie Coats & Ernest Gammon   Behind horse: George Coats & Fred Parkhouse
Lady at front door: Emily Coats (nee Parkin)   Lady in black dress: Olive Richards (nee Parkin)

Reproduced with kind permission of Mr S Knight, RL Knight Photographers.

Muddiford & Milltown

Sunnybank in Muddiford has always been home to Peter Gammon. Born in 1930, Peter was the the fifth son of Stanley (b.1897) and Ivy (b.1900, nee Parkin) and one of eight children. His four older brothers were widely known by their nicknames: John '*Cherry*', Kenneth '*Steve*', Ron '*Skiv*', Walter '*Goosey*', while Peter was known as '*Bronco*'. His sisters were Joyce, Sheila and Margaret. Reuben Tamlyn told Peter that *Sunnybank* was built in the 1920s, because he remembered watching the builders at work when he walked to school as a boy.

Above: The Gammon Family, c.1920s.
Back row: First left - Uncle Eddie Gammon, Second left - Granfer Alf Gammon, Fourth left – Ivy Gammon. Back row: First right – Uncle Ern Gammon, Second Right – Aunty Maud Gammon; Third right – Granny Ellen Gammon. Front row: Stanley Gammon.

Peter's earliest and fondest memories are of spending all the time he possibly could with farmers, especially Herbert and Archie Pugsley. He was allowed to lead the horse during ploughing and remembers taking a ferret out to go hunting for rabbits which they'd sell for ten pence a piece to a man who sent them up to London. Peter always enjoyed helping with farm work, especially collecting sheaths to make stooks at harvest time and winding the handle of the machine that chopped the mangolds for feeding the cows.

He did try milking once but chuckles at the memory, as he really wasn't too good at it! Peter remembers that during the Second World War, the older boys at school were allowed twenty-one half days off each year to help the farmers with jobs like potato picking and harvesting. More often than not they would take the whole day and in return they would receive a good meal and a few shillings in wages.

Above: Peter Gammon, c.1936.

Peter remembers on some occasions Herbert Pugsley would come by the school at lunchtimes on his bicycle, to let him know he'd be up at Metcombe that evening. Rather than going home after school, as he should, Peter would wander off to Metcombe where Herbert would be waiting for him to go rabbit trapping. It was often dark by the time they made their way home, with Peter riding on the crossbars of Herbert's bicycle. Arriving home late often resulted in him receiving a few hidings but it never deterred him from doing it again!

Peter's best friends were Alan Smith, Bill Jenkins and Cecil Gammon, and one of their favourite pastimes was to meet up at one of the Pugsleys' sheds to play cards by candlelight. On Saturdays they used to go down to the stream to catch brown trout. They would reach under a stone to tickle the trouts' tummies and then they could trap them in their hands. Peter remembers his mother being pleased when he brought a trout home as it would make a meal for the family, though Peter never enjoyed the taste particularly. Tickling or 'groping for trout' was a longstanding tradition in Muddiford, practiced by several generations who would boast of catching up to sixty within three days. The boys used to get up to all sorts of tricks. Once they tied together the shoelaces of a man called Mr Gammon from Milltown (no relation) who was drunk, and had fallen asleep in the lane! Another favourite trick was to put a drawing pin above the window and attach a piece of string with a stone to the end. Then they would cross over the road and pull the string to make a tapping sound at the window, startling the poor unsuspecting person inside who could not understand where the noise was coming from. They were chased off on more than one occasion!

All of the Gammon children made the long walk to school and back twice each day, because they also came home for lunch. Peter remembers the teachers included Miss Ashton, Mr Chugg from Ilfracombe and Miss Parkhouse. Mr Chugg would use the cane without much provocation and just failing to do as they were told would result in a sharp smack on the palm. Miss Parkhouse would also use the cane, but had another more painful habit of sticking her thumb in their ribs. Peter recalled that the teachers always maintained a strictly formal relationship with the children, there was not much fun or laughter in the classroom.

Every Sunday Peter and his brothers and sisters had to trek across the fields to the church room at Guineaford for Sunday school. Occasionally a few of them would be rebellious if they didn't feel like going and would hide in an old shed near *Crockers*. They would keep a careful look out for the others returning home afterwards, so they knew when to arrive back home! The Sunday school treat would be a walk from Marwood Hill, down the track through to Lee Woods, then on to *Lee House* where they'd be given a nice tea. Sometimes they'd have a day-school treat, which usually involved travelling by bus to Woolacombe sands.

While Peter was at school the Second World War broke out. He remembers having to take his gas mask everywhere which didn't trouble him, although he felt quite frightened by the drone of German planes overhead as they made their way to bomb Swansea. The wooden Mission Church in Lower Muddiford became the base for the Home Guard, which was led by Captain Gladwell. Members included Peter's older brother Walter, Henry Balment, Reuben Tamlyn and Jack Rashley. On Sundays, the Home Guard used to have shooting practice at the rifle range in the field opposite *Sunnybank*, giving Peter and the other boys a fine view of all the activity.

A tragedy befell the Gammon family in April 1941, when Peter's father Stanley was injured in a traffic accident and died the next day at the North Devon Infirmary aged just forty-four years old. He had been working at the aerodrome and on cycling home in the dark one evening he was hit by a motorcar. Ivy was left to raise the young family alone and Peter, then aged eleven, had to take on additional duties at home to help their mother. One of his jobs was to take a sack and an old bicycle with no tyres and cycle up the hill to gather sticks and twigs for kindling. The children also had to help with the gardening as they were dependent upon the vegetables they grew.

Peter's eldest brother John joined the army and went to fight in the Middle East, where he was shot in the hand. Later in life he became a builder, and once fell off some scaffolding during the demolition of the old Woolworths store in Barnstaple, breaking his back. Every fortnight Peter went to see John in hospital at Stoke Mandeville, where he underwent significant treatment. Second eldest brother Ken also fought in the war, driving a 'Duck' amphibious vehicle in the Normandy landings.

Peter recalls that there was no shortage of characters in Marwood as he was growing up. One of those he remembers was Ida Dobbs, mentioned earlier in this chapter, who was renowned for her eccentric ways. Her hedges were often in need of repair or cutting back and sometimes there were so many gaps in them that the livestock could wander freely in and out of the fields and lanes with no need for a gate. One night Peter's brother Ron and his pal Jim Lethaby had been to the *Ring O' Bells* in Prixford for a drink. By the time they decided to leave, it was dark outside and they mounted their motorbike and set off for home. To their surprise, they drove right into one of Ida's cows standing in the middle of the lane, throwing them both off the bike. Both men were lucky to receive only minor bruises, Evidently the cow survived, though it was somewhat dazed!

Charlie Lethaby farmed at Mill Court near to Milltown Bridge where sometimes the boys would meet up. If they misbehaved, Charlie would come down and threaten to dunk their heads in the stream! Hannah Watts ran the post office and store and would open up at any time if you wanted a loaf of bread. It wasn't unusual to see the odd mouse running along the shelf there as they always had a problem with them.

At one time there was a petrol pump at the *New Inn* (now the *Muddiford Inn*) and local gardener Sam Coats often served fuel to the motorists. He was sometimes a bit worse for wear after a few drinks at the inn and would be seen puffing away on his pipe, even whilst pumping the petrol, never realising the danger he was in! He used to live at Little Silver and would ride a pony to the Inn and tie it up round the back. Sometimes when he was leaving, he would try and mount the pony, climbing up one side and falling straight off the other, because he had consumed a few too many ciders. The pony would happily trot off home and wait for him at Little Silver.

Peter left school in 1944 aged fourteen, initially working for four years as a gardener until he was called up for national service in Malta. On his return he worked as a builder for a year before joining the South West Electricity Board where he remained for forty-one years until his retirement.

Above: Peter Gammon c.1950.

As part of his work Peter travelled all around North Devon from Winkleigh to Bideford, Merton, Ilfracombe and Combe Martin and it was through his travels that he met his wife Margaret who was working at a maternity wing in Ilfracombe. They married in 1954 and while Peter had spent his early years living in no. 1 *Sunnybank*, the couple were then able to move into no. 2 where they have lived ever since.

Lower Muddiford, c.1930s.
Reproduced with kind permission of Mr S Knight, RL Knight Photographers.

The Tamlyns - The property named *Downlyn* merges the surnames of former occupants Reuben Tamlyn (b.1913) and his wife Olive (b.1915, nee Down). Reuben was the youngest son of Richard and Alice (nee Harris), and his older siblings were Alice (b.1902), Christina (b.1904), Herbert (b.1909) and Alfred (b.1911). In the early 1900s the family lived at *Kennacott Farm*, where Richard was horseman for John Alford, and later they moved to *Rose Cottage*, Muddiford.

Reuben married Olive in 1939, settling in Muddiford, where he became the local carpenter, wheelwright and undertaker. More about his work can be found in Chapter Three.

Right: Alice, Reuben, Christina, and grand-daughters Winnie and Betty at *Rose Cottage*, c.1935.

Above: Reuben & Olive c.1993.

The Lynch Family - It may not be widely known that the North Devon Athenaeum holds the memoirs of former Muddiford resident, William Lynch (1905-1996) which provide a heart-warming insight into village affairs in the early twentieth century. It is crammed with references to local characters, including his own family members and would no doubt delight the lifelong inhabitants of Muddiford, especially his relatives who still live there.

William lived in one of the old thatch cottages that were built into the rock opposite the chapel. He was the third son of Thomas and Grace Lynch and nephew of Hannah and Charlie Watts who used to run the Muddiford post office. He fondly described spending time with Hannah, who would sit and talk to him about 'the old days'. She once spoke of the iron mines that were up at Westgate farm towards Viveham, where miners once tunnelled so close to the kitchen floor that they could hear the farmer's wife chopping potatoes. Evidently a man named Jack Gould who once farmed there, said the tunnelling accounted for the yard caving in just below the kitchen window! On another occasion, the ground collapsed near Viveham woods, dropping about twenty feet and taking a cow with it. There were also copper mines in Whitehall and an old packhorse trail used to cross the fields and hills from the mines over to Blakewell.

In the 1920s, there were many travelling salesmen regularly visiting the area to sell their wares and services. There was Mr Gillard, the mobile draper who would sell clothes and make suits; the weekly visits of Mr Elliot the butcher, Mr John Ashton the grocer and 'Cock Robins' the baker and also Mr Widlake, with his covered van and horse, who sold groceries, paraffin and sweets. Some came in their horse and traps bringing strawberries from Combe Martin and mazard cherries from Landkey.

There were many characters in Muddiford and Milltown, trading as carpenters, masons, cobblers, tailors, labourers and blacksmiths. Times were hard though with many struggling to make a living, and William's family would live on two or three rabbits a week, and lots of bread puddings. Sometimes if they were very short of money, his mother would send him down to Harry Beard's mill in Plaistow for half a bushel of meal for their pig, with a promise to pay the following week. Later in life as he wrote his memoirs, William paused to reflect how life once was compared to the somewhat lavish lifestyles of the late twentieth century. He was still finding it hard to comprehend that ordinary people owned cars, televisions and fridges and could take foreign holidays, yet they still went on strike, always wanting more.

Shortly before the outbreak of the Second World War, William went overseas to Canada where he applied to join the Canadian air force. He found that one of the conditions of entry was to have attended high school and informed the recruiting officer that he had attended Marwood, without elaborating that he had not been educated beyond the age of fourteen, confidently believing they wouldn't check. In his defence he wrote that he would have argued that the parish school was on a hill so technically it was 'high' school! After fighting in Europe during the war, William returned to Canada for several years and then settled back in Britain in 1959.

The Jenkins & The Coats - The Jenkins family lived in one of the cottages opposite the chapel, set back on the hill not far from the Lynch family. Charles Jenkins (b.1893, Ilfracombe) had moved to Marwood in 1896 with his parents and younger sister Martha.

After attending the parish school, he was employed as a horseman, initially for Mr Smyth at Hewish, and later for Mr Turner, who had taken over from the Chapples at Whitefield Barton. On Boxing Day in 1914 he married Lilian (b.1894, East Down), one of eleven children of John and Anna Coats of *Collacott*, although Charles was away for the first years of their married life as he was called up to fight in the First World War. Thankfully he returned safely and the couple went on to have nine children, Ivy, Dorothy, Tom, Fred, Nell, Edie, Bill, Betty and Margaret.

Lilian's younger brother Charlie Coats was known locally as a great character. A jack of all trades, he could turn his hand to rabbit trapping, sheep shearing, digging wells, hedging and all manner of things. Together with his brother Tommy, he would dowse[1] with a hazel stick to find the right spot to dig thirty foot wells by hand, a particularly difficult

Above: Lilian and Charles Jenkins on their wedding day, 1914.

[1] Dowsing - a spiritual method of locating ground water.

task to undertake. Charlie was known for being a highly competent sheep shearer and in 1957 he famously challenged a Barnstaple barber, Fred Edmonds to a race – a gentleman's haircut versus one sheep shear. It turned into a big event which attracted a great crowd and a reporter from the North Devon Journal even turned up. Despite managing to shear the sheep in just three minutes and twenty seconds, Fred completed the haircut within two minutes and thirty-five seconds, winning the challenge.

Above: L-R Tommy, Sam and Charlie Coats, outside the pub in Muddiford c.1960s.

The Pugsleys - Charles Pugsley (1870-1957) worked as a road contractor for several years. Horses and carts belonging to Charles, George Balment and Jack Chapple were used to carry lumps of stone, described as big as loaves of bread. The stone was taken to depots along the road, where men with fourteen pound sledge hammers would kneel on old sacks and crack the stones down to the size of tennis balls for sixpence per cubic yard. Once the stone was broken, it was spread across the road and compacted down by

Above: Charles Pugsley at work c.1930s.

steamrollers. Through his work, Charles accumulated sufficient savings to enable him to take on Milltown Farm as a tenant in circa 1910 and when the farm was put up for sale in August 1920, he managed to meet the asking price and it has remained in the Pugsley family ever since.

In 1893, Charles married Mary Mears, also known as Polly, and they had six children, Fred (b.1896), John (b.1898), Ethel, (b.1900), Archie (b.1906), Herbert (b.1908) and Daisy (b.1911). His many grandchildren remember him as very strict and there was no doubt he was in charge. He was known simply as 'The Boss!'.

Above: Charles & Polly Pugsley, c.1950s.

In December 2010, I had the great pleasure of meeting some of Charles' grandchildren and their cousins who still live in the area, to talk about parish history. This included Pam Chapple, daughter of *Henry Balment and Daisy Pugsley*; Maureen Chugg, daughter of *Fred Pugsley and May Gammon*; Stella Money, daughter of *Thomas Balment and Edith Rook*; Jean Ridd, daughter of *Jack Gammon and Ethel Pugsley* and David Pugsley, son of *Archie Pugsley and Mildred Hunt*. Having grown up together in Marwood they had many wonderful stories to tell about their relatives, local characters, life at school, the Second World War and many other matters. The banter and humour was great to see amongst these lifelong friends.

As youngsters growing up in the parish, the group were adamant that they were never bored. There was no television then but there was always something to do whether it was playing cards, dominos, going to the woods, swinging across the stream, Sunday school, not to mention the various chores they were expected to do to help their parents. As they grew older there were often events at Milltown social club, including dances, dancing classes with Wilf Dunn and his wife and magic lantern[1] or film shows. Once a year the Balment and Pugsley families would have a family day out to the beach at Woolacombe and a charabanc would arrive, drawn by two horses to transport them, with great wads of straw in the back for the children to sit on.

There were many characters in the area in those days. Everyone remembered Mr Singh, the travelling draper who they described as a real gentleman. He would ride out to all the local parishes on his bicycle, calling out 'I've got cotton!' usually balancing two or three large suitcases. If he were invited into the house, Mr Singh would lay out all his wares, materials, tablecloths, tea towels, aprons etc. He was a nice man and a bit of a favourite with the housewives! As mentioned previously by William Lynch, there were other travelling salesmen who would visit regularly, including bakers from Barnstaple, fishmongers from Ilfracombe and Clovelly selling herrings, and Mr William Ashton, the Barnstaple grocer, who would come round to take the orders and deliver the boxes

---

[1] The Magic Lantern was the forerunner of the slide projector, a popular form of entertainment during Victorian times. It began to fall out of fashion during the mid twentieth century.

two days later. It was rarely considered necessary to go into Barnstaple at that time, unless taking goods to sell at the pannier market, and neither was there much need, as long as the travelling salesmen were weaving their way out and around the parishes.

Tramps, perhaps more kindly described as 'drifters', were often seen around the area. In some cases they were veterans of the First World War who had never fully recovered from the traumas they witnessed. Locals did not fear them as they would never cause any harm but would beg for food and shelter. One well known character was called Bill Treble, who used to chat incessantly! Another drifter known as Mr Hyde would often be seen knocking on doors. Mary Pugsley would feed him and let him warm up by the Rayburn, though Jean Ridd can remember the smell becoming worse, the warmer he became! Mr Hyde felt he couldn't cope with living indoors but was genial and grateful for the help he received, even to the point where he would hand over his box of matches to assure the Pugsleys that he would not set fire to the hay rick that he slept in overnight.

Above: Milltown, with George Balment in the foreground, c.1930s.

Life in Muddiford & Milltown (1943)

And I have come to tell you folk
The news that's come to me,
About the Balments, Smiths and Borns
And Charlie Lethaby.

Perhaps you may remember
We once talked of Charlie's swine,
The patches on the washing
That hung on the garden line.

The perfume from old Charlie's pigs
How they ate poor Pugsley's wheat,
The sacks and all they ate the lot
Cos he kept 'em short of meat.

How Arthur Coats his grub missed when
His sister's young man came to tea,
How Doris fed her sweetheart full
But for Arthur no pity had she.

I've seen 'em knitting jumpers home
I've smelt 'em frying kippers,
But here the Marwood women are
Quite busy making slippers.

There's Kathy Balment's got the craze
There's Alice Jenkins now,
With Alice Smith they go home late
And what a fearful row.

They wake the folks who've gone to bed
In the middle of the night,
Their tongues they clatter such a rate
You'd think the lot were light.

Young David Pugsley breeches wears
He looks just like a farmer,
I asked him why he said because,
They keeps me bottom warmer.

Now there I quite forgot about
Old Charlie Lethaby,
His missus lost him t'other night
And wailed "Oh where is he?"

Her took the lantern went out round
The shippen and the stable,
Her searched the pig house and the barn
And under kitchen table.

But he was gone, he wadn't there
He'd vanished 'pon my word,
When suddenly an awful noise
Poor Charlie's missus yeard.

The house fair shook, the ceilings cracked
Seemed like an awful raid,
T'was up the stairs, t'was in the house
T'was just above her head.

Her knees they shaked, her heart went
thump, her yeard an awful roaring
Her creeped upstairs, looked in the bed,
And there was Charlie snoring.

A ghost, a ghost! George Balment yelled
And Herbert's knees sagged fast.
He thought the world had all gone mad
His brain was gone at last.

Says Blinker, shaking 'shall I shoot'
I think I'll wait a bit,
If I should shoot an angel I
Don't know where I should get.

For when I die and go beyond
St Peter, he might say,
You shot an angel, Blinker lad,
So you'll go below today.

Bill Lock is worried 'bout his meat
The folks say t'is too tough,
He thinks t'is hard lines Marwood folk
Should treat him quite so rough.

But Mary not to be outdone
To the telephone she runned,
Phoned up the folks at Bideford
And said her'd got the wind.

And the tale of Hilary Born is sad
She was playing with the fowls,
When a savage stag bird at her flew
And attracted by her howls

Mrs Lethaby to the rescue ran
Cocked one leg o'er the wire,
And couldn't get further back or fore
Cos her couldn't cock 'em higher.

There's an Indian pedlar comes around
A favourite of Kathleen,
Who never fails her a call to pay
When to Marwood he has been.

Our friend the pedlar, as you know
In town, has got a harem,
So as he'd not the pants she'd like
Next time she went to Barum.

By invitation Kathleen called
Romantic as you see,
And her turbaned host invited her
To stop and have some tea.

The curtain then it dropped for I
No further news have got,
Tho' Kathleen very probably
Could tell you quite a lot.

John Born and Winnie, my congrats
A son to them is born,
And this is natural you see
As rose upon a thorn.

For John is born and so is mum
They're both Born are they not,
The baby's born, all Borns are born
Us all was born - eh what!

Infectious too this born job is
T'is fact t'is not a myth,
Next door they caught it didn't they
Is that not so Frank Smith?

They copied John and Winnie's plan
And then to their great joy,
The Doctor came with his black bag
And inside a fine great boy.

There's Edie Jenkins she goes out
At nights with her true dear,
No hot water bottle does she need
With Private Kenneth Spear.

And as for Private Allen Smith
His heart is full of love,
For every damsel in the place
Is his angel from above.

Kathleen and Herbert so I'm told
Are courting strong as ever,
On weekday nights t'is just one kiss
But Sunday nights t'is seven.

And when from Chapel they come out
Old Herbert he can't wait,
Her's a bit behind but goes right on
And sits 'pon top a gate.

Murder in Milltown

The only recorded murder in Marwood in the last two centuries occurred at Milltown Bridge in September 1837. The case was heard in March 1838 at Exeter Crown Court and a comprehensive report of the hearing was printed in the North Devon Journal. As the hearing commenced, Mr Justice Bosanquet addressed the Grand Jury requesting their particular attention to this case, it being the wilful murder of a young child. He asked them to consider whether it was malicious, but to bear in mind 'of the particular motives which may in such a case have induced the prisoner to commit the offence, it was not for them to judge. They could not pry into the hearts of men – they would judge by evidence'. (North Devon Journal, March 26 1838).

During the trial, which lasted three hours, it emerged that the accused, forty year old Thomas Harper was a man of questionable sanity, described by locals as having been in the area for around two years and having a habit of laying about in linhays. When called to give evidence, local mason John Gubb told that on the morning of September 14 1837, Harper had been busy sawing marble near the bridge. John was not aware of the events leading up to the crime, but he did witness Harper stand up and swing his sharp iron shovel, striking four year old Johnny May on the forehead, causing him to fall flat on his back. As John approached, Harper remained calm, muttering to himself and made no attempt to escape.

Another witness, mason John Reed also stated that he knew Harper, who made a living from sawing marble, and was aware that he had dug out a place in Shirwell that he had thatched, and would lay beneath on some hay. John had been working near to the scene of the crime and had noticed several young children playing nearby. He was first made aware of the trouble when a young boy ran to him to say his friend was bleeding, and when John looked up he saw Harper dealing several blows to Johnny May. He immediately ran over and took Harper into custody and John Gubb's son took the shovel from him.

John Gubb junior corroborated everything that his father and John Reed had earlier said in their witness statements, adding that he knew that Harper had also been working for local farmers digging up furze brakes and breaking stones. John junior recalled that shortly before 11 o'clock that day, he heard another little boy cry out 'look to little Johnny May's head, how its bleeding'. He raced to the scene with the other men to find Harper standing above Johnny with shovel in hand, as John Reed exclaimed 'Tom thees't killed the child!'. Harper made no attempt to leave and appeared calm.

Barnstaple surgeon William Parker attended to the child who was not killed instantly, but had suffered several contused wounds, and at least three fractures to the skull. Johnny died four days later on September 18; the cause of death attributed to the wounds received to his head. Based on the witness testimonies, the Turnkey at the County Jail and a fellow prisoner, the Journal reported that it was clear that neither the judge nor the jury were in any doubt that the accused had lost control of his mind. He was declared insane and ordered to be kept in confinement at Her Majesty's pleasure.

It must have been a particularly traumatic time for the May family of Milltown, as their second eldest daughter Mary had died just six months earlier in March 1837 at the age of five. Thankfully their remaining daughter Eliza later married local farmer William Gammon and remained in the parish, living at Old Burland; their son Thomas became a shoemaker and lived with his family in Newport, Wales and their youngest son William, who was just eight weeks old at the time of Johnny's death, became a farm labourer like his father and settled with his wife and children in Cornwall.

Above: Young boys used to gather on Milltown Bridge in
the early twentieth century.

Varley

Christine Watts (nee Harris) descends from families who have lived and worked in Marwood particularly Kings Heanton, Varley and Middle Marwood, for hundreds of years. Her direct ancestors are outlined below:

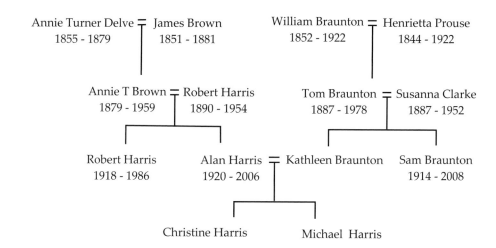

Annie Turner Delve = James Brown
1855 - 1879   1851 - 1881

William Braunton = Henrietta Prouse
1852 - 1922   1844 - 1922

Annie T Brown = Robert Harris
1879 - 1959   1890 - 1954

Tom Braunton = Susanna Clarke
1887 - 1978   1887 - 1952

Robert Harris   Alan Harris = Kathleen Braunton   Sam Braunton
1918 - 1986   1920 - 2006   1914 - 2008

Christine Harris   Michael Harris

Christine's paternal great-grandfather, James Brown was born in West Ashford. Soon afterwards his family moved to Marwood, where James and his brothers Bill, Jack and Thomas, attended the Church school in Guineaford. In the early 1870s, James worked as a farm labourer in Beara Charter and his future wife Annie Turner Delve was a farm servant at George Richards' farm in Middle Marwood. They were married in 1876, making their home in Guineaford, where their first child John was born. Tragically, Annie died while giving birth to their second child, a daughter – who was later named after her mother.

James and his two young children went to live with his parents, William and Elizabeth Brown, and sister Ellen, who had settled at Varley, where William was a farm worker. As if one tragedy wasn't enough for the family to bear, James, who was diabetic, a condition that had forced him to leave the marines, earlier in his working life, is believed to have slipped into a coma and drowned in a stream in Kings Heanton in 1882.

The children remained with James' parents and his sister Ellen, spending their formative years at Varley. John then left to join the Metropolitan police in London, while Annie remained with her aunt Ellen. The pair began a dressmaking business and further details of their work can be found in Chapter Three.

In the summer of 1915, Annie married Robert Harris, a fine stonemason, originally from Swimbridge. He had been employed by the Gammons in Muddiford, and one of his earliest jobs was to build a private house at Broomhill.

He had got as far as building the roof when the First World War broke out, and although somewhat frustrated by this interruption, he joined up and was sent to fight in Mesopotamia (Iraq), returning to Marwood after the war.

Robert and Annie rented a cottage at Varley from Alfred Kelly, where their two sons Robert junior and Alan were born. They later purchased *Varley Cottage* in 1927, previously owned by stonemason, Arthur Skinner. Robert and Annie went on to live at Varley until 1949.

Above:
Annie Turner Harris
c.1920.

Above: This cottage in Varley was home to the Harris family in the early twentieth century.

Youngest son Alan Harris first met his future bride Kathleen Braunton at the parish celebrations for the coronation of King George VI in May 1937, at nearby Swindon Down. They were temporarily apart whilst Alan had to fight in the Second World War but the pair reunited on his return, and married in 1946. At first they lived at Varley with their young children Christine and Michael, and then in 1950, Alan bought the old disused Wesleyan chapel on the border between Marwood and Bittadon, converting it into living accommodation which became the family home between 1952 and 1959. Alan also owned the nearby quarry called Little Silver.

The quarry was called Little Silver because of the iron pyrites in the stone which made it glisten like silver. There were once three cottages at Little Silver, the most southerly has since been demolished.

After the war, Robert senior and his two sons established a hugely successful building firm, Harris & Sons, who at one point employed in the region of eight hundred builders, many of them local Marwood men. Today there are many, many properties in the North Devon area, built by the family, especially within the parish. Later, younger son Alan started a separate construction business called Harris & Reed at Braunton, which was also a thriving enterprise.

Above: Alan and Kathleen's wedding, 1946.

Varley Farm

Richard Kelly (1777-1864) was farming at Varley from as early as 1815, evidenced by the Marwood Baptism Records, and later in life he was assisted by sons Thomas (1817-1908) and Robert[1] (1825-1913) until the early 1850s. In 1856, a notice appeared in the North Devon Journal announcing that Varley Farm, then also in the occupation of the proprietor, John Kelly, was to be let. John was Richard's oldest son and had previously farmed at Blakewell, however his decision to let the farm may have been prompted by a couple of matters. One may have been the imminent retirement of his father, then aged seventy-nine, and the other may have been the death of Thomas' wife Sarah in 1855. The property was described at the time as having seventy acres of very productive arable and pasture land with good farm buildings and 'thrashing' machine included.

From 1861 until 1877, Robert Moore and William Bater were tenant farmers at Varley, with seventy acres each. By 1878, White's Trade Directory shows that William Bater had left, and been replaced by Charles Kelly, youngest brother of John Kelly. Charles, having earlier tried his hand at running a public house, the *Ring O' Bells*, Prixford, returned to his family homestead to farm seventy acres, employing William Brown,

---

[1] Thomas Kelly was father of Fred Kelly well known farmer of Guineaford, and Robert Kelly, Fred's uncle, becomes his father in law when Fred marries his cousin Eliza in 1906.

Christine's great-great-grandfather, as a labourer. Charles farmed at Varley until his death in 1905, and was succeeded by his sons Alfred and Ernest. In March 1918 the freehold of the farm, then ninety-two acres, was put up for sale, and Alfred as sitting tenant, purchased it for the princely sum of £2,675.

Alfred became firm friends of Christine's grandparents, Robert and Annie Harris, and their two sons. During the Second World War when youngest son Alan was away fighting in North Africa, Annie nursed Alfred Kelly when he became very ill with throat cancer. He eventually had to go to the old workhouse building on Alexandra Road in Barnstaple. For many, this might seem to have been a horrible place to spend his remaining days, but the reality was that by the 1930s it had become a convalescence hospital, while the North Devon Infirmary was used for emergency or critical treatment. Alfred died on October 7 1942 aged seventy-nine years, and in July 1948, his farm at Varley was sold at auction to Arthur C Watts for the sum of £2,300.

Above: Members of the Kelly family at Varley, circa late nineteenth century.

Middle Marwood

The hamlet of Middle Marwood has an extremely interesting history, and despite significant research, there are still many mysteries to be solved. Until the mid nineteenth century there were various small settlements between the hamlet and nearby Whitehall, including those at Mare, Rock and Rattle Row. Early census records show that farm workers lived there, probably in very primitive dwellings, but close enough to the neighbouring farms of *Stepps, Bowen, Hordens*, Townridden Barton and Whitehall Mill, where they might have hoped to find employment. These settlements are scarcely mentioned after the 1850s, so it is likely that the old cottages were left to become derelict. Keen historian Christine Watts knows the whereabouts of these sites and can point them out along the roadside on the lane between Middle Marwood and Whitehall. Now all completely overgrown, archaeologists would delight in carrying out excavations to discover their hidden past. There were other settlements like this in secluded spots within the parish, including No Man's Land, near to the turning into Whiddon Lane, where several cottages once stood, and cottages built on wasteland that could be claimed. An example of this is a small plot of land in the verge, by the turning to Brian Balment's Dairy Farm. A small dwelling once stood there and Christine can remember seeing the remains of the old cottage garden with its gooseberry bushes that stubbornly continued to grow.

Christine's maternal ancestors first came to Middle Marwood in 1913 with the arrival of her grandparents Tom Braunton (originally from Tawstock) and Susanna Clarke. They initially rented a cottage opposite *Stepps Farm*, but as they were keen to buy land of their own, they rented in Ashford for a few years until 1918, when they were able to return to the hamlet. Christine's uncle, Sam Braunton (1914-2008), could remember the day the family moved back to Middle Marwood, riding at the back of a horse and cart on an orange box, alongside his younger sister Kathleen (Christine's mother), who was just a toddler at the time. Thomas had purchased some land and at first rented, then later bought Hordens' Cottage, now known as *Alderhurst*, which was adjacent to the dame school. In 1920, he bought another field nearby, previously owned by Fred Kelly and over the following years, Thomas patiently built up his smallholding, buying one field at a time, and selling his produce at the Barnstaple pannier market.

Other members of the Braunton family soon joined Tom and Susanna in Marwood. Tom's parents, William, a lay preacher, and Henrietta, spent their latter years at *Primrose Cottage*, Middle Marwood. His son Sam and wife Elsie (nee Lovering) settled in the hamlet, as well as his sister Kate and her husband, Tom Ward. Tom's brothers Ben and Jack Braunton farmed close by in Patsford and Metcombe.

Above:
Kathleen and
bicycle in Middle
Marwood, c.1920s.

Above:
Kathleen and Tom
c.1930s.

Above:
Sam and Elsie
Braunton.

Below:
Kathleen.

Above:
Susanna Braunton
in her heyday.

Above:
The dashing young
Tom Braunton.

When William and Henrietta died in 1922, *Primrose Cottage* was then occupied by Mr Down, followed by Mr Hammond and then Mr Mead, who left it to Gilbert Welch in his will. Gilbert was a smallholder at *Bowen Farm*, (previously run by his father George for many years).

Above: Haymaking – c.1920s. Gilbert Welch is standing on the cart; below left is Tom Braunton and right, George Chapple, pitchforks in hand.

The Isaacs farmed at *Stepps* in Middle Marwood between 1891 and 1911. They were a devout Christian family and the mainstay of the chapel for years. James (b.1844) the son of a Burrington farmer, married Elizabeth Joslin of Instow in 1868, and took on several labouring jobs to support his rapidly growing family. In the mid 1890s he purchased *Stepps*, where the family remained until oldest son William had married, at which point he was left to run the farm, while James, Elizabeth and their nine remaining children moved on to run Lilly Farm in Goodleigh.

William and his wife Lucy only stayed in the hamlet for about four years until 1902 before heading off to take a new farm in Buckland Brewer, leaving *Stepps* to be run by his younger brother Thomas and wife Annie. One of their sons, Tommy Isaac junior was born at *Stepps* in December 1902, and locals such as Andrew Chapple remember being told the miraculous tale of his birth. It seems that when Tommy was born he didn't make a sound or move a muscle, and it was immediately assumed that he was stillborn. The family laid him in an airing cupboard and left the body there whilst they went for help, but such a shock they had when they returned a short time later, to find Tommy rolling around and crying! It seems this wasn't the only scrape in which Tommy found himself.

Kathleen Harris remembers another tale concerning Tommy and an elderly lady named Harriet Down (1820-1911) who used to live in what is now known as *Whitehall Cottage*, formerly a chapel-of-ease with living quarters on the first floor. On one occasion young Tommy was passing by and Harriet offered him a cup of cider, which he readily drank. He was later found fast asleep in a hedge, much to the displeasure of his parents!

Thomas and Annie Isaac remained in Middle Marwood until 1913, when they left to start a butchers shop on Boutport Street in Barnstaple.

The new arrival at *Stepps Farm* was George Chapple, who had been farming with his family at Whitefield Barton. He purchased the farm at auction for £1,850 in July 1913, the lot being described as very superior meadow, pasture and arable lands.

Longpiece

Above: Louisa Spear outside Longpiece cottages, c.1950s.

The settlement of Longpiece was formerly known as Cross Cottages until the mid twentieth century; a terrace of three properties located on Longpiece hill, at the point where the road forks left towards Whitehall. Census records show that between the 1840s and 1890s, there were successive generations of a family called Radford living there, who were coopers[1] by trade. Over the years, the other cottages were occupied by a combination of farm workers and tradesmen including shoemakers (Hodge and Corney) and a thatcher (Gratton).

---

[1] Coopers made or repaired casks and barrels.

In the 1950s, local farmer William Spear (1891-1985) and his wife Louisa (nee Hewitt) settled at Longpiece.

Above: William Spear hard at work in the fields, c.1930s.

William married Louisa in 1915, the daughter of Fred and Ellen Hewitt of Knowle Water, Heanton Punchardon. Prior to her marriage she had been in service with a clergyman and his family in Union Terrace, Barnstaple. They had four children, Fred (b.1916), Esther (b.1917), Ruth (b.1922) and Alfred (b.1927), and for some years they lived at Seymour Villas in Ilfracombe where William built a house, before settling at Longpiece.

Above: The Spears at Longpiece, with a Ford Popular, c.1950s.

Whiddon

Members of the Balment family have lived in Whiddon for around one hundred years. George H Balment (b.1874, Milltown) initially worked as a road contractor along with his father, and Charles Pugsley, however shortly after marrying Bessie Gliddon in 1898, he took on Whiddon Farm, which has remained in the Balment family ever since. Pauline Stentiford remembers being told about her grandparents George and Bessie when they were first dating. Romantic George would write love letters to Bessie, however on one occasion he arranged to meet her at Pilton Bridge but stood her up at the last minute to go rabbiting! He was lucky to get a second chance!

George and Bessie had six sons, Robert (b.1900), Mervyn (b.1903), Walter Thomas (b.1904), William (b.1908), George Henry (b.1911) and Albert John (b.1914) and two daughters Winifred (b.1907) and Kathleen (b.1913), though tragically Winifred and William died in December 1912 within days of each other, of diphtheria and laryngitis.

Above: The Balment Family of Whiddon, c.1920s.
Back Row L-R: Thomas, Robert and Mervyn.
Middle Row L-R: George, Bessie.
Front Row L-R: George Henry, Kathleen and John.

Youngest son John eventually took over the running of Whiddon Farm, along with his wife Charlotte (nee Corney). From a young age, their children Brian and Pauline were assigned their own chores including helping their dad with milking cows, picking and chopping mangolds, collecting eggs - a job that Pauline particularly hated and 'tettie' digging. Evidently Brian took to farming, having later succeeded his father farming at Whiddon and Townridden.

Townridden

The small hamlet of Townridden was known as Marwood Barton until the mid nineteenth century. Also known locally as Old Marwood Mill, the farmstead originally formed part of the estate owned by the Leys of *Lee House*. This is evidenced by property deeds of 1772, which state that Marwood Barton included land known as The Great Square Close, The Little Square Close, The Barn Close, The Ley Close, Adderwill, Higher Ground, New Close, The East Church Parke, The West Church Parke and No Man's Land. All of the aforementioned plots were later referenced under the name of Townridden Barton in the 1843 Tithe apportionments, then owned by Henry Ley of *Lee House* and occupied by the Baments, a family of farmers who had been tenants there since the late eighteenth century.

After the Baments left in the late 1850s, a succession of farmers from surrounding parishes including West Down and Berrynarbor became short-term tenants over the years. In April 1899, Frederick Parkhouse, previously at Shirwell, became the new tenant of Townridden under unusual circumstances, having exchanged farms with his brother Will. In the early 1920s, Frederick was succeeded by new owner Joshua Joslin, whose son Thomas managed the farm from 1930. In January 1936, Thomas employed the young Harold Hopkins to work on his farm, for four shillings per week.

Above: Thomas Joslin married Gladys Thorne in 1930 and farmed at Townridden for many years, where they raised their family. The wedding gown was made by Ellen Brown and Annie Turner Brown of Varley. Gladys was a keen member of Marwood Women's Institute for years and a regular host of whist drives and meetings.

Lee House

Lee House is a fine stone-built manor house with Elizabethan origins, though the estate itself dates back to the thirteenth century. The Thorne family were resident until the early eighteenth century, when the estate passed to the Leys through the death of John Thorne, Gentleman, whose heiress daughter Elizabeth was married to George Ley Esq.

Simply travelling down the mile long driveway to *Lee House* can be breathtaking. Once the brow of the hill has been climbed, the reward is an unbroken view of the landscape with Braunton Burrows in the distance, and the glistening sea beyond. It is not hard to imagine yourself in days gone by, sitting in an elaborate horse drawn carriage, descending the winding drive which leads to the grand manor house. Lush green scenery as far as the eye can see; a view that can scarcely have changed over the centuries … that is, until the arrival of several enormous wind turbines in 2011.

Lee House has long wings projecting at right angles forming a three-sided courtyard entrance, and on approach, one immediately senses its history and wonders at the lifestyle of the gentry who made this their home.

North Devon Athenaeum keeps a small handbill within its archives, which gives a fascinating insight into the luxurious interior of the property. It lists a selection of household goods and items of furniture that were due to be sold at auction on March 6 1804, including three four-poster beds, mahogany chests and chairs with hair and leather bottoms, some handsome prints and good paintings.

Left: Notice archived at North Devon Athenaeum B87-01-66.

To be SOLD by Auction,

At LEE-HOUSE,

In the Parish of MARWOOD,

PART OF THE

HOUSEHOLD GOODS

AND

FURNITURE,

CONSISTING OF

Three Four-Post and one Tent Bedsteads, with Linen and Check Furniture, Feather Beds and Bolsters; Mahogany Chests of Drawers, Bason-Stands and Night-Stools; Pier and Swing Looking-Glasses; a Set of Mahogany Dining and Card Tables; three dozen Mahogany Chairs with Hair and Leather Bottoms, Brass Nailed; an easy Chair which occasionally forms a Bed; Mahogany Camp Chairs and Tables; some handsome Prints and good Paintings.

The Sale will commence on Tuesday the 6th. Day of March next, precisely at three o'Clock in the Afternoon.

N. B. The Furniture may be viewed the Day previous to the Sale.

J. CHAMBERLIN, Auctioneer.

Dated, February 13th. 1804.

In her book *Not Many Years Ago – Memories of My Life* (1881) Emma Augusta Bridges describes *Lee House* as 'a weird, melancholy place' with its 'well-stocked' wall gardens, copse wood and plantations. The two wings of the mansion housed the domestic offices and stables, and the main living quarters were described as lacking the type of decoration expected for such a grand property. While Miss Bridges described the furniture as 'scant and shabby', and walls adorned with portraits of ancestors in naval or military uniforms in much the same condition as the furniture, she affectionately described the Leys as providing a warm welcome for all guests, with good food and fine wine.

The first census of 1841 records the head of the household as George Ley (b.1811), a gentleman of independent means, residing with his brother Francis (b.1821), Naval officer, and sister Elizabeth (b.1816), also of independent means. As well as the obligatory three house servants and two farm labourers, a cousin of the Leys, John Sampson (b.1806, Colyton) was also visiting. George left Marwood to join the Navy, leaving his younger brother Henry (b.1812) to lead the household, as a gentleman farmer, and he was joined by older sister Mary Ann (b.1809).

In June 1856, the North Devon Journal-Herald reported the tragic news that George shot himself at the house. The article stated:

> By one of those events so appalling to human nature, but which it is greatly to be lamented are of so frequent recurrence, the respectable family of Lee House, are involved in the deepest distress; George Ley Esq., the proprietor of the Mansion, has for some time past betrayed considerable aberrations of mind, and it is rumoured that he has more than once before attempted self-destruction.
>
> Between the hours of eight and nine o'clock on Tuesday morning he retired into the drawing room, from whence a report was soon after heard of the discharge of firearms; his son, in the most utmost alarm, instantly ran into the room, where a most horrid spectacle presented itself to his view, his father lay extended on the floor, a breathless corpse.
>
> Source: North Devon Journal-Herald, June 1856.

After George's death, his son Francis inherited the property, and became known as a great socialite, rarely without an invitation to some dinner, dance, whist table or picnic. Sadly at the age of forty, he broke his neck and died following a hunting accident, forcing the sale of the house and land. A notice of the auction was placed in national newspaper *The Times* in August 1874, revealing the full extent of the estate which then included Prixford Barton, Townridden and hundreds of acres of land.

MESSRS. MANNING and SON are instructed to SELL by AUCTION, at the Golden Lion Hotel, Barnstaple, on Friday, 11th September, 1874, at 4 o'clock precisely, in one lot, the valuable FREEHOLD ESTATE known as the Lee Estate, comprising a modern residence, containing entrance-hall, three reception rooms, 10 bed rooms, and all convenient domestic offices ; stabling, coach-house, and small farm-yard, with paddocks, flower and kitchen gardens, in the occupation of Henry Dene, Esq. A farm called Prixford, with farm-house and set of farm buildings, and 254a. 1r. 37p. of good arable, orchard, and pasture land, in the occupation of Mr. Thomas Western. A farm, called Townridden, with farm-house and set of farm buildings, and 158a. 3r. 31p. of excellent arable, orchard, watered meadow, and grazing land, in the occupation of the representatives of the late Mr. John Alford. Two cottages and several gardens, and 65 acres of wood land. The property is beautifully situate on gentle slopes, possessing very fine views of the river Taw, the Bristol Channell, and a very large expanse of picturesque country, it is well stocked with game, and is particularly attractive to sporting gentlemen, and also well worth the attention of capitalists as an investment. Particulars with plans and conditions of sale, may be obtained of the Auctioneers ; of Messrs. Pearse and Crosse, Solicitors, South Molton ; and of Mr. George Brown, Barnstaple.—Dated Barnstaple, 10th August, 1874.

Source: *The Times*, London, Saturday August 29 1874, price 3d.

Over the years that followed, several affluent families came and went, including the Montagues. John M Montague (1853-1922) and Violet Lind (1866-1930) married in 1886 and spent the early years of their marriage in India, where John was heavily involved in managing railway construction and where their daughters Violet and Marjorie were born. They returned to England at the turn of the century, initially living in Fremington for several years where third daughter Elizabeth was born, before moving to *Lee House* in April 1904 (source: *Marwood Church Monthly*) where two new additions to the family, Joan (b.1905) and Nancy (b.1908) were welcomed. In 1911, the census reveals that two housemaids from Barnstaple attended the family, one cook named Lily Jenkins from Guineaford and also a nursemaid/governess, responsible for the five daughters.

Above: *Lee House* in the early 1900s. This photograph and those below were
among a number given to Sheelagh and Michael Darling
by a descendant of the Montague family.

The Montagues left the Lee Estate to live at Broomhill House, now a hotel, which was built by mason Bob Harris and carpenter, George Worth.

Lee was again put up for sale and an advert was placed in the North Devon Journal in October 1919. The estate was described as a Gentleman's residence, together with excellent walled gardens and pleasure grounds, several closes of pasture and arable land, an excellent wood 'Lee Wood', in all 77 acres. It boasted twelve bedrooms, three WCs, two bathrooms (hot and cold water), entrance hall, dining room, drawing room, morning room, smoke room, library, kitchens, lobby, dairy and storerooms. The outbuildings included stables with stalls for 4 horses, piggeries, cowsheds, poultry sheds, carpenters shop and coach house.

Above: One of the Montague girls in her pony and trap outside *Lee House*.

In 1927, Mrs Burgess bought the property which then had just eight acres of land, with most of the estate having been purchased by local farmers. As the parish celebrated the coronation of King George VI in 1937, Mrs Burgess invited all the Marwood school children to visit *Lee House* for an afternoon tea; a great treat for all involved. The wonderful photograph below captured the event:

Above: Marwood Schoolchildren at *Lee House*, with Reverend Skene and Mrs Burgess, 1937.

In his memoirs, William Lynch of Muddiford mentioned Mrs Burgess who was known for her love of woodwork and carving. William's father Thomas was a carpenter, and in 1923 he did some work for her at *Lee House*, constructing an 'oak' room, with oak frames and sash for each window, made of oak beams reused from an old barn – sawed up by Rawle, Gammon and Baker, timber merchants. At that time, William remembered that his father had gone to Appledore dockyards, where they were breaking up one of the last wooden warships called *HMS Revenge*[1]. He bought the fine old oak balustrade, which they then fitted beneath the handrail of the first floor balcony in the oak room, to the delight of Mrs Burgess. When William did some work at *Lee House* he found an old rapier[2], mysteriously placed on top of a wall under the roof, and he later got the local blacksmith to make the thick end into a chisel. William also reported that he had spotted an old stone on a wall in the central courtyard, engraved with the date 1508.

When Marwood Parish Church was in need of a cupboard for the clergy to hang their surplices, Mrs Burgess donated some carved wooden panels and other pieces of old wood. She requested William Lynch use the pieces to construct a cupboard and this now stands at the west end of the Nave.

In 1946, the Pitts-Tucker family moved to *Lee House*, where they lived for around thirteen years. Mr Pitts-Tucker was a former solicitor, who used to travel into Barnstaple to work, and if the weather was fine, Harold Hopkins remembers he would bring out his old pony and trap. The jingle of the bells could be heard for miles around.

In 1959, Sheelagh and Michael Darling became the new owners and immediately had their hands full with major renovation work to rectify a very primitive domestic environment, featuring an antique stove, a brass copper for boiling water for the laundry, a kitchen without a water supply and a scullery containing the original open hearth with bread oven.

---

[1] HMS Revenge was the 70 gun, 800-horsepower flagship of the Channel Fleet. Launched in 1859, she never engaged in battle but sailed to far flung lands such as North America and the West Indies.

[2] A rapier is a slim, sharply pointed sword; used mainly in the sixteenth and seventeenth centuries. Fashionable with the wealthy, it was often used during duels!

Marwood Hill

Marwood Hill House, known today as *Marwood House,* has a long and colourful history, and like *Lee House,* an entire book could be written about these ancient properties alone. This section concentrates mostly on the occupants of the mid nineteenth to the mid twentieth century.

Prior to the arrival of the Bridges family in 1843, *Marwood Hill House* had been leased by Thomas Downes Esq. It is not known exactly how long he was in residence, however Vestry records of 1827 show that he played an active part in local affairs during his stay, which appears to have been a decade at least. Thomas took the opportunity to exercise his influence at a Vestry meeting in February 1828, when he requested permission to divert the road leading from Marwood lane to the church around the shrubbery in front of his house. This seems to imply that prior to the erection of the existing boundary wall, parishioners would walk close to the front of the property as they made their way to church. The chairman agreed, and later the lane was redirected around the outskirts of the newly built dry stone wall. Shortly before he left, Thomas placed a notice in the North Devon Journal in March 1841 announcing the sale of household furniture, farming stock and other effects, which were to be sold by auction at the premises on March 23 and 24.

A useful insight into the furnishings can be seen in the advert, which seems to all intents and purposes to be a house clearance:

> *In the Dining Room – will be found a handsome mahogany pedestal sideboard; set of eight mahogany chairs, covered with hair; an elegant easy chair, reclining back, spring, stuffed with down cushion; two tables on claws; Turkey carpet, 18ft by 15ft – 3in; Hearth Rug; Fender and Fire Set; large folding screen.*

> *Drawing Room: - an upright Piano-Forte; two Music stools; six solid Rosewood chairs; rosewood couch; round rosewood table; two small tables; Chimney glass in a gilt frame, plate 42in by 34in; excellent Brussels carpet, 22ft by 17ft – 6in; Register Stove; Fender and Fire Set.*

> *Entrance Hall: - two oak tables; four oak chairs' hat and umbrella stands; handsome hall lamp; blue dinner and dessert services; china tea set; cut glass decanters; tumblers and wine glasses; twenty-four blue finger glass; tea and coffee urns; tea trays; plant baskets; stair carpeting etc.*

> *Book room: - six hair seat chairs; two mahogany tables; carpet 15ft by 13ft; moreen[1] window curtain; Fender and Fire set.*

---

[1] A sturdy ribbed fabric used in upholstery.

Bed Rooms: - neat Tent and other Bedsteads; feather beds; hair and wool mattresses; Japan chest of drawers; wash stands and dressing tables; rush seat chairs; night commodes etc.

Kitchen: Eckstain's kitchen range, with self-supporting cistern; steaming apparatus and stove; roasting apparatus; set of dish covers; iron boilers and saucepans; dresser and shelves; Baker's patent mangle; a general assortment of kitchen requisites.

A quantity of Green House plants and shrubs.

Farming stock: - two horses; two fat bullocks; an excellent milk cow; a sow and six small pigs; a sow and a farrow; a good market cart; butts and wheels; ploughs and harrows; chaff cutter; stone roller and stage; gig and cart; harness; a large quantity of cider and casks; tubs and kieves; part of a good rick of hay.

Source: North Devon Journal, March 18 1841.

Thomas Bridges Esq. (b.1805, London), a gentleman farmer, arrived with his wife and family in the autumn of 1841 intent on managing the eighty acres, with the assistance of seven locally employed labourers. Thomas was an influential man, and soon after his arrival he began to attend Vestry meetings, and for ten years undertook the role of churchwarden, committing his own money and time to improve the interior of the church. As mentioned earlier in this chapter, one of his daughters, Emma, wrote a book chronicling some aspects of life in Marwood in the late 1840s and 1850s. More about the Bridges' stay in the parish can be found in Chapter Four.

When the Bridges left in around 1856, the elderly spinster daughters of the late Charles Newell Cutcliffe and his wife Margaret (nee Mervin) moved to Marwood Hill.

Mervin Family

Marwood was formerly the seat and property of the Mervin family, until it passed to the Cutcliffe family by inheritance. Margaret (daughter and co-heiress of John Mervin, former Lord of the Manor of Marwood) inherited the family home where she had spent her formative years and after her marriage to Charles Newell Cutcliffe in 1776, the couple lived at Marwood Hill. In 1780 they moved to Pilton where their eight children were born, later returning to the family home. Charles was a solicitor and banker, descended from another wealthy Devon family, and he was known for being one of the founders of the first Barnstaple bank, known as Cutcliffe, Roche, Gribble and Co, in 1791. Their eldest daughter, Frances Cutcliffe, married Zachary Hammett Drake at Marwood in 1803, and later inherited the estate in 1822.

The last surviving Cutcliffe daughter, Harriet, died in 1867 and thereafter the property remained under the ownership of descendants of the Cutcliffe family, Drake and later Landon & Goodban, until the mid twentieth century.

In the interim, the house was let to several tenants. In March 1882 an advert was placed in the North Devon Journal, announcing that *Marwood Hill House* was available to let with immediate possession. It was described as having thirty acres of good meadow, pasture and orchard land, together with shooting over six hundred acres. The interior boasted spacious hall, drawing, dining, breakfast and housekeeper's rooms, kitchen, scullery, larder, storeroom, wine and beer cellars, dairy, wash-house, W.C., six good bedrooms, two dressing rooms, linen closets and six good servants' bedrooms. The outbuildings included a three-stall stable, loose box, carriage house, harness room, barn, cow house, piggery and other buildings, all well supplied with good spring water, and walled gardens stocked with fruit trees.

The well-to-do tenants included the Griffiths family in the 1880s and the Arthurs at the turn of the twentieth century, with each household boasting four to six servants to attend to their every need. In the mid 1920s, Caroline and Emily Boucher James, known locally as the Misses James, became the new ladies of the manor, taking residence at *Marwood Hill House* from around 1926, where they remained for several years, known for their fine hospitality and support of local causes. Later in 1947, Commander Robert Martin, (b.1882, Sidmouth) and his wife Lilian moved to Marwood Hill for a brief period. Commander Martin had served in Her Majesty's Navy during the First World War, and was awarded the 1914-15 Star, Victory & British War Medals. The couple were a big hit with the local children because they allowed them the use of the billiard room to watch old movies – a real treat in those days.

In February 1948, a sale notice was printed in the North Devon Journal in respect of the property at Marwood Hill. Described then as having vacant possession, a Georgian House with six to eight bedrooms, two bathrooms, three to four reception rooms, cottage buildings and garage, excellent walled garden and pleasure garden, pasture and orchards, the whole extending to twenty acres, seventeen acres let to good farmers. The estate was later purchased by a gentleman of the medical profession, known as Dr James Ambler Smart.

Dr James Ambler Smart (1914-2002)

Dr Smart, known as Jimmy, was the only surviving son of Alfred and Dorothy Smart (nee Cox). Educated at the historic Charterhouse School in Surrey, Jimmy was determined to pursue a career in medicine from a young age and went on to train at St Thomas' Hospital, London, where he qualified in 1937.

On the outbreak of the Second World War in 1939, he joined the Royal Naval Volunteer Reserve as a ship's doctor. Over the years that followed, Jimmy experienced a series of intensely dramatic events which would have tested even the most experienced medical practitioner. Within just three months of joining up, Jimmy was aboard the minesweeper *HMS Adventure* which suffered major damage when it detonated a magnetic mine, killing twenty-four and wounding sixty-nine. Less than six months later Jimmy was serving on *HMS Curacoa* near Norway when she sustained heavy aerial attacks from German planes and suffered major damage, killing thirty and wounding another thirty. In April 1941 he was aboard *HMS Capetown* when it was torpedoed off Mersa Kuba in the Red Sea, hitting the boiler room causing severe damage and many casualties.

Above: Surgeon Lieutenant
James Smart, c.1939.

In 1942 Jimmy was on board *HMS Hermes*, a state of the art aircraft carrier with capacity for twenty planes. While in the Indian ocean in April 1942, the ship came under a colossal attack from Japanese aircraft. *Hermes* was deluged and sunk by over forty 250 pound bombs, killing over two thirds of her ship's company. The men were flung into the water which was strewn with wreckage, corpses and black with oil. With immense courage, Jimmy managed to swim between rafts, administering morphine and comforting the dying and wounded. For this act of bravery he was awarded the MBE. Jimmy's nephew, John Snowdon quoted a newspaper announcement that described the events:

> *The full story has just been released of the circumstances under which Surgeon-Lieutenant-Commander James Ambler Smart of the Royal Naval Volunteer Reserve has been awarded the MBE, which, it is officially stated, was the only decoration made to the ship's company of HMS Hermes, when she was sunk in the Bay of Bengal in April, 1942. Referring to his decoration, Smart, who was a Surgeon-Lieutenant at the time of the sinking, said 'I was only doing my job'* [He'd been treating a rating so he wasn't in the sick bay when it got a direct hit]. *'I realised we were going down and I slipped over the side with the rating whom I had been attending. As I went in, a flagpole became tangled around my back and the ropes twisted round my legs. I thought my end had come.*

Then I struggled loose. I got away completely safe, with only a bit of shrapnel in my pocket ...' Smart swam around in the water from one Carley float to another, tending to the wounded men.

Press report, 1945: source unknown.

Above: Camellia 'Jimmy Smart'.

After the war Jimmy returned to civilian life and joined the Bear Street practice in Barnstaple as a general practitioner and anaesthetist, alongside well known Doctors Harper and Brook. He bought *Marwood Hill House* in 1949 establishing his own GP practice, and his sister Barbara Snowdon and her young son John lived there with him for several happy years. Jimmy always said that Marwood Hill Gardens first began in May 1949, at first within the walled garden where he tended to his camellias, and gradually evolved as he tackled old misshapen trees and hedges and tidied up the lawns of the big house. The gardens were initially opened only on one Sunday each year as part of the National Garden Scheme, and Jimmy used this as an opportunity to raise money for nurses.

In 1953, Jimmy employed Beatrice Brooks (nee Holland) as his housekeeper, a very important role for a young girl. Amongst her many duties, she was required to take calls for the doctor, often noting down complicated and unfamiliar medical terms, arranging home visits and reporting all urgent matters to Jimmy. Beatrice remembers with a wry smile that sometimes he would be busy at work on his camellias and would seem a little reluctant to be torn away to attend to his patients, such was his growing passion for gardening. On many other occasions Jimmy demonstrated his great dedication to medicine, including one case where he donned a pair of skis in order to reach a young woman in labour in Challacombe who was cut off by a snow drift.

Beatrice recalls that one of the most difficult tasks she had to deal with occurred on Monday evenings. As the attending anaesthetist at Bideford Hospital on Tuesdays, Jimmy would require a list of the planned surgery. The night before, a surgeon would call with a list of the operations to be carried out and Beatrice would write down all the terminology with great difficulty, as the words were not familiar to her. Unfortunately, the doctor was never there to help because Monday nights always meant a trip to the cinema for Jimmy and his sister Barbara!

In January 1966 Jimmy was dealt a tragic blow when his father and sister were killed in a car accident and later that year he lost his mother at the age of eight-eight. Rather than live alone, Jimmy decided to let the house and move into a flat in Barnstaple.

Marwood Hill House was let for ten pounds per week to the emerging sculptor, John Robinson, who moved in with his wife and young family in January 1969. John created several superb sculptures during his time at Marwood, some of which are on display in the gardens today and the font cover 'Nunc Dimittis' in the parish church.

Above: *Marwood Hill House* c.1969, described by John Robinson as 'the perfect example of a two-storey Georgian house, coated with white stucco and south-facing'.

In the meantime Jimmy continued to pursue his ambition to 'ensure the garden is a source of pleasure to visitors' (1998). He purchased more land, some of which was formerly glebe and the rest from a retiring farmer. Much of the pasture land was rough and neglected and Jimmy quickly set to work planting trees such as pines grown from seed which he had brought back from Portugal, silver birch, magnolia, cherries and a variety of rhododendrons and other shrubs. In 1969 he built a large greenhouse specifically for camellias in the walled garden and commenced damming the stream to create the two lakes. Jimmy had the greatest attention to detail and even took care to choose trees with yellow or gold foliage to border the lakes, creating enchanting reflections.

Around this time, *Marwood Hill House* was put up for sale with a change of name to *Marwood House,* enabling Jimmy to retain the name *Marwood Hill.* He had a separate property built overlooking the valley only a hundred yards away from his former home and he became deeply involved in its architectural design to ensure full advantage was taken of the surrounding scenery. This included a magnificent balcony and huge windows carefully designed to offer panoramic views of the ever developing gardens.

1970 saw the arrival of head gardener Malcolm Pharoah from RHS Wisley, who worked with Jimmy on the continued development of the gardens. Over the years Jimmy travelled far and wide to collect a variety of plants, trees, shrubs, herbaceous and alpines, which meant they could propagate and sell plants from their own unique stock.

Jimmy shared his seemingly effortless approach to cultivation during the many lectures he gave, revealing:

> I am very inclined to follow nature as far as possible and to plant where the plant is likely to be happy and, although I can admire it when practised by others, I do not want to have what I describe as a contrived garden with very carefully arranged colour.

> Taken from the lecture notes of James A. Smart, 1999.

One of the next phases of development of the gardens came when Jimmy retired and purchased another twelve acres of land downstream from the bottom lake. This enabled the creation of the Bog Garden; a delightful feature that greets visitors with a carefully selected display of primulas and astilbes, accompanied by Rodgersias and Iris Ensata, followed by Hemerocallis, Lythrum, Lobelias, Ligularia and Inula. A stream flows through the garden, cascading in occasional waterfalls.

As the gardens evolved, Jimmy's horticultural expertise literally blossomed. He had become internationally respected and to this end in November 1994 he was awarded the prestigious Victorian Medal of Honour by the Royal Horticultural Society. This is an honour only granted to sixty-three people at any one time, in commemoration of the sixty-three years of Queen Victoria's reign. At the presentation it was said:

> Your chronicle of horticultural achievement has many pages and in particular we single out your great knowledge and collection of Camellias including those that you have bred, some of which have been given an Award of Merit. You have travelled much in Australia and New Zealand and we owe to you the introduction from these countries of many plants to Britain.

> The Royal Horticultural Society has benefited from your presence, both from the legendary quality of plants you have shown, and from your experience in judging. In addition, we have learnt from your wisdom as a member of the Camellia and Rhododendron Committee.

> But your finest achievement is at Marwood Hill in Devon where you have created a great garden, combining your deep knowledge of plants with a sense of taste and artistry. There your many important plant collections, including the National Collection of Astilbes, are enjoyed by thousands of visitors who may be lucky enough to be infected by your enthusiasm and joie de vivre and an energy which at 80 promises well for the continued expansion of Marwood Hill Garden.

> This Victoria Medal of Honour is given to you because we recognise you both as a supreme plantsman and a great gardener whose generosity has given pleasure to thousands of other gardeners.

Jimmy died at the age of eighty-seven in May 2002. He had been sitting in his living room overlooking his pride and joy, Marwood Hill Gardens. He left the gardens to his nephew John Snowdon, safe in the knowledge that he would oversee their continued development.

Jimmy was described as a man of great character and immense generosity whose ambition was to share his passion for gardening and create a source of pleasure for people. Perhaps the real testimony to Jimmy's work is best represented by the reaction of the thousands of visitors attracted to the gardens each year, who describe the experience as 'inspiring', 'real', 'timeless' and 'magical'. Long may they continue to come and enjoy all that Marwood Hill Gardens have to offer.

Above: Images from Marwood Hill Gardens, 2011.

Chapter Three:
Making Ends Meet

Farming

As a rural parish, farming has played an integral role in the lives of Marwood folk for centuries. Between the years of 1841 and 1911 there were approximately forty farmers recorded on the census returns at any one time; roughly half farmed over one hundred acres and numerous smallholders held between ten and fifty acres. During this period most farmers in North Devon were tenants, paying rent to landowners rather than purchasing their own land. Pivotal to the community, tenant farmers provided guaranteed income for landowners, employment to labourers and business to tradesmen such as blacksmiths and carpenters.

Over the course of the nineteenth century, farming went through dramatic change due to a combination of great advancements in tools and the mechanisation of farming practices. Times were still hard for farmers however, especially in the 1870s when they faced new challenges such as successive poor harvests and competition from cheap grain imports from the United States and Canada, factors which contributed to the beginning of a nation wide agricultural decline.

As in other parts of the country, these developments impacted job security for all whose work was connected to farming although in North Devon, the impact was less severe. For one thing, there was an ample supply of cheap labour so there was less need to invest in expensive new equipment. In addition, local farmers rarely specialised and most combined keeping livestock with crop growing, principally wheat, oats and barley. This diversity meant that when prices were low on one commodity, others held their value, maintaining some financial stability.

Above: Tom Braunton driving his cattle to the water pump in Middle Marwood c.1930s.

As sung in the lyrics of the old nursery rhyme, the farmer needed a wife. Typically he would hope to marry a farmer's daughter who knew the ropes and was already accustomed to hard work. Examples of farming unions in Marwood are as below:

William Down (Stepps Farm) & Hannah (daughter of William Beard, Bowen Farm).

William Alford (Kings Heanton) & Emily (daughter of John Rudd, Higher Muddiford).

Hayman Brailey (Metcombe) & Elizabeth Irwin (daughter of Joseph Irwin, Metcombe Farm).

William Fairchild (Prixford) and Jane (daughter of Charles Kelly, Varley Farm).

Above: Emily Alford (nee Rudd), c.1936.

Left: The Alfords' farmhouse in Kings Heanton, c.1930s.

It was usually a husband's responsibility to look after matters relating to crop growing, sheep and cattle, while his wife would often single–handedly manage the farmhouse, dairy, farmyard and their children. Older children would be tasked with chores as soon as they were able, particularly with feeding livestock, milking and collecting eggs. David Hey (2002) author of *How Our Ancestors Lived* explains that the farmer's wife was critical to the success of the farm, creating readily available income to maintain the household through the sale of eggs, milk, cream and butter. Charles Pugsley's wife worked so hard at Milltown Farm in the early 1900s, that she only took one day off per year and that was to do the Christmas shopping!

When it came to harvest time the whole household was involved, together with neighbouring farmers and other volunteers who would provide a helping hand. This was a time of hard work and heavy drinking with plenty of barrels of cider on standby!

Above: Standing on cart (L – R) Phoebe Dennis, Gilbert Welch, Sam Braunton.
Below (L-R) Eddie Chapple, Tom Braunton, George Welch c.1930s.

Harvest Time in Marwood

Above : Gilbert Welch, Mr Chapple, George Welch & Tom Braunton c.1930s.
Below: William Spear and his children at work during harvest c.1925.

Farm Labourers – 1800s

Farm labourers had an arduous existence and many struggled to scratch out a living. They often worked ten to twelve hour days which would be even longer during lambing and harvest time. Labourers and other agricultural workers or tradesmen were taken on for periods of six months to three-years but work was seasonal and they risked being laid off during the winter months. In some areas, farm labouring was only ever on a casual basis and men would go off 'jobbing' each day in search of a day's wages.

Until the 1880s, it was common for all members of a labourer's family to work to make ends meet. This was essential as a labourer's wage could be as low as seven shillings a week, supplemented with a daily allowance of cider which represented some of the worst wages in the entire country. Before schooling became compulsory, labourers' children would work from the age of six. Boys would sometimes work especially long hours alongside their fathers, weeding, picking stones, picking potatoes, trapping rabbits, bird scaring or raking hay, for which they would receive just one shilling a week. Girls helped their mother with household chores such as caring for younger siblings and feeding animals.

A labourer's wife dealt with a myriad of household chores, like fetching water from the well or spring, washing, mending clothes, sweeping floors, cleaning soot from the open hearth and might even take on some of these activities for other households for a few pence in wages. She would grow vegetables in the garden, look after any small livestock that they could afford such as chickens and prepare meals from the most meagre ingredients, all whilst looking after the youngest children. On top of this, some labourers' wives were bound to join them in the fields as a condition of the husband's employment, particularly if they lived in a tied cottage (Hey, 2002).

Cambridge graduate, Reverend Frederick Collison was incumbent at Marwood Parish Church between 1853 and 1886. On his arrival, he was astounded by the way of life of the 'illiterate folk' of Marwood and wrote memoirs to record his observations, including the sight of women and children working in the fields:

> Girls were set about the same work as boys to plough and harrow the ground, and would ride the farm horses astride like the boys, with less clothing than decency required. Once or twice I have myself seen a woman with a rope over her shoulder dragging a sort of plough which her husband was thrusting before him to cut the sod in order to break up a field for tillage. This was called "spading" and was extremely hard work.
>
> Source: NDRO 3398A/PV1.

Women were expected to undertake the same type of hard labour for very little pay, although developments in farming eventually led to a decline in women working the fields. Continuing mechanisation reduced the amount of labour required and new machinery was often heavier and too difficult for women to operate.

By the late 1800s, most women in the parish were only employed as labourers on a seasonal basis to assist with harvests and picking root vegetables.

Farm Labourers – 1900s

Labouring was still the chief source of employment in the parish by the turn of the twentieth century. Marwood school log books show that the vast majority of boys left to be engaged as labourers, although this might also have been in road construction or building work. Others may have taken an apprenticeship in carpentry or other trades.

Harold Hopkins left Marwood school at the age of fourteen in December 1935 and became a farm labourer, working for Thomas Joslin at Townridden. Beginning on a wage of four shillings per week, Harold recalls that by the end of his first week he was working a team of horses to sow a six-acre field. When his granfer Bob Hopkins asked Thomas if his grandson was doing a good job, the wily response was that he was very pleased but he still wasn't going to give Harold a pay rise!

Right: Harold's granfer Robert Hopkins c.1920.

Harold continued his farm labouring until he was called up to fight in the Second World War. He travelled to Bristol to enlist, only to find he was rejected as his eyesight was below the minimum standard. Frustrated by this, he then attempted to join the police force but was again declined, this time due to his height. Harold came to the conclusion that farm work was his best option, so he applied and was accepted to take on Chapel Farm between Prixford and Guineaford, owned by the Devon County Council. He was quoted in the book 'Memories of Barnstaple Cattle Market'[1], recalling the days when he drove flocks of sheep three miles to market in Barnstaple each Wednesday, along with his Uncle Tommy, at a time when the price of six tooth closewool ewes was six pounds apiece. Owning just a small number of sheep in those days, it was scarcely enough to make a living so Harold also started milking cows for regular income and built the shippen near *Homeleigh Farm* on the lane leading to the parish church. His next venture was the buying and selling of cattle, and he went to markets in Taunton on Saturdays, Bideford on Tuesdays and Holsworthy on Thursdays. In those days, cows cost eighty pounds apiece, so he had to have close to one thousand pounds in the bank to enable the purchase of eight cows. Harold sold the only land he had to Mr WTJ Beaman to raise the necessary funds and continued trading for many years.

---

[1] 'Memories of Barnstaple Cattle Market' by Ruth Larrea (2003).

Left: William Spear instructs his son Fred on the plough c.1930s.

Females and Farm Work

As mentioned previously, by the late 1800s female farm servants were no longer expected to undertake the gruelling tasks in the fields; instead they were based in the dairy or as a domestic maid in the farmhouse.

It was at this time that the Devon County Travelling Dairy School was established, which visited rural parishes around Barnstaple with the objective of educating locals on the latest dairy techniques, particularly in the art of butter and cream making. In February 1931 the North Devon Journal reported that Marwood had 'again been favoured with a visit from the Devon County Travelling Dairy School' with classes held at Marwood Hill, thanks to the generosity of Miss James and organisation of Percy Brailey. Ten lessons in butter making were given after which a competition was held for all participants. The winners were reported as (1st) E Vanstone, (2nd) W Webber, (3rd) R Balment, (4th) M Hunt and runner-up, N Watts. The following were classified as Very Highly Commended: Mrs Nicholls, Mrs Joslin, O Down, V Brailey, G Quance, D Jenkins and K Braunton.

Above: Marwood Hill Dairy School, 1931.

Prizes were presented by Miss James who spoke of her pleasure in watching the students at work, and Colin Ross who judged their efforts and complimented all on the high standard of work achieved. Miss Eva Mattinson, gave a small speech about her passion for dairy work and her past successes in County Dairy competitions, where she had been a silver medallist.

After the ceremony, the committee led by E and W Alford, A Brailey, F Smyth, N Shephard, Misses James, E Mattinson and Miss J Worth, provided tea for everyone who participated and came to watch the competition.

Above: Marwood Hill Dairy School, February 1931.
L-R (standing) - Robert Balment; Mildred Hunt; Kathleen Balment; (unidentified); Gladys Joslin; (unidentified); Nancy Watts; Olive Down; Flo Nicholls; Kathleen Braunton; Percy Brailey.
L - R (seated) - (unidentified); (unidentified); (unidentified); Colin Ross; (unidentified); Eva Mattinson; Dorothy Jenkins.

Many a Marwood maid mastered the art of cream making, which was enjoyed by parishioners and customers at the pannier market in Barnstaple. Before retiring to *Meadow View*, Guineaford, the Hockin sisters, Ethel and Minnie, managed a small dairy farm in Higher Muddiford. Herbert Tamlyn's granddaughter Helen Knight, remembers visiting the ladies as a young girl to collect scalded milk for her Nan to make puddings. Ida Dobbs of Kings Heanton was another former pupil of the Devon County Travelling Dairy School and later became a prize-winning competitor and member of the Devon Young Farmers Association.

Above: Ida, second from left, in the second row, with the Devon County Dairy School, c.1905.

Blacksmiths

The blacksmith was indispensable in a rural parish like Marwood for as long as horses remained critical to farm work, and in 1881 they could be found hard at work in every hamlet in Marwood. As well as tending to horses, work included making and repairing tools and equipment for farms and households. It was a trade that was often passed down from father to son and Harold Hopkins, now a retired farmer, discovered his direct ancestors were blacksmiths over several generations, from the middle of the eighteenth until the beginning of the twentieth century. His great-granfer John Hopkins was a blacksmith in the nearby hamlet of Whitehall for almost fifty years.

In many villages it was usual for the blacksmith's shop to be situated at a crossroads with running water nearby, just as it was in Guineaford. The old 'smithy' still stands there today, now used as a garage. One of the blacksmiths who worked at the Guineaford forge was James Taylor (b.1864, Shirwell).

James was married to Mary Ann, and they had five children, though their second born, Georgina (b.1890) sadly died aged only twenty months in 1891. Mary Ann was then dealt an even more devastating blow, when James died in November 1896, shortly after being admitted to North Devon Infirmary.

The official cause of death was described in the *Marwood Church Monthly* as perityphlitis and the rupture of an abscess (appendicitis). It was quoted that James had attended the Parish Church on the previous Sunday and had been *deeply impressed by the Sermon (on our heavenly citizenship) and by the hymn 'For all the Saints'.* He was buried alongside his daughter Georgina, on Thursday November 19 1896, aged just thirty-two years. By the time of the next census in 1901, the Taylor children were living with their blind grandmother, Mary Ann Taylor of Prixford. Their mother Mary Ann had gone into domestic service, almost certainly to earn money for their keep.

Above: James Taylor, shoeing what is believed to be the Reverend Pryke's horse, c.1895.

Ernest Harding *(pictured right)* was a blacksmith in the early 1900s who lived in Guineaford but walked to Milltown every day to work. David Pugsley remembered that Ernest was quite a character who was determined to warm his stiff leather apron in front of the fire before he would start work. On one occasion a frantic farmer was waiting for assistance at the forge because his horse had lost a shoe at a critical point of harvest, but old Ernest wouldn't lift his hammer until his apron was warm!

Above: Ernest Harding, c.1940.

By the early twentieth century, there was a fall in the number of blacksmiths in the parish, from eleven in 1881 to three in 1911. The heavy reliance on horses had ensured a regular supply of work for centuries and as farming practices developed, the farmers' needs changed, creating more demand for the repair of new farm tools and machinery. After the First World War there was a vast decline in the use of horses for transport and labour. The arrival of the motor car in the parish, followed by the first tractors meant the rural smithy had to diversify to make his living and it was common for blacksmiths to broaden their skills and become mechanics for vehicle repairs.

Samuel J Born of Milltown was one tradesman who perfected the art of diversification, by running a sawmill, blacksmith's shop, carpentry and wheelwright's shop in his enterprise of farm machinery repair. His team could repair anything from mangle pulpers to chaff cutters to Lister engines.

Above: The old smithy in Guineaford is now used as a garage.

Carpenters

Carpentry was another trade that was often passed down through generations and one example of this is the Worth family. John Worth (b.1781) was a carpenter and his eldest son William (b.1821) soon followed him into the trade. William married Elizabeth Bament, and their five sons John (b.1850), George (b.1852), William junior (b.1855), Henry (b.1863) and Robert (b.1865) all became carpenters. William junior married Ellison Born, and one of their sons also became a fine fourth generation carpenter.

George Worth, William's second son, was brought up in Guineaford and began his married life with Mary Ann (b.1854) in Kings Heanton. In 1882 they moved to *The Nook* in Guineaford and George became the village carpenter and undertaker. In the event of a death, he would spend all night making the coffin, occasionally with the help of his able assistant, Harold Hopkins who lived next door in *The Old Inn*. Harold would carry buckets of steaming water to help George with the shaping of the wood. Upon completion of a coffin, Harold would borrow his Uncle Tommy's horse and cart to deliver it, much to the irritation of his uncle who would complain that the mare was tired next day.

George was very active in the community being at different times a member of the choir, bell ringer, churchwarden, sidesman, census enumerator and parish councillor, amongst other responsibilities.

Above: George B. Worth, c.1920.

Reuben Tamlyn was a well respected carpenter who was born in 1913 at *Rose Cottage*, Muddiford, the youngest son of Richard and Alice Tamlyn. He was both carpenter and wheelwright by trade, although like George Worth, he also took on the necessary role of undertaker. The wooden built Mission church was located at the bottom end of Reuben's garden and when it was no longer needed by the community, it was sold to him for use as a workshop. The building still remains today at the roadside below *Downlyn*.

Reuben married Olive Down of Guineaford and they settled in Muddiford, where their children Gillian and Gordon were born. Gordon fondly remembers those halcyon days of growing up in Muddiford when he and his friends would play cricket in the road without the fear of speeding motorists.

Above:
Olive Tamlyn,
c.1935.

Above: Reuben Tamlyn outside his workshop, c.1940s.

When he was in his late seventies, Reuben designed and constructed a fine pair of wooden gates for Marwood Parish Church. There is a small engraving on a brass plaque, which reads 'These gates were designed, made and given to the Church by Reuben J. Tamlyn of Muddiford, February 1989'.

Right: Reuben's gates at Marwood Parish Church.

Reuben was related to the Lynch family of Muddiford. John Lynch (b.1770) used to boast that he had wealthy Irish ancestors, and on one occasion he was finishing work in Little Silver and having drunk a large amount of cider, he boasted that his Irish forefathers had a castle in Ireland. His workmates were most amused, crowning him King Lynch and pushing him back down to Muddiford in a wheelbarrow!

John is mentioned frequently in Vestry records from the 1820s for his much respected role as overseer of the poor and for his carpentry work. His great-grandson William Lynch, later wrote that every Christmas John used to walk miles around the parish to distribute charity money to the poor, which he continued until he was well over eighty years old. On March 10 1828, it was reported that two ash trees on the bowling green, at the west end of the parish churchyard, should be felled and the wood sold to raise money to repair the church-house. John paid two shillings per foot for one of the trees and Thomas Challacombe bought the other. In March 1835 it is recorded that John agreed to make coffins for the paupers of Marwood for ten shillings and three pence, over the ensuing year.

John's grandson, Thomas Lynch, was another carpenter who undertook lots of work in the parish. Once he was asked to carry out some repairs at *The Dell* in Higher Muddiford and on knocking down a wall, he discovered several silver spoons stashed in a rat's hole. This find was met with some embarrassment by the owners who admitted that some years earlier a maid had been accused of stealing them and lost her job as a result!

Millers

Marwood was once well populated with watermills, most of which were in operation by the mid eighteenth century. Valerie Porter, author of *Yesterday's Countryside (2006)*, explains that the mill would have been a hectic place:

> … noise of horses whinnying, wagons rumbling, men shouting, hoists creaking, all against the background sounds of the wheel turning, the stones grinding and the busy working water splashing and rushing over its wheel.
>
> Source: Valerie Porter, 2006, p174.

There were at least six working watermills in the parish during the 1800s, grinding corn for flour and cutting chaff for animal feed. There were mills at Blakewell (said to have been destroyed by a fire in 1867 and rebuilt), Metcombe, Milltown, Westcott Barton, Whitefield Barton and Whitehall.

Colin Pearse, author of *Mill to Mill and Stook to Flour* (2008), revealed that the waterwheel and millhouse at Whitehall were built in the early eighteenth century and served the local community for over three hundred years. Records of the first millers there are scarce, but from 1870 onwards, generation after generation of the Herneman family ensured the smooth running of the mill until its wheel finally stopped turning in the mid 1900s.

Above: James Dennis, holding his great-grand-daughter Ruth Herneman; to the left, his daughter Rebecca and to the right, his grandson Fred Herneman c.1915.

Richard Herneman (b.1838) was the only surviving son of James and Priscilla Herneman, respected millers of Bradiford. Perhaps it was inevitable that Richard chose to follow in his father's footsteps and become a miller in his own right and by 1870 he had secured the tenancy of Whitehall mill in Marwood with his wife Ann and daughter Eliza (b.1863). In the years that followed they had seven more children; James (b.1864), Emily (b.1866), William (b.1869), Annie (b.1870), John (b.1872), Samuel (b.1876) and Elizabeth (b.1877). Richard was the resident miller and farmer at Whitehall for over twenty years, eventually leaving in 1890 when he was succeeded by a third generation of Herneman millers when his oldest son James stayed on to manage the mill. James, his wife Rebecca and son Fred, ran the mill for over thirty years until James' untimely death in 1924 at the age of sixty. After a brief tenancy by Ernest Conibear (1924 to the early 1930s), remarkably, a fourth generation of the Herneman family, Fred (b.1888) and his wife Elizabeth took over the running of the mill and it was to remain their home, long after the mill had closed. Today there are still descendants of the Hernemans living at Whitehall mill.

Inns/Hotels

It seems that Marwood was never short of inns where exhausted labourers could buy a mug of beer after a long days' work. There were a combination of alehouses and inns, the former being an informal arrangement where ale or beer brewed on the premises would be sold, normally in the front room of the cottage.

There was at least one alehouse in Guineaford in the early 1800s, run by the Chugg family who lived opposite *The Nook*, as mentioned in the previous chapter. The 1841 census records reveal that the head of the household, Thomas, was formally employed as a farm labourer, leaving his wife and elder daughters to brew and serve those in need of a pint. Interestingly, the alehouse appears to have been established before the *North Devon Inn*, which did not start trading until circa 1849.

The Chuggs' alehouse may have opened following the introduction of new legislation called the Beer Act of 1830, which allowed individuals to brew and sell beer in their own homes on purchasing a licence costing two guineas[1]. The only caveat was that the licence did not permit the consumption of wines or spirits on the premises, spirits being considered the cause of alcoholism and poor health among the working classes. Beer on the other hand, was considered to be harmless and nutritious and was even given to young children because of fears about the cleanliness of water drawn from wells and springs.

Alehouses sprang up across the nation with some making huge profits, so that by 1834 they outnumbered the inns, taverns and public houses. The sheer numbers of alehouses opening meant that new licensing laws were introduced in 1869, far more akin to the laws we know today. In Middle Marwood however, there had been some particularly informal arrangements in place in the 1800s and early 1900s, due to the presence of a brewery opposite *Bowen Farm*. It is thought that thirsty locals could obtain a swift pint at *Bowen* and *Stepps Farm* during this period, although one suspects that no licences were held!

Inns were often considered to be more comfortable establishments, some were purpose built and others only identifiable by the large sign above the front door of the cottage. They were typically larger in size, providing accommodation and stables and commonly found along busy roads for the relief of weary travellers. In rural areas, inns became part of the social fabric where perhaps the only alternative meeting place was the church. In Marwood the local inns were used for celebrations following community events such as ploughing matches and sports days. Locating historical information about any of the licensed premises in Marwood has been particularly difficult, with the most reliable records being census and trade directories.

---

[1] 1 guinea = £1 1s
1 pound = 20 shillings
1 florin = 2 shillings
1 shilling = 12d

The table below details the landlords of the six known inns trading between 1841 and 1911, with any gaps indicating their closure or absence of trading records.

Inn	Landlord 1841	Landlord 1851	Landlord 1861	Landlord 1871	Landlord 1881	Landlord 1891	Landlord 1901	Landlord 1911
Ring O' Bells *Prixford*	Joseph Goss	Joseph Goss	William Hancock	Charles Kelly	William Smyth	George Rodd	James Dennis	Horatio Lean
New Inn *Muddiford*	John Redmore	Elon Harris	Elon Harris	Elon Harris	John Gubb	John Gubb	John Prance	Henry Tucker
Maltster's Inn *Middle Marwood*	George Richards	George Richards						
Fry's Hotel *Burland*	Edwin Shapland	James Pearce	James Pearce	James Pearce	Susanna Pearce	Susanna Pearce	Susanna Pearce	Emma Pearce
Mervin Arms *Milltown*	William Corney							
ND Inn *Guineaford*		Francis Fairchild	John Fairchild	William Gammon	William Gammon	Henry Yeo	William Taylor	James Dennis
Blue Ball Inn *South Burland*	James & Mary Hussell							

The *Blue Ball Inn* at South Burland was trading late in the eighteenth century, as evidenced by the notice dated September 22 1796 *(pictured right)*. It probably served those travelling along the turnpike road over Swindon Down, though it was last referenced on a map in 1827.

The last known landlords were James and Mary Hussell, and it appears the inn ceased trading when Mary was declared bankrupt. The London Gazette reported on September 6 1842, that 'Mary Hussell, Beer House Keeper, formerly of Burland and late of Muddiford' was imprisoned at Barnstaple

TO BE LET,

BLUE BALL INN,

And also a MEADOW,

Right: 'To Let' notice at South Burland, dated September 1796.

gaol on account of her insolvency or inability to cover her debts. She was requested to attend the court-house in Exeter on November 20 1842, but the outcome of that hearing is not known. The *Blue Ball Inn* never resumed trading and later became known as Burland Farm.

The *North Devon Inn* at Guineaford was serving locals in the 1840s initially from one room, with the later addition of a first floor clubroom and skittle alley with stables below. In June 1916, after almost eighty years of trading, landlord Ralston J Watts applied to the magistrates to renew his licence on behalf of the brewery, Edwin Petter & Sons of Barnstaple. The magistrates were informed that the population of the parish was declining (then 654) and that some people in Guineaford no longer wanted a public house. In light of the fact that there were already two other licensed houses in the parish and the number of residents was falling, the magistrates decided to refuse the licence renewal on the grounds of redundancy. It was declared that there would be no hardship on the tenants as they would be awarded compensation, and all should bear in mind that there were no guarantees that either of the two remaining establishments, the *New Inn* at Muddiford or the *Ring O' Bells* at Prixford would have their licences renewed. Ultimately both were permitted to continue trading and by 1919 Ralston J Watts had become landlord of the *Ring O' Bells*. Both establishments continue to serve both locals and tourists today.

In August 1920, a former sixteenth century coaching inn, known as the *New Inn* at Muddiford, came up for sale at auction. It formed part of a number of lots including the freehold of Milltown Farm, several cottages and plots of land including Knowl Park, Westward Piece and Swindon. The *New Inn* was described as a 'slated licensed house, with bar, bar parlour, kitchen, scullery, cellar, wash house, coal house, four bedrooms, together with tiled shippen, slated three stall stable, large club room, closet, piggery, garden and meadow' and it was sold to Mr Prescott for seven hundred and fifty pounds. Only a few years after this sale, Charles and Winifred Marston made the bold decis ion to relocate from Rochford, Essex to Muddiford, where they ran the *New Inn* as a small hotel for ten years. The inn was used as a base for the Army Catering Corps during the Second World War.

Right: Winifred Marston (centre)
with daughters Betty and Joan c.1930s.

In more recent years mysterious sightings have been witnessed at the premises, now known as *The Muddiford Inn,* which suggest some kind of ghostly presence. Landlady Pearl Powell has documented these observations and they certainly make some frightening reading, particularly the apparition of a girl holding a baby and what is thought to have been a coachman dressed in a long cloak. Fortunately Pearl has been assured that these are 'friendly ghosts' who are just interested in the goings-on in the pub!

Above: The New Inn, Muddiford c.1930.
Reproduced with kind permission of Mr S Knight, RL Knight Photographers.

Women at Work

In the early censuses, many women were not recorded as having an occupation of their own, listed instead as 'labourer's wife', 'rector's wife' or 'carpenter's wife' and so forth, though they often played a hugely supportive role behind the scenes. Later in the 1800s, more females found gainful employment, typically through occupations such as dressmaking, teaching, shop keeping and going into domestic service.

Almost without exception, as soon as young women became married, they were expected to give up their employment, irrespective of their trade - excluding farmers' wives of course, whose work was only just beginning! Census records show that between 1841 and 1911, less than five per cent of all females in paid employment were married, a practice which continued until the outbreak of the Second World War when women were called upon to undertake the work traditionally done by men who had left to fight for their country.

Domestic Servants

It was most common for young unmarried girls to go into live-in domestic service when they left school. In Marwood, the wealthy families at *Marwood Hill*, *Muddiford House* and *Lee House* would employ several servants and others may have found work at the rectory or with prominent farmers at Townridden, Westcott and Whitefield Bartons. When the Bridges family were resident at *Marwood Hill House* in the 1850s, there were no less than five live-in servants, comprising a housekeeper, housemaid, laundry maid, parlour maid and kitchen maid. In 1901 when Mr Arthur was resident, he employed six live-in servants including housemaid, nurse, parlour maid, cook, kitchen maid and coachman.

Hilda Watts (nee Carter) was one of five daughters, raised on a farm in High Bickington by parents John and Ellen. In January 1936 just a few months after her fourteenth birthday she remembers a lady named Mrs Wansbrough arrived at her school to select a girl for domestic service. Hilda was fortunate to be chosen for what was seen as a great placement 'in gentleman's residence' for the Reverend Cecil Wansbrough of High Bickington. Her mother Ellen negotiated the wages with Mrs Wansbrough and they agreed upon seven shillings and sixpence per week, inclusive of keep, which was a very good salary at that time. Hilda remembers having to wear a blue dress with a white apron and cap and be immaculately turned out. She was only allowed out on Tuesdays, her day off, and had to be back by nine o'clock in the evening. She would normally spend this time visiting her parents and helping them with chores. Hilda had every other Sunday off but she was always expected at church whether or not she was working, because her employer was a man of the cloth. Hilda remained with the Wansbroughs until 1941 when she volunteered to join the Wrens. She was assigned as a cook and posted to *HMS Raleigh* for training, and was later stationed at Falmouth and Plymouth.

Grocers

In Guineaford like many other hamlets, people would open up their own homes to run informal shops and in the 1851 census, a grocery shop was run by spinster, Miss Harriet Slocombe (b.1808, Heanton Punchardon). Harriet, with the help of an errand girl, ran various services from her cottage in the village including a bakery, drapery and tea dealer, until the 1870s.

Right: Beryl and David Pugsley (centre) with
Doris Baker in the field opposite Oaklands, c.1940.

In the 1890s, Eliza Summerfield (b.1843, nee Hill) opened a grocery shop in the front room of her home in *Oaklands* which she continued to run until the early twentieth century, later succeeded by her daughter Mary Jane (b.1864) who continued serving her loyal customers until the early 1940s.

Harold Hopkins remembers taking out a ferret with his friend Ernie Watts to catch rabbits. This would earn them a few pennies so they could go and buy sweets from Mary Jane's. David Fairchild and Lou Spear remember calling by on the way home from school, perhaps to purchase a sherbet fountain or bottle of dandelion and burdock if they clubbed their pennies together. Mary Jane's niece Ivy Baker and her husband Henry ran the shop in later years.

Dressmakers

Orphaned at the age of three, Annie Turner Brown of Kings Heanton had a sad start to her life but was fortunate to have grandparents nearby in Varley, who raised her and her older brother John. Following the death of their grandparents in the early 1890s, John moved to London where he became a policeman and Annie remained at Varley with her Aunt Ellen, who began to teach her to sew. As Annie's needlework expertise grew, the pair started to take on dressmaking work and their services were soon in great demand. Annie and Ellen were often asked to take up temporary residence in the houses of upper class families, while they tailor made entire wardrobes for them all. They were also known for the fine wedding gowns they created.

Between the years of 1851 and 1891, on average there were fifteen women making a living as dressmakers in Marwood however at the turn of the twentieth century, this number had dwindled to three, as the independent tailors and dressmakers struggled to compete with emerging mass produced lines of 'off the peg' clothing (Source: Marwood census returns 1851-1911).

Above:
Annie Turner Brown
(b.1879) with her
aunt, Ellen Brown.

Poverty

Poverty was an ever-present worry, particularly for agricultural labourers in receipt of low wages. In most cases there was seldom opportunity to put money aside for unemployment or old age so understandably there were occasions when households were unable to make ends meet. Other than seeking support from relatives who were often in no position to help, the labourer had no option other than to apply to the parish for assistance.

The Vestry controlled both ecclesiastical and civil matters arising within the parish until late nineteenth century legislation brought the latter under the control of county, district and parish councils. At the annual Marwood Vestry meeting, members were elected to undertake roles such as churchwardens, parish constables, surveyors of the highways and overseers of the poor, and it was normally the farmers, tradesmen or minor gentry who were appointed. These overseers were responsible for setting and collecting the poor rate, distributing payments to the needy, tracking down fathers of illegitimate children and helping the poor find work, amongst other tasks.

As a means of minimising the cost of poor relief, the parish arranged for children from poor labouring families to be bound as apprentices from the age of nine upwards. In return for a one-off payment made by the parish, farmers' or tradesmen's households were expected to take on one child or more, to feed and clothe them and to teach them a vocation. Once agreed, the apprenticeship became legally binding in the form of an Indenture, of which one copy was kept by the master and another by the Vestry.

The Marwood Parish Apprentice Register reveals that children were bound in their apprenticeships either until they were married or reached the age of twenty-one. Most boys were apprenticed to a farm and were expected to learn to plough and harrow the ground and other equally physically demanding tasks usually undertaken by grown men. According to records made by Reverend Frederick Collison, some girls in Marwood were also sent to work in the fields, although in most cases, their role was to serve within the farmhouse. For the younger children this must have been a distressing time, removed from their family home, perhaps to a household some distance away and subjected to hard labour. If the family declined to send their child to be apprenticed, they could be excluded from receiving further support from the parish.

An interesting example of an apprenticeship is noted in the Vestry records. At a meeting on February 7 1843, the case of pauper child William Edwards was debated. Disabled through the loss of a leg, the only trade considered fit for the boy was tailoring. It was proposed that the boy be apprenticed to William Lovering of Braunton, who would receive the sum of twenty pounds for teaching him the skills of a tailor. For this sum, William Lovering was expected to find 'meat, drink, clothing, medical attendance or any other necessaries that may be wanting for him during his apprenticeship'. The money was to be paid in two instalments of ten pounds from the outset, and ten pounds when half of the apprenticeship had been completed. Although twenty pounds was an enormous sum of money, the boy would be removed from Marwood parish, taught a trade and ultimately cease to be an ongoing liability.

People could apply to the parish for what was known as 'outdoor' poor relief, which had to be approved by the overseers. Specific and legitimate reasons for the application had to be given, such as periods of unemployment or illness, which could result in a temporary weekly payment of a few shillings, enabling the labourer to support his family at home until his circumstances changed. Other means of support included the provision of blankets, shoes and clothing or under more serious circumstances, paupers were ordered to the poorhouse for 'indoor' relief, which usually applied to the elderly or infirm, and abandoned or orphaned children. Extracts from Vestry records demonstrate the extent of the poverty faced by many Marwood labourers and their families:

Vestry Records

24 September 1827 *Ordered that shoes be given to the two eldest children of Anne Browne.*

17 December 1827 *John Jenkins disabled by an accident applying for casual relief, ordered that the clerk do pay him 2s. Anne Blackmore and Mary Worth jnr were ordered to have each a pair of shoes.*

25 March 1828 *Resolved that it is expedient that additional accommodation be provided in the poor house for the necessitous poor of this parish and that the house be put into repairs preparatory thereto – and that W Gilbert of Pilton, Carpenter and Joiner, be instructed to make a survey and estimate of the necessary repairs to be done.*

7 April 1828 *The smallpox having made its appearance in the neighbouring parishes, ordered that Mr Newbolt do vaccinate such of the poor inhabitants of this parish as should apply for that purpose and that the expense thereof at 2s 6d per head including medicines be defrayed out of the poor rate.*

2 June 1828 *Mary the wife of Humphrey Wilkey of Barnstaple, having applied for relief stating that her husband had run away on Sunday 1st June, she was told she might come to the poor house where she would receive proper relief.*

11 August 1828 *Robert Dyer having applied for relief on the ground of his age being 69 and his incapacity of earning his living, he was ordered to come to the poor house where he would be maintained.*

25 August 1828 *William Jostling of Pilton having applied for relief to enable him to bury his child, his application was rejected on the grounds of his keeping at home two children above 9 years of age who he refused to have bound apprentices.*

4 May 1829 William Trick having applied for relief on the grounds of his wife having been ill for the space of six weeks, his application was rejected by reason of his insolence.

11 January 1830 John Pugsley applied for a pair of shoes, his application was rejected on the grounds of his refusing to have his son bound an apprentice.

8 March 1830 Anne Lemon made an application for relief; she stated that her husband John Lemon was in the infirmary at Barnstaple with a shattered hand, caused by a chaff cutter at Mr Rock's at Blakewell Mill. Ordered 1s 6d per week til further order.

28 March 1831 John Worth, Carpenter, agreed with the parishioners to make good elm coffins for such paupers as should die in the ensuing year at 12s each – memorandum, great and small included.

September 10 1831 Mary Gammon applied for a gown; her application was rejected on the grounds of her refusing to deliver to the overseer a blanket which he had lent her in her sickness. John Pugsley was granted a pair of shoes, Nicholas Williams a pair of stockings.

Source: Marwood Vestry Book 1827 – 1855.

These records demonstrate the incredibly difficult position that families could face in times of need. Consider the dilemma of William Jostling whose child had died yet he was denied financial help with the burial on the grounds that he would not have his two daughters bound as apprentices. The Parish Register reveals that by the following year, perhaps under even more difficult circumstances, William eventually consented and eleven year old Elizabeth was bound to James Laramy in Whiddon and nine year old Jane was sent to John Tucker at Herder's in Kings Heanton. William's eligibility for poor relief would have subsequently resumed.

The Marwood census of 1841 shows that there were still thirteen 'paupers' residing in poorhouses, ranging between the ages of three and seventy-five:

Name	Age	Name	Age
Judith Bowden	50	James Wilkey	35
William Bowden	8	Jane Wilkey	35
William Ward	4	Mary Wilkey	11
William Groves	75	Joseph Wilkey	9
Fanny Smyth	70	Richard Wilkey	7
Jane Jenkins	65	James Wilkey	5
		Anne Wilkey	3

The Wilkey Family

The presence of the Wilkey family in the poorhouse in the 1841 census is unsurprising as they had been mentioned in Vestry records from 1830 onwards, facing various financial and medical problems.

James Wilkey was born in Marwood in 1804, the son of Richard and Ann. He was bound as an apprentice to William Corney in 1817 at the age of thirteen at Thornes in Kings Heanton. On January 4 1830 he married Jane (nee Geer) and settled in West Down, but within a month of their marriage the parish issued a Removal Order because they had become chargeable (in need of poor relief). The order specified that the Marwood churchwardens and overseers of the poor were responsible for the transfer of the couple and to receive and care for them in their parish.

Vestry records show that the couple were brought to Marwood poorhouse on February 8 1830 and James had immediately applied for work in the parish. Interestingly, James also requested the sum of thirteen shillings to redeem his household goods which had been withheld in West Down. The parish clerk was ordered to inspect his belongings to ensure they were worth redeeming, and if so, to bring them to the poorhouse. Unfortunately for James, the clerk inspected the goods and reported back one month later that they were not.

In July 1841, the Vestry ordered Jane Wilkey to bring her eldest son Joseph to be examined by the parish surgeon in respect of a 'dry scurf'[1]. It seems that his condition caused such concern that Mr Mackaral, a chemist in Barnstaple, was asked to dispense medicine for it, with the charges covered by the overseers of the poor. The following year in March 1842, the 'scurf' mentioned earlier had developed into a more serious condition requiring hospitalisation. The overseers were ordered to make an application to send Joseph, then aged ten, to the North Devon infirmary, describing him as a 'poor child afflicted with an infectious disease in the head'. To make matters worse, Joseph was very poorly clothed, forcing the overseers to obtain suitable clothing and linen to ensure the boy was admitted to the infirmary in a respectable state.

Clearly Joseph was becoming costly to the parish and it was noted at the time that as soon as a cure had taken effect he was to be placed in Barnstaple Union Workhouse until arrangements could be made to bind him as an apprentice. The nature of Joseph's condition remains something of a mystery however, because it seems he was still not cured by the beginning of June 1842.

At the Vestry meeting John Lamprey proposed and John Bament seconded that Joseph should be placed under the care of Mr Facey[2] of Combe Martin 'for an effective cure of

---

[1] Scurf is known today as dandruff; however it appears that Joseph's condition was in its worst form, possibly causing his hair to fall out and pus to seep from sores in his head.

[2] William Facey of Combe Martin is listed in the census as a former schoolmaster, and later 'Vendor of Medicines'.

that disease called the scaled head' and that the costs of treatment would be defrayed out of the church rate.

Two weeks later on June 20 1842, a certificate was provided stating that Joseph had been successfully cured and he was immediately ordered to become bound as an apprentice. Later records show that Joseph succumbed to the disease again and this time his siblings had become afflicted which meant Mr Facey was asked to provide further medical treatment. To meet the cost of the medicines, the overseers of the poor went from house to house in Marwood requesting voluntary contributions.

By October 1843, the overseers reviewed the register of people who were due to take an apprentice, with a view to binding Joseph Wilkey and his younger brother Richard. Clearly the ongoing health issues of the family had by now become common knowledge in the parish and people refused to employ either of the boys. Despite the Vestry issuing a summons to enforce the apprenticeships, the magistrates ruled that Richard could not be bound on the evidence of several witnesses who stated he was not fit for work. In despair, the Vestry ordered the overseer John Lamprey, to apply to the Guardians of the Barnstaple Union Workhouse to take both Joseph and Richard. It is unknown whether John Lamprey's conscience troubled him or the workhouse refused entry but in December 1843 it was reported that he had offered to take Joseph as his own apprentice at his farm in Blakewell. Joseph's brother Richard was apprenticed to John Joslin of Prixford Barton and the original Indenture papers which record this transaction are now archived at the North Devon Record Office. It reads:

> Richard Wilkey a poor male child, of the age of eleven years, belonging to and having a settlement in the said parish of Marwood and whose parents are not able to maintain this child, and the said overseers have proposed to us, the said Justices, to bind such child to be an apprentice to one John Joslin of the parish of Marwood in the county aforesaid, and residing within the distance of forty miles from the parish and place to which the said child belongs; and as an apprentice with him, the said John Joslin, to dwell and serve until the said Richard Wilkey shall come to the age of twenty-one years. For his estate in the said parish called Prixford, according to the statutes in such case made and provided.

Source: NDRO 3398-4/100 (image reproduced on the following page).

The apprenticeships of Joseph and Richard Wilkey are significant because they were the last to be arranged in Marwood. This was due to the introduction of the Poor Law Amendment Bill of 1844 which abolished the compulsory apprenticeship system. Subsequently only private apprenticeships arranged between parents and masters were permitted and these were not recorded by the parish.

It might be imagined that these would be the last references made to the Wilkey family in the Vestry records, but this was not the case. The England & Wales Death Index reveals that James Wilkey, Joseph's father, died in January 1845 and it appears that Jane and the younger children remained at the poorhouse. However at a Vestry meeting in October 1845 it was proposed by Henry Ley Esq. that notice should be given to Jane Wilkey for her disorderly conduct, ordering her to leave the poorhouse within a fortnight. This she did and within a matter of weeks she married Robert Creedy of Wiveliscombe, who later died in 1849. Curiously the Vestry records state that at a meeting on December 24 1850 it was proposed that Mr Carder should go to Wiveliscombe to ascertain whether the reputed wife of Robert Creedy was 'dead or living at the time of his marriage with Jane Wilkey'. Unfortunately there were no further references to this matter in any records, but it suggests that either Robert was guilty of bigamy or that Jane had laid claim to his estate upon his death.

The exact date of the closure of the Marwood poorhouse is unclear however Vestry records suggest that it was late in 1845, as there are no further references to its upkeep following the expulsion of Jane Wilkey.

Above: The formal documentation used to confirm the apprenticeship agreement for Richard Wilkey. Source: NDRO 3398-4/100.

Chapter Four:
All Things Ecclesiastical

The Domesday Book of 1086 indicates the presence of a church in Marwood as early as the eleventh century, where it refers to the settlement of 'Cherchemerewode' (Church Marwood), possibly constructed from wood as was characteristic of the period. Some of the fabric of the stone built parish church which stands today has thirteenth century origins, although the greater part of the building dates from the fifteenth century onwards. There is an interesting reference to the church in the Episcopal Registers of Walter de Stapledon (Bishop of Exeter 1307-26), which reveal that on January 1, 1309, the Bishop demanded that it be enlarged to accommodate its growing congregation:

> At Marwood the Lord Bishop ordered the Parishioners of Marwood Church under a penalty of ten pounds to enlarge their church within a year from the Feast of St Michael so that whereas a certain part of the Parishioners are now during Divine Service excluded from the Church because of its narrow dimensions and want of room, they may for the future be able to enter and thus the Parishioners may together be able at the same time and in the same building hear the Services of the Church.

Source: Translated from Latin in *Marwood Church Monthly*, October 1897.

Marwood Parish Church was formerly dedicated to St Michael the Archangel, later amended to St Michael & All Angels and is thought to have been founded by the Martin family. For hundreds of years it remained the sole place of worship in the parish with the exception of small private chapels built on the Westcott and Whitefield estates. According to Zachariah Smyth (b.1829), the son of a Metcombe farmer, there was a small chapel-of-ease[1] in Patsford in medieval times, which is mentioned as having long been in ruins in the 1868 National Gazetteer of Great Britain and Ireland. Zachariah wrote to the North Devon Journal and his letter, printed on March 19 1896, revealed that in the mid nineteenth century, a quantity of human bones had been dug up in what was then known as Chapel Field, causing local people to suspect that it was a former burial ground. A recent archaeological report undertaken by Exeter Archaeology also indicated the presence of a chapel, northeast of Patsford Farm.

The nineteenth century brought the first signs of division among the parish when the first non-conformist places of worship were built. This began with the Methodist movement in Prixford, followed closely by the Independents in Muddiford. There were also small chapels in Middle Marwood and Whitehall, although only limited information exists particularly concerning the latter.

---

[1] Chapel-of-ease: built within the boundaries of the parish, to accommodate those who lived a long distance away from the main parish church.

With such an abundant history of worship, it will be of little surprise to learn that it has been said of Marwood:

> Tribute should, perhaps, be paid to the fact that the great cause of religion has always been most worthily upheld in the Parish, being indeed, a widespread family tradition in many cases.

Source: North Devon Journal, January 1937.

Marwood Parish Church

St Michael & All Angels is an ancient building of early English and perpendicular style, of architectural interest for its craftsmanship dating back to the thirteenth century. It is positioned on high ground, overlooking Marwood Hill Gardens.

According to Victorian architect Edmund Sedding of Plymouth, the original thirteenth century plan of the building was cruciform, with nave, chancel, north and south transepts. The existing south transept, also known as the Lady Chapel, was erected around the middle of the thirteenth century, though the north transept was extended into the north aisle in the fifteenth century. The north aisle is divided from the nave by four bays with decorative columns moulded from bere stone, and at its east end is a late sixteenth century vestry.

Church Tower

At the western end of the church lies the fifteenth century bell tower. There is a legend associated with its origins, which mentions a laundress from Westcott Barton. Evidently, the woman found a quantity of money hidden in the old mansion, and believed its divine purpose was to enable the construction of a tower at the parish church, which she duly arranged to be built as high as the belfry window. According to Morris' trade directory of 1870, a figurehead of a woman was carved into the tower's stonework on one side of the window, and an ironing box on the other side, which it states 'gives a colouring of probability to the tale'. Today these carvings are no longer visible, possibly as the result of later restoration work.

The tower initially boasted five bells cast by Thomas Bilbie of Cullompton in 1771 and later a sixth bell, the treble, was cast by John Warner & Sons of London. In 1890, Reverend Torry, who described the bells as 'remarkable for sweetness of tone' (*Marwood Church Monthly*, February 1894), ordered restoration

Above: Marwood Parish Church: 2011.

work the following year, which involved the repair and re-hanging of the bells at the cost of one hundred and twenty-five pounds. Harry Stokes 'Church Bell Hanger & Builder' of Woodbury carried out the work and the belfry was officially reopened in October 1891.

Each bell is individually inscribed, in most cases with the names of their generous benefactors, as shown below:

(1) Thomas Watts, John Kelley, William Berry, George Smyth, Thomas Heath. J Bilbie fecit 1771.
(2) Thomas Hartnoll, John Lamprey, John Mules. J Bilbie fecit 1771.
(3) Mr Thomas Sharland & Mr George Horwood, church wardens. J Bilbie fecit 1771.
(4) Thomas Bilbie of Cullompton cast us all 1771.
(5) George Ley senr, George Ley jnr Esq. J Bilbie fecit 1771.
(6) The Rev Richard Harding, rector, 59 years. God preserve our church and King.

In February 1901, *Marwood Church Monthly* reported that the parish bell ringers had met in the Belfry in January to organise themselves into a formal band and establish a set of rules, as shown below:

1. The band shall consist of a president, leader and ringers.

2. The Rector shall be ex-officio president. The office of the leader shall be annual, but the retiring leader is eligible for re-election.

3. All new members shall be elected by a majority of existing members, subject to the approval of the Rector.

4. There shall be a meeting held annually in the month of December, for the election of the leader, and other business.

5. The leader shall be responsible for the entire management of the Belfry.

6. The ringers are expected to attend punctually when their services are required.

7. No person beside the ringers shall be allowed to be present in the Belfry during any ringing, without the permission of the president, or leader.

8. The ringers are expected to attend punctually when their services are required.

9. The ringing on Sundays shall commence at 8.30 in the morning. In the evening it shall commence not later than 6 o'clock and continue until ten minutes before the service begins. There shall be a weekly practice on Wednesday evenings.

10. A register of attendance of ringers on Sundays, and at practices shall be kept by the leader. All members absent from ringing without giving notice shall be fined one penny.

11. Any ringer who shall be absent from the Belfry for more than four consecutive weeks without the permission of the leader shall be considered to have resigned.

12. After ringing on Sundays, the ringers are expected to attend Divine service in the Church.

13. In the case of dispute as to matters connected with the Belfry, the decision of the president shall be final.

Signed:
George B Worth, Leader
Robert Worth
William Taylor
Fred J Kelly
Charles Smith
Frederick Yeo
Henry Manning

In 1905 it was reported in *Marwood Church Monthly* that the bell ropes were in dire need of repair and had only lasted in the meantime due to the skilful repair and dedicated care of Robert Worth and William Lovering. It was estimated that each rope would cost fifteen shillings to replace, though fortunately the following gentlemen pledged to pay for one rope each, the Reverend Alfred Johnson; W E Arthur Esq. *(Marwood Hill House)*; T Joslin Esq. *(Westcott Barton)*; General Sturt *(Muddiford House)* and the fifth, jointly by Messrs C J Harris and W J Gear of Kings Heanton. The sixth rope was funded by contributions from J M Montague Esq. *(Lee House)*, J R Morris, F J Morris and H G Hastings Shaddick.

1905 also saw the formation of a Ringers' Association for the Deanery, which was celebrated with a festival at Marwood Parish Church in October of that year. Bands of Ringers were sent from Ilfracombe, Pilton, West Down, Mortehoe and Heanton Punchardon to attend the inaugural service, following which a hymn 'Praise Him upon the loud Cymbals' (sung to the tune of 'Melcombe') which was written by Reverend Johnson of Marwood. *Marwood Church Monthly* reported 'The singing of so many male voices sounded very impressive'.

It is one hundred and ten years since the Belfry rules were passed and many of them still apply, perhaps with the exception of the one penny fine for unauthorised absence! Bell ringing continues to be a popular pastime for Marwood parishioners who strive to maintain this great tradition.

The ringers still meet for their weekly practices, and it is heartening to know that the peal of the bells has echoed around the parish on Wednesday evenings for so many years and continues to do so into the twenty-first century.

The Ringers Hymn
Marwood Festival 1905

"Praise him upon the loud cymbals"

O thou whose praise all creatures sing,
And from whose love all blessings spring,
O bless our efforts when we ring,
Lord God Almighty!

O bless the music of our bells,
That loud in rhythmic cadence swells,
And far and wide, Thy message tells,
Lord God Almighty!

It bids Thy children come to pray,
Within Thy house on Christ's own day,
And all their griefs before ye lay,
Lord God Almighty!

It summons them on festal days,
Their strains of joy to Thee up raise,
And glorify Thee by their praise,
Lord God Almighty!

O when our ropes we downward ply,
And loud our bells peal forth on high,
Let all to Thee in love draw nigh,
Lord God Almighty!

To cherish and revere the place,
In which we worship, give us grace,
And help us there to seek Thy face,
Lord God Almighty!

To please all ears we'll ring, but most,
To praise with the angelic host,
Thee, Father, Son and Holy Ghost,
Lord God Almighty!

Former Marwood ringer Lou Spear*(pictured right c.1955)* remembers 'learning the ropes' from former captain Noah Passmore in the late 1940s and later from Jack Watts, another celebrated captain, who recently celebrated his ninetieth birthday.

Above: Marwood bell ringers c.1969, L-R Frank Hommel, Denzil Spear, Bernard Brooks, Jack Watts, Freddie Manning, Frank Quick, George Manning, Allan Watts, Donald Quick.

Right: In the late 1960s the Marwood church bells were due for re-casting. With the assistance of Harold Hopkins and his tractor and trailer, the enormously heavy bells were transported out of the churchyard for their long journey to Loughborough for recasting.

Left: A young Fiona Brooks and her dog Rusty, demonstrate the immense size of the bells.

Churchyard

An extension to the original churchyard was added in 1878, taking over land formerly known as the Revel Ground or 'Bowling Green' where parish revels had taken place during the annual fair and festivities. Vestry[1] records mention that the 'present generation' preferred to play skittles rather than bowls, although other sports such as wrestling took place there. In fact it was said that a stone was once erected at the site, inscribed with words of praise for sport.

In an article in the North Devon Journal in April 1987, local historian and author Peter Christie, refers to historical accounts sent to the newspaper in 1896 again by Zachariah Smyth. He described the Marwood fair held annually just after Whitsun, which involved sideshows and wrestling matches, with silver spoons for prizes – evidently accompanied by heavy drinking. If the wrestlers became too inebriated, they were placed in the stocks located by the churchyard wall. Zachariah described the lead up to a wrestling match:

> A ring of men would form and the challenger would literally throw his hat into the middle shouting "A man! A man!" To take up the challenge, another hat was thrown in and the two wrestlers would strip to the waist and put on loose jackets of coarse material to fight in.

> Source: Peter Christie, North Devon Journal (1987).

Regrettably, the sports were so frequently accompanied by incidents of drunken and disorderly behaviour that they were discontinued in 1828. The 'Bowling Green' was temporarily granted to the occupiers of the poorhouses for use as a garden and later let to the adjacent farm for five shillings per year with the income added to church funds.

In 1876 the churchwardens recognised the growing need to enlarge the existing graveyard, the obvious solution being to utilise the former revel ground and terminate the farmer's lease. In August 1878, Lord Bishop Frederick of Exeter declared the ground to be consecrated, formally extending the churchyard at the lowest end beyond the War Memorial.

The Church-house (also known as the Lychgate Rooms)

Robert Bovett (1989) explains that parish church-houses were usually built of stone and thatch, and located close to the church. The Marwood church-house still stands today, adjacent to the lychgate adjoining the churchyard. It was once thatched, as evidenced by the churchwardens' accounts, which detail the cost of reeds to repair the roof, and while its exact date of construction is unknown, it is likely to be at least sixteenth century.

---

[1] The Vestry controlled both the ecclesiastical and civil matters arising within the parish until legislation brought the latter under the control of county, district and parish councils.

The church-house could be described as an early equivalent of the Church Hall. It was used for social activities that were not appropriate within the church itself, such as preparation of food and drink for the feasts and fairs that were held to celebrate saints' days. Although these festivities raised funds for the church, in the seventeenth century, the Puritans put an end to what they considered to be irreverent behaviour on consecrated land. So began a number of different uses for the building. For example, there were two church services on Sundays, and for those parishioners who lived a long distance away, it was unfeasible to travel home in-between. The church-house provided those people with shelter, and stabling below for their horses.

Right:
Marwood
Church-house and
Lychgate in 2011.

Until the sixteenth century, it was the responsibility of the churches and other religious charities to care for the poor. Following the dissolution of the monasteries during the reign of Henry VIII, this duty passed to the parish. Under Elizabethan law, a poor rate or tax could be charged to those in the parish who could afford to pay it, to cover the costs of supporting those in need.

Substantial amendments to English Poor Laws in 1723 required each parish to provide accommodation for their poor, particularly the old and infirm and as a result, many parishes including Marwood, initially adapted their church-houses for this purpose. In 1779, the Marwood Episcopal visitation returns stated that 'we have no Hospital or Alms-House other than what we call a Church House, for keeping & Lodging some Parish Poor'. In the 1906 Charity Commission report however, it was revealed that in addition to the church-house, there was also a cottage situated at the roadside in front of *Marwood House*, which may have been converted to a poorhouse in the late eighteenth century. This is supported by notes in the Vestry records, which make a clear distinction between the church-house, also known then as the schoolroom and the poorhouse.

In 1834, the Poor Law Amendment Act introduced further changes to the welfare of the poor, one of which led to the formation of Poor Law Unions. This meant that local parishes became part of one larger Union, which retained responsibility for the management of a central Union workhouse. A Board of Guardians oversaw the operations of the Union, each guardian being elected by the constituent parishes, although each parish vestry would remain responsible for levying poor rates for the upkeep of the workhouse. Given the provision of a central workhouse, a later act passed in 1836, meant all redundant parish property, church or poorhouses, were ordered to be sold.

> The Barnstaple Poor Law Union was formally established in December 1835, and guardians from thirty-nine local parishes (including Marwood) were duly elected. It was agreed that a purpose built workhouse should be erected, and this was completed in 1837. Situated in Alexandra Road, it was designed to accommodate almost three hundred people, at a cost of four thousand eight hundred pounds. The layout incorporated four separate wings and courtyards, which allowed for the segregation of men, women, boys and girls.
> Source: www.workhouses.org.uk/index.html?Barnstaple/Barnstaple.

Although the 1834 act intended to assist parishes with the burden of looking after their poor, ultimately the Vestries had a responsibility to limit those costs which would fall to their local ratepayers. Under the terms of the Poor Law Amendment Act, the provision of local outdoor relief was not banned, therefore at Marwood, and many other parishes across England, the Vestry elected to retain their local poorhouse and to continue paying outdoor relief, which would equate to approximately half the cost of sending their poor into the Barnstaple workhouse.

At a meeting chaired by George Ley Esq. of *Lee House*, the Marwood Vestry unanimously agreed that 'the poorhouse, school room and all the rights, tithes, privileges and appurtenances thereunto belonging, shall be kept in all respects as it usually and formerly had been kept, and not in no respects to be sold as directed by the Poor Law Commissioners, but for the shelter and comfort of aged and impotent people and such who are by large families incapacitated to pay a cottage rent'. At first glance, one might perceive this to be a great act of paternalism, a sense of wanting to 'look after their own' rather than dispatch people to the rather daunting Union workhouse. Perhaps a more realistic explanation was the Vestry's concern for the potential financial burden of paying for the upkeep[1] of their parishioners in the workhouse, and felt a more practical solution was to care for them locally and control the cost.

---

[1] The cost of keeping a pauper in the Union workhouse could be several shillings per person, per week.

By 1839, the Marwood poorhouse was still in use and at a Vestry meeting in April, it was noted that the building was in a very bad state of repair. It was proposed that the necessary work be undertaken, and a fortnight later at a further meeting chaired by George Ley Esq. it was confirmed that local mason Henry Hill of Guineaford had attended to the repairs at a cost of one pound and ten shillings. Evidently, the parish intended to continue using the poorhouse for the foreseeable future.

One year later at a special meeting in April 1840, the Vestry met to discuss the 'disorderly conduct of some of the pauper occupiers of the poorhouse. It was ordered that the several occupiers thereon be directed to provide themselves with other lodgings, on or before Midsummer next, and that the said house be then closed, and that notice hereof be forthwith given to such occupiers'. Yet, this threat to close down the poorhouse was not followed through because in November 1840, records reveal that local man William Groves was ordered to come to the poorhouse as he was 'by age and infirmities incapacitated from paying house rent'.

In October 1841, the Vestry learned that a great number of local and able bodied labourers had made applications to the Board of Guardians for outdoor relief in the event that they had been unable to find work. To the indignation of the Vestry, the Board instructed that those labourers should be admitted with their families into the Barnstaple workhouse, and that outdoor relief would no longer be paid to able bodied paupers. The Vestry quickly took action, instructing all labourers who were out of work, to apply to the overseers of the poor of Marwood, who would find them work with local farmers rather than send them to the workhouse.

The last mention of the poorhouse being occupied was in late 1845, however it was not until 1858 that the Vestry approved the sale of the parish property, church-house and dilapidated poorhouse, under the terms of the act of 1836, and on condition that when the latter premises were pulled down, no new buildings were erected on the same site and the land returned to the Lord of the Manor.

The 1906 Charity Commission Report confirms that in 1859, the Lady of the Manor, Miss Harriet Cutcliffe of Marwood Hill, purchased the church-house together with the poorhouse for the sum of two hundred and fifty pounds. Miss Cutcliffe instructed William Worth to pull down the old, dilapidated poorhouse which stood close by her impressive Georgian manor house but to retain and renovate the church-house[1]. Upon completion of the works, she generously presented the building to the parish, to be used, as before for parochial purposes. The ground floor of the church-house being partially open at the side, was once again used for stabling horses for those coming to church and the upper floor remained for the use of the school and the Vestry.

---

[1] The church-house was designated a Grade II listed building in November 1984. The existing building is described as nineteenth century with fragments of walls from the earlier building, reflecting the renovation work carried out by carpenter William Worth in 1859.

In 1906 there was an enquiry to ascertain the rightful ownership of the church-house (Lychgate Rooms) – the Reverend Alfred Johnson believing it was the property of the church and the council believing it belonged to the parish. The building had many earlier purposes, being known as the 'school room', 'church house chamber', 'church house', 'vestry room' and 'parish room', and stood partly on land belonging to the parish and partly on land held by the feofees of the Lord of the Manor, at a nominal rent - churchwarden accounts show that in 1801 '8 years chief rent of the church-house due Michaelmas 1s 4pence'. As a result of the enquiry, Reverend Johnson decreed that ownership of the property should be granted to the parish council.

Inside St Michael & All Angels Parish Church

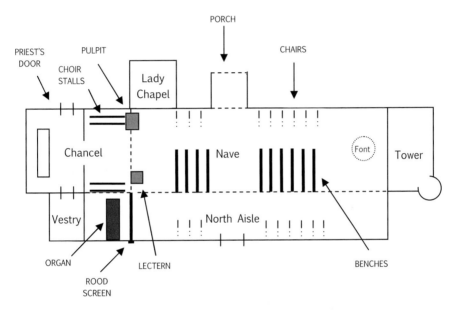

Craftsmanship

Prior to the fifteenth century most churches had little or no seating, leaving the congregation either to stand or kneel upon earthen floors scattered with straw and herbs. The need for seating grew as sermons became more common and longer in length, and initially some benches were set up around the edge of the nave for the elderly and infirm to rest. Open benches were later installed in the fifteenth and sixteenth centuries with exquisite carved ends. The carvings are seen in a range of styles, some denoting shields, saints or musical instruments, each framed by floral or foliage design.

Right: One of the ornate bench ends at Marwood.

According to Emma Augusta Bridges (1881), some of the carved ends were destroyed. She described the interior of the church; 'There were handsome carved oak ends to the few open seats still left; the others, some fifty years before the time of which I write, had been burnt in the village poorhouse for firing, and replaced by the wretched, incongruous deal erections in which the people, hidden from view, sat and slept away the hour for worship'.

'Deal' pews were in effect enclosed wooden boxes with high fronts and backs, commonly found in parish churches during this period. They were arranged to accommodate all levels of society, and could be leased or bought like property at varying costs, for use by families. An example of this custom was illustrated in the Vestry book in September 1840. The record describes the lease of the box pew in the north aisle, next to the north door, to John Lynch of Muddiford, for the sum of three shillings for the year ending in Easter 1841.

Being a relatively wealthy family, the Bridges of *Marwood Hill House* owned their box pew. Emma Augusta Bridges described the brass rails that ran along two sides of their pew, on which two green baize curtains were hung for privacy and to keep the draughts out. This meant the children could not see out of the pew unless they climbed upon the hassocks! The local gentry had their box pews located in the chancel, alongside Reverend Riley's family pew, to symbolise their status. The rest of the congregation were seated in the nave, positioned in order of importance.

In 1858, restoration work saw the chancel box pews dismantled, the remaining oak panelling being reused to form the reredos[1]. The central decorative panels of the Marwood reredos were taken from the old Whitefield family pew.

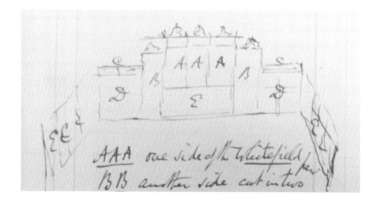

Above: Sketch by Reverend Collison, showing the layout of the wooden reredos surrounding the altar, indicating where former box pew panels had been reused, c.1858.

Source: North Devon Record Office: 3398-4/266.

---

[1] A screen usually made of wood or stone, which stands behind the altar table,

When Devonshire architect Edmund Sedding listed his recommendations for the restoration of the church in 1897, thankfully he suggested that all remaining box pews were dispensed with and replaced with oak benches or chairs.

Rood Loft and Screen

The beautifully carved wooden rood screen in the north aisle *(pictured right, c.1920)* is one of the last remaining examples of sixteenth century craftsmanship, many having been destroyed during the reformation of Henry VIII. Originally this medieval screen extended right across the church, from the north to the south wall, which meant that the mass would be mostly celebrated out of sight of the congregation. Not long before his death in 1853, the Reverend Richard Riley ordered the removal of the south end of the screen. Vestry records show that local carpenter, William Worth, had been tasked with taking the screen down, describing it as being richly carved with images. William said he thought the fragments of the screen were stored under the tower but later nothing was found. In July 1903, the Reverend Alfred Johnson issued a plea in *Marwood Church Monthly* for parishioners to come forward if they knew the whereabouts of the remains of the screen. He had been advised that some may have been stored in the old tithe barn, and 'Even the smallest fragment of such an archaeological

Above: The Rood Loft at Marwood c.1930.

treasure would be invaluable' though his appeal was futile. In the many titles written about the churches of Devon, there is still a great sense of sadness expressed at the loss of this historic woodwork at St Michael & All Angels.

In her notes on 'Devon Churches in the Deanery of Barnstaple', Beatrix F Cresswell notes that the carving on the existing rood screen 'is of a most delicate type' and 'above runs a graceful cornice and the groining is filled with ornaments of renaissance character'. The doors of the screen are inscribed with 'Sir John Beapul, parson of Merewode', who was rector from 1520, during the reign of Henry VIII.

The rood loft was built on a platform above the screen, upon which the rood (crucifix) would have been placed. In previous centuries it could be accessed via a small staircase, tucked just inside the Lady Chapel. The entrance to the stairs is actually set high into the wall and in the past, there would have been wooden steps to allow access.

Right: The elevated doorway in the Lady Chapel, which would have provided access to the former south end of the rood loft.

Today, there are some remains of the carvings at the back of the rood loft, which can be seen from the chancel, yet sadly the front was removed in the early 1850s.

In 1904 it seems that the remainder of the screen was in a sorry state, having been taken down and stored at the rectory. Reverend Alfred Johnson engaged architectural carver, Walter Thetford of Litchdon Street, Barnstaple, to restore the screen 'in the most neat and workmanlike manner, taking away all parts affected by dry rot, and making good with oak of best quality and carving same where required to match the old work'. Given the intricacy of the work required he was paid thirty pounds for his services, which included re-erection of the screen in the church. Walter was also commissioned to create the lectern using old oak recycled from another part of the church.

Pulpit

Along with the altar, the pulpit has long been seen as one of the most important features of the church, particularly following the Reformation when Christians first came to hear the bible preached in English, making the pulpit a place of immense authority. The existing Marwood pulpit has Jacobean carvings, dating to the mid seventeenth century and is found to the east of the transept. Vestry records suggest that it was originally placed west of the Lady Chapel and described as being 'surmounted by a sounding board connected to the pulpit by wainscotting'. It was also set four feet higher than the existing platform, emphasising its place of authority to the congregation.

Church of England services follow the Common Book of Prayer which involves the rector reading out a series of statements, followed by responses made by the congregation. In the early nineteenth century, Reverend Richard Riley read his statements from the high pulpit, beneath a sounding board which projected his voice further around the church.

Above: The pulpit at Marwood parish church.

In the mid 1800s the parish clerk would sit in front of the pulpit, vigorously encouraging the largely illiterate congregation in their responses. When Emma Bridges started attending Marwood church in the 1840s, the incumbent Reverend Riley was already in his eighties and quite frail, which meant the congregation often struggled to hear him, even with the aid of the sounding board.

It was only the responses loudly prompted by the parish clerk, Henry Hill, that would enable them to keep track of the progress of the service.

According to James Coulter (1996), author of *Tawstock & The Lords of Barnstaple*, the walls of medieval churches were covered with large pictures depicting scenes from the bible. After the reformation, it was common for the walls to be whitewashed and text from scriptures painted in pertinent places. At Marwood, Reverend Torry discovered scripture from the book of Proverbs, painted in black letters on the wall behind the pulpit, which he suspected had been there for at least three hundred years (Source: NDRO 3398-4/266):

> *My son, keep my words, and hide my commandments with thee.*
> *Keep my commandments, and thou shalt live, and mine*
> *instruction as the apple of thine eyes.*
>
> *Proverbs 7:1, 2 Geneva version.*

In 1891, the old pulpit was dismantled, restored and re-erected to its current position east of the transept chapel. Slender wooden pillars, which had once formed part of the staircase required to reach the higher pulpit, were removed and reused as decorative support around the stone base.

Misericords

There are wooden stalls in the chancel with seats known as Misericords or mercy seats *(pictured right)*. According to Vestry records, three Misericords originally faced the altar and would have backed on to the former rood screen.

In 1859 local carpenter William Worth moved the stalls to their current position on the north side of the chancel, at right angles to the altar. They remain in this position today, used by the choir. William also carved six new Misericords in the same style as the original ones and these were placed to the south side of the chancel where the rectory family box pew was previously located.

When a Misericord seat is lifted, it reveals a small shelf with intricate carving beneath *(pictured below)*, just large enough to have propped up clergy who might have stood for long periods during prayer, in days gone by.

Left: Beneath each Misericord seat, a secret carving is hidden.

Lady Chapel

Within the Lady Chapel or South Transept, two stained glass windows have been erected.

Above: The stained glass window dedicated to Reverend Pryke.

In August 1904, *Marwood Church Monthly* reported that the parish church could boast, probably for the first time in its history, a stained glass window *(pictured left)*. This was prompted by the recent discovery during restoration work, of an original thirteenth century lancet window within the east wall of the South Transept, which had been walled up and covered with a tombstone. Mr Henry Burgess had restored the window, adorning it with plain glass, however after a visit to the church by Arthur W Hunt Esq. of Lancaster, a contemporary of former incumbent Reverend Pryke and stained glass architect by trade, the Reverend Alfred Johnson was asked to accept the gift of stained glass for the lancet window.

The window depicts the infant Jesus, his mother and John the Baptist and is aptly dedicated to Reverend Pryke, instigator of the restoration fund, and popular with parishioners during his incumbency between 1893 and 1900. The inscription reads:

To the Glory of God and in memory of
the ministry of William Emmanuel Pryke
Rector 1893 – 1900.

A brief history of Reverend Pryke's residence in Marwood follows later in this chapter.

The second and larger window is dedicated to the son of Colonel and Mrs Heyworth, formerly of Whitefield Barton, who lost his life in Gallipoli during the First World War. The inscription within the panels reads:

In loving memory of Captain Heyworth Potter Lawrence Heyworth of the 2nd Battalion North Staffordshire, who was killed in action at Gallipoli August 6 1915.

The window was unveiled at an evening service at the church in August 1916, by churchwarden Mr W.Harris, assisted by sidesmen Noah Passmore and Robert Worth. Reverend Johnson then dedicated the window with the following words:

In the faith of Jesus Christ, we dedicate this window to the glory of God, and in memory of his servant, Captain Potter Lawrence Heyworth, in the name of the Father, the Son and the Holy Ghost.

Source: North Devon Journal, August 6 1916.

Above: Stained glass window dedicated to Captain Heyworth in the Lady Chapel.

The left hand light bears the image of St Lawrence, with the words 'Be thou faithful unto death'. The central light is of 'Christus Consulator' (Christ the Comforter), with the words 'Come unto me, ye that labour' and on the right, is the familiar image of St George, in defeat of the dragon, with the poignant words 'I have fought the good fight'.

Piscina

In the south wall of the chancel, close to the altar is a thirteenth century, trefoil headed piscina, a small stone basin set into a recess originally used pre-reformation for the washing of sacred vessels following mass.

The Marwood Piscina was one of a number of adornments that caught the eye of renowned architect William Richard Lethaby (b.1857). Born and raised in Barnstaple, William was educated at a grammar school in Paternoster Row and later apprenticed to Alexander Lauder. He had a hugely successful career, designing some notable buildings nationwide, and later in life he became Professor of Design at the Royal College of Art and Principal of the Central School of Arts and Crafts in 1902 (which he founded), as well as Surveyor of Westminster Abbey in 1906. In the North Devon Athenaeum, one of William's sketchpads can be found (dated 1896) which contains a series of rough pencil drawings of Westminster Abbey and the interior of St Michael & All Angels Parish Church in Marwood. Perhaps he was looking for inspiration?

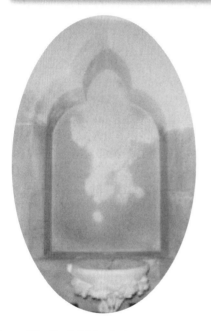

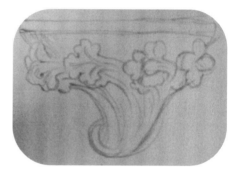

Above: William Richard Lethaby's rough sketch of the Piscina at Marwood Parish Church, c.1896. With kind permission of North Devon Athenaeum (B70c-05-11).

Above: The Trefoil Headed Piscina at Marwood.

Font

The original font dates to the twelfth century, a very simple rectangular design. Reverend Collison wrote rather disparagingly in the Vestry book in 1858 that it resembled a horse's trough. Mounted on a circular stone shaft which is now placed underneath the pulpit as a support, the font was previously situated in the north aisle, at the point where an indentation has been cut into one of the pillars. The indentation can still be seen and it is the exact measurement of the depth of the font. Emma Augusta Bridges described the old font with similar disdain as 'a plain sort of trough, resembling those which in times past stood beneath the pump, in which potatoes and other roots were washed'.

When baptisms were performed, the rector preferred to keep a small white basin within the font, containing the holy water rather than fill the entire vessel.

In 1859, when Reverend Collison was informed that a new font had been donated, he ordered the removal of the old singing gallery that had previously stood at the west end of the church, to enable the new font to be positioned there (just as it is today). The gallery had blocked the entire west window, with the exception of one section, which had been filled with stained glass by Emma's father, Thomas Bridges, who was churchwarden for ten years.

Above: The original Norman font, which is said to be older than the church building.

Above: The current font carved in an ornate medieval style during the early Victorian era.

In May 1859, Ann Tyrell of Ilfracombe, sister of Bishop William Tyrell, former graduate of St John's College, Cambridge, donated the new circular font. It was made by Pulsford Masons of Barnstaple and carved from French Caen stone, supported by four Devonshire marble shafts which were the gift of Reverend Collison's mother. The font has beautiful foliage decoration and mitred priests carved around the bowl.

The old 'trough' font was initially buried in the ground beneath the new font, supposedly a Victorian tradition, but it was disinterred in 1940 and can now be found just outside the belfry.

On the lid of the font sits a sculpture by John Robinson (1935-2007), who also created some of the eye-catching statues on display at Marwood Hill Gardens. The sculpture was donated in 1970 and depicts the Prophet Simeon blessing Jesus. A brass plaque is fixed onto the base, engraved with the words of 'Nunc Dimittis' translated as 'Simeon's song'. In the book of Luke (2:29–32) Simeon is described as a devout old man who was promised by the Holy Ghost that before he died, he would see the Saviour. When Mary and Joseph brought Jesus from Bethlehem to the temple in Jerusalem for a customary ceremony, Simeon realised the child was the promised Messiah and is said to have taken Jesus in his arms and chanted a song of thanksgiving:

Lord, now lettest thou thy servant depart in peace, According to thy word For mine eyes have seen thy salvation Which thou hast prepared before the face of all people. To be a light to lighten the Gentiles and to be the glory of thy people Israel.

Nunc Dimittis - Luke 2:29-32.

Left: 'Simeon's Song' by John Robinson.

Sundial

Above the church entrance, upon the embattled south porch, an ornate sundial is placed, dating back to 1762 *(pictured below)*. It is a beautiful example of the craftsmanship of John Berry, a former parishioner of Marwood. An edition of *The Exeter Daily Gazette* in 1891 described John Berry as a mason from Muddiford 'who is still remembered, as the local masons trace their skill through two or three generations back to him. His sundials may be seen over the church porches in the neighbourhood, and in the gardens of private houses.' Upon his death in February 1796 aged seventy-three, John was buried near to the south porch of the church.

According to Stephen Friar (2001) sundials were often used to remind the congregation of their own mortality and the need for repentance. This is substantiated by the Latin inscription on the Marwood sundial: TEMPUS FUGIT, MORS VENIT, NOS UT UMBRA, which translated, means *"Time flies, death comes we (are) as a shadow"*.

Above: One of John Berry's finest sundials sits above Marwood Parish Church porch.

It shows the approximate time at various places including Berlin, Paris, Vienna and Jerusalem, and another interesting feature is the lower pointer, which by its shadow shows the position of the sun in the zodiac at different times of the year, indicated by the signs engraved on the dial.

Regrettably, the sundial was badly damaged during a terrible gale in May 1897, and the incident was reported in *Marwood Church Monthly*:

> Among the disastrous effects of the gale on Ash Wednesday morning, was the destruction of the interesting sundial over the Church porch. The slate, of which it was composed, was smashed to pieces. There must be many persons interested in Marwood affairs, who would be glad to contribute towards the cost of replacing our ancient dial. The old one cannot be mended, but an exact copy will be made of it.

> Source: *Marwood Church Monthly*, May 1897.

Although the article suggests that the sundial was beyond repair, it seems that later an attempt was made to salvage this historic ornament. As can be seen in the photograph, the sundial is now in situ with several large cracks, which would have been a more economical solution than replacement.

Gifts

There have been many magnificent items that have been donated to the church over the centuries, and often in remembrance of loved ones. The fine litany desk which sits in front of the oak clergy chair, was given in memory of Wilfred and Emily Main of Guineaford, by their four children. The Main family lived at *Byeways* in Guineaford between the 1880s and early 1900s. Wilfred (b.1857), originally from Cornwall, was schoolmaster of the Church school for twenty-four years, before his eyesight began to deteriorate. As Wilfred's retirement approached, a party was held in his honour in the rectory garden in June 1901, with tea provided by the Reverend and Mrs Barlow. A cheque was presented to him for the sum of thirty-two pounds which had been donated by almost one hundred subscribers in the parish, indicating the great respect with which he was held. As the guests gathered underneath the chestnut tree, the Reverend Barlow described Wilfred as having always endeavoured to develop the characters of his pupils rather than 'merely cramming their heads with facts', and that he should be thanked for 'his constant and ungrudging help' for the good of the school, Church and the Parish (*Marwood Church Monthly*, July 1901).

Above: The Litany Desk donated in memory of Wilfred & Emily Main.

Wilfred's wife Emily (b.1858, nee Skinner) was born and raised in Marwood, as were their four children, Frederick (b.1881), Hilda (b.1884), Reginald (b.1890) and Mildred (b.1892). The children attended the Church school and they all fared extremely well both in terms of attendance and academic achievement, often receiving honourable mentions in the *Marwood Church Monthly*. After Wilfred died in 1906, the family initially relocated to Exeter, although later, both Reginald and Mildred returned to Guineaford, with their respective spouses. Reginald, a retired school master of Worksop College, was married to Edna and known for his beautiful playing of the organ in the parish church. As a boy, David Fairchild remembers his mother persuading him to have singing lessons with Reginald, a talented chorister. Mildred married Alfred Underwood, and many parishioners including Harold Hopkins and Lou Spear have fond memories of the kindness of Mrs Underwood, who would hold parties every Christmas, with gifts for the local children.

In April 1896, *Marwood Church Monthly* reported that 'A handsome new Cross for the holy table has been presented bearing the following inscription - To the Glory of God and to the dear memory of Thomas and Ellen Bridges, once residents in this Parish, this Cross is given, in gratitude for a happy childhood, by their two surviving daughters, Ellen McGhie Hesse and Emma Augusta Bridges, 1896'. The cross *(pictured left)* was first used in a church service on Easter Sunday in that year, and is still in use in the church today, positioned at the centre of the altar.

Thomas (b.1806) and Ellen (b.1807) Bridges were residents of *Marwood Hill House* from 1843 to the mid 1850s, where they raised a large family of six daughters and two sons. Their third eldest daughter, Emma Augusta Bridges (mentioned earlier), wrote a book called *Not Many Years Ago: Memories of My Life*, under the nom de plume 'An Elderly Bachelor, E.A.B', first published in 1881, and providing a fascinating insight into life in Marwood and North Devon, particularly in respect of church affairs during the 1840s and 1850s.

Spurred on by curiosity, I managed to track down a copy of this book and upon reading it initially, was unable to see the connection with Marwood. After more months of parish research and at the second time of reading, it became clear that Emma wrote the book using fictitious place names and character names, to preserve anonymity of the people involved including herself. For example, Marwood itself is 'Woodley', Barnstaple is 'Stapleton' and the Rector (at that time Reverend Riley) is known as 'Mr Smith'. Emma portrays herself as a crippled boy, named Sinclair.

Having spent so many months immersed in research of the parish, the real life Marwood characters being portrayed became apparent, and many of the stories relayed by Emma are authenticated in other archived documents, such as Vestry records and newspaper articles. The book is a truly fascinating piece of history.

In September 1898, an article in *Marwood Church Monthly* encouraged parishioners to purchase their own copy of the book, hinting that 'many Marwood characters, clerical and lay, will be easily recognised', although by that time, fifty or more years had passed since the period described in the book. The author, then known only as 'An Elderly Bachelor' had pledged that 'profits made through the sale of these true memories will be given to the Restoration fund of Marwood Church', and over the years that followed, several pounds were received.

Emma's interest in religious affairs had significant bearing on her own calling in life when she joined the Clewer Sisters of Mercy. She spent the rest of her life working to provide spiritual support for women trapped in poverty and prostitution, the sick, infirm and orphans, particularly in impoverished inner city areas, until her eventual death in 1918 at the House of Mercy in Highgate, London.

There were many significant gifts listed in the Vestry records, which had been kept in an iron safe in the rectory due to their immense value. These included the communion plate and registers, a silver flagon – a bequest of William Bourchier, Rector, bearing the coat of arms of the Earls of Bath and hallmark 1671. An alms dish dated 1678; a large paten - bequest of Reverend John Sommers 1713-14; a silver communion cup with cover (no date but Elizabethan in period, similar to items found at churches in Braunton and Ashford) and a silver dish. More recent gifts include a silver paten and wafer box donated in 1944 by Mr Alfred and Mrs Mildred Underwood (nee Main) and in 1948 the Marwood Women's Institute donated a pitcher for use with the font.

Restorations
Vestry books reveal the continual challenges faced by the many rectors and churchwardens in maintaining the parish church over the centuries. Some of the earliest reported restorations commenced in 1858 following the arrival of the Reverend Frederick Collison, who commented upon the neglected appearance of the church following Reverend Riley's long tenure. There are extensive notes in the Vestry records which detail the works carried out at a cost of four hundred and fifty pounds, some of which are shown below. It is interesting to see the local gentry criticising some of the changes taking place, although the rector appears quite unperturbed!

In the first place the vaults were arched over or bricked up – a proceeding which greatly offended Miss Cutcliffe, and the altar was raised from being level with the floor to its present height.

The chancel was drained and its future dryness ensured by digging down and leaving a space of nine inches all round clear of the wall, so as to keep the soil from touching the wall.

The oak roof was found to be too rotten a condition to be maintained and was replaced by one of similar design.

All of the windows were replaced with the exception of two lancets, against one of which the Vestry had been built, while the other was covered by the Mules' monument which was removed to its present position in the aisle.

The gravestone of John Marwood of Westcott, the oldest dated in the church, was removed from the aisle to its present position in the centre of the chancel to the indignation of the Chichesters. Those of former rectors were placed nearer to the altar.

On removal of the singing gallery, the present platform was constructed in consequence of the complaints of the bell ringers.

Source: North Devon Record Office 3398-4/266.

Close to where the bell ringers gather today there was an open singing gallery, hung with thick green curtains of a coarse woollen fabric. Here the village choir would sing, supported by a group of musicians playing their flutes, clarinets and violins. Evidently the congregation would turn to face the gallery while they were singing hymns, allegedly giving rise to the saying 'face the music', then turning eastwards towards the altar during the Gloria carne (Bridges, 1881). Churchwardens' records show that between 1820 and 1837 William Warren of Guineaford was paid two pounds and two shillings for 'teaching the singers' and there are notes concerning the purchase of instruments including a clarinet at a cost of one pound and sixteen shillings.

In 1858 the singing gallery was pulled down, relocating the choir to the stalls in the chancel and replacing the musicians with the harmonium. Emma Augusta Bridges of *Marwood Hill House* wrote sorrowfully that it was 'a pity that throughout our village churches the poor harsh-toned, brass-voiced little harmonium has ousted all those stringed and wind instruments of times past'.

Further restorations took place during the term of Reverend Alfred Torry in 1891, including the repair and re-hanging of the bells as mentioned earlier. At the same time, William Allen of Barnstaple glazed the windows in the nave, the stonework being restored by Youings of Barnstaple. An interesting discovery was made in the vestry room when builders uncovered an old stone staircase which can still be seen today. It is believed that this may have led to private quarters used by priests in medieval times.

In 1897, it was reported in *Marwood Church Monthly*, that Plymouth architect Mr Edmund Sedding, had made a careful examination of the parish church. He had found the roof in an even worse condition than he had anticipated and was forced to report it as unsafe. Mr Sedding wrote a long letter to the churchwardens, detailing his recommendations and advising that an extensive restoration should be undertaken, with a shocking estimation that it would cost five hundred pounds to repair the roof and fifteen hundred pounds to restore the church.

Reverend Pryke was incumbent at the time and he made a renewed appeal to the parish to encourage fund-raising in aid of the restoration, asking all to 'work together for its restoration as a legacy to our posterity and the children which are yet unborn'.

The Reverend personally pledged one hundred pounds towards the roof repairs, and promised a further one hundred pounds when the restoration was finalised. He arranged for collections at every service, collecting boxes, fund-raising entertainments, 'and every other step, which seems possible and desirable, will be taken to arouse and test the interest of the Parishioners in the work. Effort will be needed - earnest, self-denying, persevering effort.'

The passionate Reverend also published an earnest plea in *Marwood Church Monthly* October 1897, mournfully acknowledging that the congregation had depleted over the centuries since the church was first built and that at the same time 'we have allowed the fabric of God's house, which our forefathers built, to fall almost into ruins.' He continued:

> Shall we not again see our ancient Church filled with reverent crowds, not on Harvest Festivals only and on special occasions, but whenever it is open for worship, and especially on Sunday mornings? Let us give God the first hours of every week, rising with Christ to newness of life. The morning hymn supplies the exhortation, which many of us need - "Shake off dull sloth, and early rise, to pay thy morning sacrifice". And let us deny ourselves superfluities, things which we can do without, that we may be able to repair and restore the church, which our fathers used and valued in the old time, not now "under a penalty of ten pounds" but for the Love of God.

> Source: *Marwood Church Monthly*, October 1897.

So began years of fund-raising activities, including summer fetes, concerts in the Church school and collections during church services and door-to-door. Profits from the sale of *Not Many Years Ago: Memories of My Life* were also added. Gradually, the restoration fund grew, allowing some building work to begin, however the major refurbishments did not take place until September 1903. The sheer scale of those renovations meant that the church had to be closed for nine months; therefore it was with great joy that in May 1904, it was reopened with a divine service held by the Lord Bishop of the Diocese, during the incumbency of Reverend Alfred Johnson. A fully choral service was held, including the anthem of psalm 122 'I was glad when they said unto me'.

In more recent times, further restorations were required during the incumbency of the Reverend Claude Benson Skene in 1938, after it was discovered that the dreaded Death Watch beetle had invaded the ancient woodwork. The Reverend initiated a new restoration fund, reaching out beyond the parish for support by putting an article in the *Western Morning News* on November 19 1938. In the interview, he described how the beetle had started to eat away at the sixteenth century carved oak bench ends and that the anticipated cost of repairs would be in the region of one thousand pounds. This restoration work included resurfacing of the floor and in one place Reverend Skene noted that in the foundations there were fragments of bone and a tooth in a perfect state of preservation. He also described the removal of the old singing platform at the west end of the church, which allowed the bells to be rung from floor level and the windows reglazed with plain glass, making it considerably brighter inside.

Above: Marwood Parish Church c.1930s.

Muddiford Mission Church

With Marwood being a large parish with small hamlets and farms scattered throughout, some members of the congregation faced an arduous journey to get to the parish church. As WG Hoskins (1954) wrote 'even a walk of a mile or two along the deep lanes in winter from home to church was a difficult proceeding because the high hedge banks prevent the lanes from drying out, and for several months of the year there would be deep and liquid mud everywhere'. In order to meet the needs of those people and perhaps in a subtle response to those who had chosen to attend the more conveniently located Congregational church in Muddiford which opened in 1846, the Reverend Frederick Collison cemented his plans to build a chapel-of-ease, known as Muddiford Mission Church.

Reverend Collison negotiated the lease of a plot of land owned by Mrs Frances Drake, Miss Harriet Cutcliffe and Miss Emma Cutcliffe, taking effect from September 1863 for a term of twenty years at a cost of two shillings and sixpence per year. Permission was given to erect a building 'for the performance and divine worship according to the rites and ceremonies of the Church of England, under the Rector of Marwood'. At the Reverend's own cost, a timber structure was duly built to accommodate one hundred and twenty sittings, with a stage, vestry, nave and a tortoise stove for warmth. This was an outstanding example of Reverend Collison's devotion to his work and to the parish, having already planned and established the Church school and ordered major restoration work at St Michael & All Angels.

The church was still in use at the turn of the twentieth century as evidenced by the *Marwood Church Monthly,* although it is evident that at times it was a struggle to sustain a satisfactory congregation. In 1902, the church was closed between April and September because the offertories being made were insufficient to cover running costs, though it was later re-opened in the winter. Locals and friends of the parish rallied to support the church including Henry Collison, son of the late Reverend Frederick Collison and Mrs Heyworth of Whitefield Barton, who were generous benefactors, together with Mrs De Guerin of *The Dell* who played the organ and her daughter who led the Sunday school.

Almost fifty years after the church was built, the incumbent Reverend Alfred Johnson examined the paperwork that was drawn up when the land was originally leased. In the Vestry records he wrote of his belief that the lease should have expired in September 1883 and that no rent had been paid since that time. It had been built at the expense of Reverend Collison and restored by the Prykes and now that it had effectively become redundant, Reverend Johnson decided to sell it and use the funds raised to restore the parish church. Unfortunately there are no records to confirm the details, but it seems that the building was initially purchased by the parish council.

The building had a number of different uses in the early twentieth century, including being the designated headquarters for the Muddiford Home Guard during the Second World War and also the young men of the parish used it as a clubroom where they could play darts and skittles. Eventually, Reuben Tamlyn was permitted to purchase it for use as a workshop in his occupation as carpenter, wheelwright and undertaker.

The old wooden church still stands today in Muddiford, now almost one hundred and fifty years old – funny to think it was only intended to be in use for twenty years!

Patronage

Parish churches were mainly built on land owned by the Lord of the Manor and typically near to his residence. This ensured him and his descendants the title of patrons of the church and ownership of the advowson, which is the legal right to nominate a person for the incumbency of a parish. An advowson could be bought and sold.

Records of the patrons of Marwood Parish Church are written in the Vestry book and later mentioned in a paper written by Miss Daphne Drake in the 1940s. These wealthy nobles had strong royal connections and owned significant Devonshire estates, including Tawstock[1], with which Marwood was closely connected. Details of the former patrons of Marwood from 1263 to 1715, can be found in the appendices.

> In Medieval times the King leased land to his Barons, bestowing them the title of Lord of the Manor. They were given complete autonomy and the right to establish their own system of justice, mint their own money and set taxes.
>
> In 1293, King Edward I granted William Martin permission to host an annual fair at Marwood, dedicated to the Feast of St Michael (September 29). The fair was usually held over three days, attracting large numbers of worshippers. Attractions would include trading stalls, archery tournaments and performances by singers, musicians and acrobats to entertain the crowds.
>
> Source: www.medieval-life-and-times.info/medieval-life/medieval-fairs.htm.

St John's College, Cambridge

Marwood Parish Church has been in the patronage of St John's College, Cambridge, since 1715, following the bequeathal of a senior Fellow and first Professor of Moral Theology, Thomas Smoult. In his will, Thomas left his executor Edward Chester, the sum of five hundred pounds to buy an advowson, which would enable St John's to nominate scholars for the incumbency of that parish, subject to the approval of the Bishop of the Diocese.

In 1714, an act of parliament was passed which enabled the trustees of the late Lord of the Manor Sir Bourchier Wrey, to sell off parts of his Marwood estate including the patronage of St Michael & All Angels Church and rectory. On July 27 1715, acting on behalf of the late Professor Smoult, Edward Chester purchased the advowson of Marwood for four hundred pounds. Edward conveyed it to the trustees of the college on November 12 1715, recording then that he had paid the remaining balance to St John's. By the late eighteenth century, the college was in possession of many advowsons across the country, including those at Marston Morteyne and Houghton Conquest in Bedfordshire, Staplehurst in Kent, Aldworth in Berkshire and Wootton Rivers in Wiltshire. Marwood was the only advowson held by St John's in Devon.

---

[1] Tawstock was often referred to as Marwood's sister church in *Marwood Church Monthly*.

Possessing the advowson gave St John's the ability to influence matters relating to the running of the church. It also meant that scholars who wished to retire from their fellowships at the college, perhaps through wishing to marry, which would mean automatic loss of their fellowship, could be appointed to clergy positions within the parish and provided with a benefice (rectory).

The Rectory

The Old Rectory in Marwood village is believed to have been successively rebuilt on the same plot of land over many centuries, most latterly in around 1715 by the Harding family of nearby Upcott House. The benefice was considered to be a fine acquisition with over twenty-six acres of glebe[1] land, providing incumbents with a very good living. This was valued at four hundred pounds per annum in 1878, while nearby benefices Heanton Punchardon and Shirwell were valued at four hundred and thirty-one pounds and five hundred and sixty-one pounds respectively. Emma Augusta Bridges described Marwood as one of the best livings in the Diocese of Exeter.

Former Marwood Rector, Reverend Richard Harding, described the rectory and church in the Glebe Terrier in 1727:

Our parsonage house containing a kitchen, hall and parlour in yet front, all floored with earthen floors and not wainscoted but plaistered and whitened. A pantry and scullery, a back kitchen or brew house, a dairy and cellar with six chambers, a cider cellar and lyme house adjoining with two chambers over them all built chiefly with stone and covered with stone or slate. Our outhouses are two large barns consisting of thirteen bayes covered partly with stone and covered partly with straw or thatch, the one built with stone, the other with stone and earth.

A stable consisting of five bayes built partly with stone, partly with earth and covered with stone and a linhay or cow stall covered with thatch. Our Glebe containing one close of land called Culver close (arable) about three acres bounded on the east by the lands of Richard Mervin Esq and on the north and south by the King's highway. One other close of land called Adwell (arable) about four acres and a half of an acres, bounded on the north and west by ye lands of the said Richard Mervin Esq and on ye east and south by the King's highway. A large cottage, walled, an orchard and a garden with a dove house therein built and covered in stone in all about an acre.

A Bible of ye largest volume and ye last translation together with two common prayer books. A book of Homilies, a font of stone for ye administration of baptism and two tables of wood hung up with ye Ten Commandments fairly written therein. In the chancel we have a convenient table for ye celebration of ye Holy Communion with a carpet of silk to cover it and a fair linen cloth to spread at ye ministration of ye Holy Sacrament, on each side of which is a table of wood hung up with ye Lords' Prayer and ye creed.

Source: NDRO/3398-4/102.

---

[1] The glebe was the portion of a manor assigned to yield profit in support of the parish church and clergy.

In 1730, Reverend Harding wrote to the Lord Bishop of the Diocese, to complain that a cowshed, barn and brew house had fallen down following a violent windstorm. He observed that they had been built without permission during the incumbency of Reverend Sommers, and requested permission to have the remains of the buildings removed.

Source: NDRO/3398-4/102.

Should any repairs or renovation work to the rectory have become necessary, the incumbent was able to apply for a loan obtained through mortgaging income from their benefices at low interest rates. This was sanctioned through the introduction of the Clergy Residences Repair Act of 1776, and enabled the building, or in many cases rebuilding of many attractive Georgian rectories that still stand today, including Marwood.

In the Vestry records, it states that former Reverend Samuel Weston Ryder undertook some major rebuilding work at the Rectory in 1782. Accounts suggest that Ryder was perhaps responsible for adding 'the eastern part, as the thickness of the partition wall indicates that once it was an outer wall. The old entrance was possibly at the west side where the study is now'. Records show that St John's College lent the Reverend four hundred and eighty pounds towards the renovations, through a mortgage in 1783.

When Reverend Henry Barlow came to Marwood in 1900, he purchased a number of fittings from the previous incumbent, Reverend William Pryke, who was moving on to the parish of Ottery St Mary. These included:

Bookshelves and cupboard – study	£2 15s
Dresser and shelves – kitchen	£5
Phoenix stove – laundry	£ - 12s 6d
2 two-door cupboards - nursery landing	£1 10s
Carriage lift – stables	£ - 6s
Coachman's coat, hat & gaiters	£ gratis
Whalebone brush	£ - 2s 6d
Grinding stone – farmyard	£ - 10s
2 wheelbarrows	£ - 12s
2 Hay forks	£ - 4s
4 trestles for platform for use at the day school	£1 10s
Bath, lavatory & basin, hot & cold water apparatus with tank & cylinder	£25

Source: NDRO 3398-4/17.

This was such luxury for the Rector and his family to have a bath, lavatory and basin with hot and cold water, when the rest of the parish were using their outdoor privies and fetching water from springs and wells!

By the latter half of the twentieth century, the Church of England recognised that the escalating costs of maintaining large rectories were becoming unmanageable. This led to the sale of thousands of predominantly Georgian and Victorian rectories, which were considered too large and expensive to be retained. Marwood rectory was eventually sold to private buyers in 1973.

Above: Marwood Rectory, c.1928. Sunday school scholars enjoying their annual treat involving fun games and a lovely tea in the rectory garden. Some are ready for croquet, with mallet in hand! The little boy in the foreground facing the rectory is Harold Hopkins.

Rectors of Marwood Parish Church

Between 1804 and 1943, eight Rectors and former scholars of St John's College, Cambridge, have been incumbent at Marwood Parish Church:

Richard Riley b.1766, Staffordshire d.1853, Marwood Incumbent 1804-1853 (49 years)	A noted academic and former fellow of St John's College. He was known for being a difficult character and unpopular with his parishioners. Richard married Sarah, only daughter of Benjamin Gower of Cobham, Surrey in August 1805. Their two sons attended Cambridge – Richard (junior) became curate in Cornwall though Edward sadly died whilst studying, aged twenty-five years. One of the longest serving Rectors, incumbent until his death in April 1853 aged ninety. His term is well documented in the book "Not Many Years Ago: Memories of my life" by E. A Bridges.
Frederick W P Collison b.1815, London d.1889, London Incumbent 1853-1886 (33 years)	Awarded two scholarships while at St John's College, where he also held the offices of Librarian and Hebrew Lecturer. Married Mary, daughter of Dr Thackeray, of Cambridge, in January 1855, raising two daughters, Mary and Margaret, and three sons, Charles, Henry and Frederick. Henry preached at Marwood church in 1896. As Rector of Marwood and Rural Dean, Frederick was an influential man who supervised major church restorations; erected a Mission Church in Muddiford and established the Church school in 1857. Author of a widely read account of some manners and customs prevailing in the parish when he arrived. his notes have offered a valuable insight into nineteenth century Marwood.
Alfred F Torry b.1840, Lincolnshire d.1906, Buckinghamshire Incumbent 1886-1893 (7 yrs)	Born and raised in Lincolnshire, the oldest son of James Torry, a Turnpike Surveyor and Ann Freer. He was a noted academic gaining First Class Theological Honours at St John's College. Ordained Deacon in Ely in 1864, ministering in Worcestershire, Yorkshire and Cambridgeshire before arriving at Marwood in 1886. Shortly before arriving in the parish, he married Elizabeth, eldest daughter of the Reverend Charles Goldie, Vicar of St Ives, Cambridgeshire, in February 1886. After seven years at Marwood, Alfred later became Rector of Marston Morteyne in Bedfordshire, until his death whilst in service, in January 1906. (Photograph by permission of the Master and Fellows of St John's College, Cambridge).
William Emmanuel Pryke b.1843, Cambridge d.1920, The Close, Exeter Incumbent 1893-1900 (7 yrs)	Ordained deacon 1867; priest, 1868; Curate of Stapleford, 1867-71. Headmaster of the Royal Grammar School, Lancaster, 1872-93. Vicar and Rural Dean of Ottery St Mary, 1900-8. Chaplain to the Bishop of Exeter, 1903. Canon-residentiary of Exeter, 1908-20; Treasurer of Exeter Cathedral, 1910-16; Chancellor, 1915. Married Harriet, daughter of Dr George Adams, of Clifton in August 1883. Only son, Maurice Pryke became Rector of Risby parish, Suffolk. He was much liked and respected in the parish and returned as often as he could, after taking his new position in Ottery St Mary

Henry T E Barlow b.1864, Bristol d.1906, Lawford, Essex  Incumbent 1900-1902 (2 yrs)	A noted academic and Lecturer in Ecclesiastical History, 1896-1900. Ordained deacon 1889. Principal of Bishop Wilson Theological School, Isle of Man, 1889-93. Married Margaret Brown of Chester in 1894. His youngest son Montague also became a Rector. Being in poor health, he spent only a brief time at Marwood, later becoming Rector of Lawford and Honorary Canon of Carlisle, from 1902 until his untimely death in 1906. A leather bound Bible was presented to the church, with the following inscription inside the front cover – 'Presented to the Church of St Michael and All Angels, in memory of Henry Theodore Edward Barlow, Rector of Marwood 1902-1904, by his youngest son'. (Photograph by permission of the Master and Fellows of St John's College, Cambridge).
Alfred R Johnson b.1861, London d.1937, Dartmouth  Incumbent 1902-1917 (15 yrs)	Born in London and raised in Cambridge, Alfred was the son of Charles H Johnson and Maria Jane Millar, both cooks and confectioners. By 1880 he was an undergraduate of St John's College, Cambridge, and was living with his family above a baker's shop. He gained his Masters qualification by 1886, and was a Fellow of the college for six years. Alfred was ordained deacon at Exeter in 1898 and Priest in 1899, while working as Second Master at Exeter School. He married Katherine Burch in 1900 at Exeter, and shortly afterwards, was appointed as Rector of Marwood in 1902. They had two sons, Kenneth (b.1902) and Eric (b.1906). After sixteen years at Marwood, Alfred went on to become Rector of Marston Morteyne until his retirement in 1935.
George F Mattinson b.1862, Salford d.1941, Barnstaple  Incumbent 1918-1936 (18 yrs)	Ordained deacon at Exeter in 1885; becoming Curate of Barnstaple, 1885-6 and later at Merton, 1886-8, where he met his future wife, Henrietta Kempe. Several incumbencies in Yorkshire and Berkshire before returning to Devon as Rector of Marwood. His adopted daughter Eva was chairwoman of the Marwood Women's Institute. On February 20 1941, the North Devon Journal reported the death of Reverend George Mattinson, who had devoted half a century to ministerial work, and was described as a brilliant theological scholar. At his funeral; amongst many mourners assembled were Daniel D Pill (former headmaster of Marwood School), PC Josiah Sanders, Fred Kelly, Harry Bourne, Henry Balment, William Worth, Claud Gammon, Richard Brooks and representatives of Marwood Women's Institute – Miss Jenkins, Sadd, Joslin and Cook.
Claud M Benson Skene b.1884, London d.1958, Devizes,  Incumbent 1937-1943 (6 yrs)	The youngest son of Reverend Samuel S. Skene and Charlotte Skene, he was born in Kensington, London but raised in Yorkshire. He was educated at Pocklington School as a boarder, before studying at St John's Cambridge, and like all three of his brothers, he gained a BA in theology before he was ordained. After his marriage to Charlotte Judge in 1916, Claud was appointed as chaplain to the forces in the First World War, and also ministered in churches in South Africa before returning to England in 1922. Claud spent a relatively short time in Marwood, steering the parish during the early years of the Second World War and working tirelessly to raise funds for restoration of the ancient church. (Photograph by permission of the Master and Fellows of St John's College, Cambridge).

Reverend William Emmanuel Pryke (1843-1920)

Whilst undertaking research into the past rectors of Marwood, I came into contact with Jo Clinton, great-granddaughter of Reverend Pryke, who was incumbent at Marwood between 1893 and 1900. Jo very kindly agreed to share photographs and her personal account of William's life. He was a man credited with many attributes and held in high esteem, and his obituary written by his friend of fifty years, C.E Graves gives a remarkable testimony to his ceaseless energy and faith in God despite the many difficulties he faced through his life.

He was born in Cambridge in March 1843, the eldest child of Joseph Pryke and Elizabeth (nee Holcombe, of South Molton). William was educated at Perse School, Cambridge and later entered St John's College in 1862 with a minor scholarship. He was ordained as a priest of the Church of England in 1868.

Above: Reverend Pryke, 1870. By permission of the Master and Fellows of St John's College, Cambridge.

In 1872, during William's thirtieth year, he applied for the post of Headmaster of Lancaster Royal Grammar School. As he explained in his application, he was in a very difficult position. He wished to marry. He could hardly expect to become Headmaster of a boarding school unless married, but if he married he would automatically lose his Fellowship at Cambridge but without the certainty of obtaining the post.

The logic appealed to the Grammar School Committee and William was duly appointed as Headmaster having married his fiancée Ellen Collier before he took up his post. Ellen was the sister of Henry Collier, one of William's students at St John's who was studying theology, which is possibly how the couple met. Sadly their life together was cut short; for Ellen and their infant son Kenneth died in child birth, within 2 years of the marriage. William was left devastated. It is recorded that he contemplated leaving Lancaster but fortunately for the school he remained and made many improvements to it, often at his own expense. (See 'The Royal Grammar School, Lancaster' - A History by Athol Laverick Murray).

Ten years later in 1883 William married again, unfortunately we do not know how the couple met but it may have been through the bride's brother, Reverend Charles Adams who was also a cleric and based in Lancaster from 1874-6. Harriet Adams was fifteen years younger than her husband, being twenty-five years old when she married and very young to take on the responsibilities of being a headmaster's wife. They were to have one child, William Maurice born in 1886.

In 1893 after 21 years as headmaster, William resigned from the school having decided to resume Holy Orders. During his time in Lancaster he had been much in demand as a preacher and public speaker. On leaving

Above: Harriet Pryke c.1885.

the school he was presented with a fine grandfather clock, in gratitude for his generosity in providing free tuition for Wane and Moon scholars. The family moved to Marwood in Devon, where William was appointed rector. He was a popular and charismatic preacher and soon had a devoted congregation. In recognition of his many talents, William was encouraged to accept the prestigious living of Ottery St Mary in 1900, also being appointed rural dean.

Left: Reverend Pryke (seated) with his wife Harriet, and son Reverend Maurice Pryke, at Ottery St Mary.

William's last move came in 1908, when he took up residency in The Close as Canon of Exeter Cathedral. He was later appointed as Treasurer in 1910 and then Chancellor in 1915.

William Emmanuel Pryke died Feb 1 1920 aged 76 and his funeral service at Exeter Cathedral was very well attended. He was later interred at the churchyard of Ottery St Mary. His wife Harriet survived her husband by 30 years, dying in 1950 at the grand old age of 91.

Left: The Prykes at Ottery St Mary, c.1910.

An edited account of Reverend Pryke's life, with kind permission of Jo Clinton.

Reverend Pryke was indeed a popular rector during his time in Marwood. In the first ever edition of *Marwood Church Monthly* in January 1894, it was reported that almost the entire adult population attended his induction ceremony and later, a tea at the rectory. In the article the Reverend printed a warm and sincere letter of thanks to his parishioners:

> … let me thank you for the kindly welcome which you have given me as Rector of the Parish. I have already made the acquaintance of most of the Parishioners, and I feel assured, that we shall live together, and meet together in the House of God, not merely as acquaintances but as friends. I was specially gratified to see so many Parishioners present at the service connected with my induction, when almost the whole adult population of Marwood filled our ancient church.

Source: Marwood Church Monthly, January 1894.

Amongst his many achievements at Marwood, Reverend Pryke was the instigator of the monthly parish newsletter, *Marwood Church Monthly*. Frequently quoted in this volume due to its rich content, the first edition was issued within a few months of his arrival. Parishioners were asked to subscribe in advance for six or twelve months to ascertain the numbers to be printed which were sold for one penny each.

Each edition included comprehensive updates on events within Marwood particularly those concerning the parish and Muddiford Mission churches, such as births, marriages and burials, amounts collected at weekly offertories and dates of services with hymn numbers. Other local matters were also recounted such as weather, social activities, parish council meeting minutes and ploughing match results. The newsletter was in circulation for eleven years, spanning the incumbencies of the Reverends Pryke, Barlow and Johnson, however it appears to have been dropped in 1906 because no issues later than December 1905 have been found.

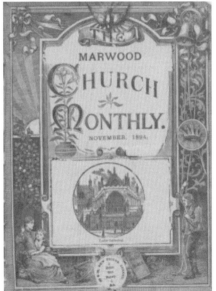

Left: The original front cover design, 1894.

Right: The revised front cover design, 1904.

In addition to their many secular duties, there are countless reports of Reverend and Mrs Pryke being enthusiastically involved with the community, organising parish events and hosting annual parties to show their appreciation of the churchwardens, choir and bell ringers. Evidence of festivities and the strength of the bond between the Prykes and the parish were reported in the *Marwood Church Monthly* newsletters:

Harvest

The Harvest Festival was held on Thursday September 7th. It was preceded, as usual, by a Public Tea in the National School, and games were played on the rectory lawn and in the meadow. Football and quoits were the favourite pastimes. October 1894.

Church School Treat

The children of the National School reassembled, after the summer holidays, on July 20th, and held their annual treat in the afternoon. They walked in procession to the Church singing "Onward Christian Soldiers". After tea, games and races were held on the rectory lawn, and a very happy evening was spent. August 1896.

Sunday School Treat

At the Sunday school, the Star Register has been introduced, and has already produced a good effect as regards punctual and regular attendance. The forty one Sunday Scholars enjoyed their annual treat on Tuesday 29th. After tea, the Christmas tree was displayed and its fruits distributed. Twenty three children recited pieces of poetry. Games were played with true Marwood energy and spirit. The parents of the scholars were invited, and were happy witnesses of their children's joy. January 1897.

Easter

A good audience assembled on April 20th, in the National School, for an Easter Entertainment, which was greatly enjoyed. Mr Bowling's original reading "The Prize Village" was greatly appreciated, and we must try to live up to his description of us. Copies of Mr Bowling's verses may be had, for one penny each, on application to the Rector or Mr Main. Performances included: Song & Chorus "My Uncle's Farm", Maurice Pryke; Song "A jovial monk am I", Mr R Worth; Tambourine March and Drill, Marwood girls; "Reuben and Rachel" Mrs Passmore and Mr F Kelly; God save the Queen. May 1897.

Epiphany

On the evening of January 6th, the feast of the Epiphany, the Rector and Mrs Pryke entertained a large body of church workers - the choirs, ringers, teachers, church officers and friends - at supper in the National Schoolroom. The room was then cleared for games and entertainments. The Rector read A Horse's Dream a poem by our friend the Rev E W Bowling. Good songs from Messrs GB Worth, FJ Kelly, WW Main, H Hill, R Worth, FT Main and others, helped to fill up a bright, delightful evening, which passed too quickly. Maurice Pryke performed some conjuring tricks. About 1.30am, two grand old traditional Cornish carols were sung, and the party broke up with cheers and kind greetings. February 1899.

On Tuesday June 26th, more than six hundred parishioners and friends assembled at the Rectory, by invitation of Mr and Mrs Pryke, and had tea in the garden. The weather was beautifully fine and warm. The Rector was presented with a silver inkstand and to Mrs Pryke, an oak writing table. With these was given an illuminated address, bearing the names of about three hundred subscribers. July 1900.

Reverend Edward Woodley Bowling (1837-1907)

Reverend Edward Woodley Bowling was never rector of Marwood, but being a close contemporary of Reverend Pryke, he often spent time in the parish, occasionally preaching and taking part in local activities.

Born on Christmas day 1837, Edward was the son of a physician, who was practicing in Nice, South of France. Edward received some of his schooling there and later enrolled at St John's College, Cambridge in 1856. His first role as curate was in Newton, Cambridgeshire and he was later Rector of Houghton Conquest, Bedfordshire for six years. St John's Alumni records describe him as an 'accomplished writer of light verse' who later published his own work *Sagittulae; Random Verse*. He was a regular contributor to *Punch*, *The Globe* and the college journal *The Eagle*, under the signature of Arculus.

In September 1897, *Marwood Church Monthly* reported that Edward had arrived in Marwood on August 3 and stayed for the entire month whilst Reverend Pryke was attending to other matters in Lancaster. He preached at several church services and also gave lessons at the Church school on Mountains and Rivers of the Bible, later donating a map of the Holy Land for use in the school.

In April 1898, Edward returned to Marwood, preaching occasionally and assisting with raising funds for the Church school. He offered to write a poem dedicated to Marwood, and recite it at a concert. The poem provides an intriguing insight to Marwood affairs at that time, as Edward skilfully portrays many local characters.

The Prize Village

Of all spots under heaven the County of Devon all judges declare is the best,
For Nature's kind bounty this beautiful County with good things unnumbered has blest;
And we all of us deem that Devonshire cream all delicate dainties surpasses;
And who, as he knelt at their feet, has not felt the charms of the Devonshire lasses?
And for fighting and sporting, and also for courting, all history clearly has shown
Again and again that the Devonshire men for their brilliant successes are known.

There's a Devonshire village, renowned for its tillage, its wheat, and its oats and its barley?
For its sheep and its lambs, and its Gammons and hams, above all for John Gammon and Charlie.
Shall I tell you the name of this village of fame? You shall know what it is by and bye;
In the meantime attend to my rhymes to the end, and you'll guess it yourselves, if you try.
For woods and wild flowers and sunshine and showers, green meadows and streams of pure waters,
And fresh bracing air, and maidens as fair as the fairest of Eve's many daughters,
This place wins the prize; you need only your eyes and ears on a tour of inspection,
And as sure as a gun, when the tour you have done, you will look at the place with affection.

If you wander in search of a beautiful Church, you may travel for miles upon miles,
And believe me that, though you may rush to and fro, over hedges and ditches and stiles,
No Church you will find that is more to your mind than the Church of this place, and the Rector
Is an excellent teacher, and eloquent preacher, whose words are far sweeter than nectar.
He has got a good wife, who's the pride of his life, for she makes it her duty and joy
To be doing good work for the Parish, and Kirk, and Maurice, her twelve year old boy.

If you happen to call at the Rectory Hall, I'll bet you a penny that you see
Either neat Annie Gore come and open the door, or the queen of all parlour maids, Lucy,
And Rose – she's the cook – knows her cookery book, for her dinners are really Parisian,
And the soup, and the fish, and the joints and each dish that she sends up are almost Elysian.
If you wish to explore and go on next door, new treasures you'll soon be discovering,
For you'll see a fair dame and her husband, whose name I am sure you all guess must be Lovering.

Then there's Billy a terrier, I've ne'er seen a merrier, and Mr John Gammon and Charlie –
John Gammon's the master, and Charlie goes faster than steam, but his temper is snarly.
Then you come to the Schools in which Mr Main rules, he is quite the humanest of Mains,
Though Rodds he has many, he uses not any, but with a light hand holds the reins.
The Church has good ringers and beautiful singers – their names are too many to mention,
But to all in the choir – it's the best in the shire – we would all, if we could, give a pension.

Then the organ to play there are good Miss Barclay and Mrs De Guerin – their playing
Is, we all shall agree, at the top of the tree, an opinion which goes without saying.
This place was delighted, and somewhat excited, I'm told by a recent Election;
But peace and good-will prevail in it still, and hearty regard and affection;
The Councillors two are good men and true, and each of the sound to the core is;
If you wish to be told their names, I'll make bold to name Messrs Joslin and Morris.

There's nothing on earth that can vie with true worth, and of Worths in this place there are plenty,
There are Pugsleys and Yeos, and if you want clothes there's a Westcott, sufficient for twenty.
Other names may be found which in plenty abound, Down, Hill, Pearce, Smith, Hancock and Kelly,
Better names you will ne'er find in Devon elsewhere, from Ilfracombe down to Clovelly.

Then where can you find a Doctor so kind, from prescribing a pill to trepanning,
As the hearty young giant, so strong, self-reliant, and skilful, our friend Dr Manning?
Shall I tell you the name of this village of fame? Try to think – you will easily guess it:
Without the least doubt, you have all found it out. Yes! Marwood's the village. God bless it!

POSTSCRIPT

You all will be glad of a post-script I add, to thank all the Messieurs and Madams
Who have charmed us tonight – you have heard with delight Messrs Fixsen, Smith, Taylor and Adams,
And we all of us like to hear young Master Pryke, and the two Messrs Worth and Fred Kelly,
My old rhyme to repeat, singers none are so sweet from Ilfracombe down to Clovelly.

No birds in a cage beat the two Misses Page, and the two nightingales from the Dell
Are so sweet that I think they must each of them drink from the spring that you call Honey-Well.
And what shall I say of your friend Miss Barclay? We all on her help are dependent,
For piano and son would, I fear, have gone wrong without her as superintendent.

I'm sure that the Rector will thank the Inspector of Schools in the County of Devon
For the musical treat of the violin sweet from his daughter, the eldest of seven.
Let me mention one lass more; she's now Mrs Passmore, but was once on a time Miss Jane Gore;
She has all our good wishes, of happiness, riches, and peace may she have a good store!
To the place she loves best, like a bird to its nest, she has come back, which proves to you clearly
That no village on earth is the equal in worth of the village you all love so dearly.
I've finished my task, and your pardon I ask for the rhymes which I've ventured to write,
Long life to you all, young and old, great and small. I wish you good luck, and good night.

Source: *Marwood Church Monthly*, May 1898.

Above: Edward Woodley Bowling c.1880s.
By permission of the Master and Fellows of St John's College, Cambridge.

164

In June 1898, Edward sent a guinea to the church towards the provision of a bench in the churchyard. *Marwood Church Monthly* reported 'The seat will be placed on the terrace below the tower, looking westward towards Lee Woods and the beautiful Whitehall valley'.

The churchyard at Marwood must have had a special place in Edward's heart, as it inspired him to write further poetry. Imagine him sitting in the churchyard, appreciating the solitude and scribbling down the verses as they came to his mind:

Thoughts in Marwood Churchyard

"Lift up your hearts!" O Lord, to Thee
Our hearts we lift, nor only we
But all Thy works their heart and voice
To Thee lift upward, and rejoice.

The running rills of water clear,
The lark whose song makes Heaven more near,
The whisp'ring breeze, the rustling tree,
The murmur of the passing bee.

The bleating lambs, the lowing kine,
See all to tell Thy Love Divine;
And, blent in harmony, to raise
From earth to Heaven their song of praise.

Yet down beneath the flowers we tread
Sleep their last sleep the silent dead:
"They praise Thee not" – the Psalmist sings;
But the glad news of better things

Tells us that they in peace who rest
Shall one day wake to rapture, blest,
And, rising, in Thy presence raise
One song of universal praise.

Therefore, O Lord, to us who live
Thy purifying Spirit give,
That when beneath green earth we lie,
Though soul and body seem to die,

Above: One of the impressive
monuments in Marwood churchyard.

We, from past sins and sorrows free,
Thy glory face to face may see,
And with Thy Saints and Angels raise
The song of everlasting praise.

E. W. Bowling

Published in *Marwood Church Monthly*, June 1898.

Lines in Marwood Churchyard

Stranger, or native of this peaceful spot,
Who'er thou be, whate'er may be thy lot,
Pause - 'neath thy feet, each in his hallowed bed,
Sleep, until Christ shall give them light, the dead:
Around thee, both in shower and sunshine fair,
Wood, hill and valley, blend their beauties rare;
While, all embracing in the arms of love,
The Eternal Father reigns supreme above:
Then shalt not thou who on this scene dost gaze,
Lift up thy heart to God in prayer and praise.

E. W. Bowling

Published in *Marwood Church Monthly*, September 1898.

Above: Edward Woodley Bowling c.1860.
By permission of the Master and Fellows
of St John's College, Cambridge.

When the news came that the Pryke family were to leave Marwood in 1900, there was a real sense of sadness as his ministry had been compelling and the family had shown a deep affection for the parish.

Edward composed another charming poem which he dedicated to the Prykes, partly to commemorate their time in Marwood, but also to acknowledge his deep fondness for the parish. A copy of the poem was found purely by chance at the North Devon Record Office.

Farewell to Marwood

There's a word we have all of us spoken,
Though we love not upon it to dwell,
For oft 'tis of sorrow a token
The word which I mean is "Farewell".
This word I must now say to you,
Sweet Marwood and Kind Marwood friends,
Though to bid you a final adieu,
My heart-strings distressingly rends.

O where in the world are there flowers
That equal the wild flowers that grow
In Marwood's delectable bowers,
And where are there breezes that blow
So fresh and so soft as the air
That blows from wild moor and salt wave;
And where are there maidens so fair,
And men so devoted and brave?

Marwood people are sober, no doubt.
For the spring they love best is called "Honey-well".
And it takes one no time to find out
That in Marwood they all spend their money-well.
"Little Silver" they own, it is true,
But the silver they have is well spent;
And though "Guineaford" guineas are few,
They enjoy them without discontent.

And where in the world will you find
A Rector and Rectoress like
The Rector and Rectoress kind,
Whose name as we all know, is "Pryke"?
And where will young Maurice their son
Enjoy a more excellent wicket,
Than the Rectory Lawn where he won
His spurs in the grand game of cricket?

All Marwood is sorry they're going,
But feels that wherever they live
They will always kind feeling be showing,
Kind sympathy ready to give.
And whoever succeeds them, we trust,
That both he and his may be like
Those friends so kind-hearted and just,
Mr, and Mrs, and young Master Pryke.

Farewell! yet there's no separation,
Sweet Marwood, between me and you,
For daily in imagination
I shall picture of Marwood a view.
The Rectory, Church, and the Village,
The charms of each hillside and dell;
The fields of green pasture and tillage,
Will with me in memory dwell.

I shall think of the children's bright faces,
In the Village, the Church and the Schools;
Of the Marwood fair women, whose graces
Compel us to bow to their rule.
I shall think of the men – the stout ringers,
Each of whom is a match for six Boers;
Of the Choir, and its excellent singers,
And the views of the Devonshire Moors.

Farewell – in all truth and sincerity,
Though at Marwood I'm only a guest,
With plenty and peace and prosperity
I pray that you all may be blest.
May you all in all goodness be nourished,
All wrongs may you strive to amend;
And, as Marwood has hitherto flourished,
May it flourish henceforth to the end.

May, 1900   E.W.B.

Source: North Devon Record Office, 3398-4/270.

Above: St Michael & All Angels, Marwood, c.1920s.

Marwood Methodist Church

The birth of the Methodist movement dates back to the eighteenth century, a digression originating mostly from the Church of England. Two of the most influential instigators for change were John and Charles Wesley, the sons of an Anglican minister, both of whom studied at Oxford University where their interest in faith first took root. Originally ordained as Church of England clergymen, John in 1725 and Charles in 1735, the brothers were later described as having undergone a 'profound spiritual experience' (www.methodist.org.uk), after which Charles wrote the first of over six thousand hymns and John wrote or contributed to the publications of hundreds of articles.

Together, the Wesleys were instrumental in founding a preaching organisation in 1739 that would later evolve as the framework for a global Methodist Church. The Wesleyan theology sought to broaden Christians' awareness not only of their faith, but of a responsibility to attend to the welfare of those in need, the poor, infirm, widows and orphans, urging followers to 'Make all you can, save all you can, give all you can' (www.methodist.org.uk).

The Wesleys were soon banned from speaking in many Anglican churches due to their evangelistic methods. Despite an initial discomfort to preaching in the open air or non-religious buildings, John recognised that many working class people felt alienated from the liturgy and hierarchy of their Anglican churches and went on an extended journey preaching and reaching out to people of all backgrounds in villages and towns across the country. Others also trained as preachers and travelled around 'field preaching'. Their sermons praised God's eternal faithfulness and were well received by those who had previously felt undeserving of a relationship with the Lord. As the number of preachers grew, so the movement became accessible to people in rural areas such as Marwood.

Emma Augusta Bridges (1881) reinforced the opinion that the attitude of nineteenth century Church of England clergy in some cases hastened the growth of the non-conformist movement. Clergy, who were university educated and mostly from privileged backgrounds, could hardly be further removed from their congregations in rural parishes. If they knew nothing about farming or did not partake in hunting or other game activities, they often failed to relate to either the working classes or local gentry. This was exactly the state of affairs in Marwood, when the Reverend Richard Riley began his incumbency in 1804.

It is perhaps therefore unsurprising that the Methodist movement was first introduced at Marwood in 1806, when a local preacher held services at Blakewell Farm, the home of the Laramy family. From there farmers Mr Philip Rock and Mr John Lamprey, formed a small community, which had soon attracted fourteen members.

Over twenty years later in 1828, the decision was made to build a chapel. The Charity Commissioner's Report of 1905 made reference to an agreement that was made between the landowner Philip Laramy, Philip Rock and ten charity trustees, in relation to part of a field known as Furze Rick or Dughill Field in Marwood, on which it was intended a chapel be built for 'divine worship'. Evidently, the land was donated for the token sum of one guinea, under terms 'to permit such persons only as should be appointed by the Methodist Conference under the Model Deed of February 1784, to have the benefit of the chapel and premises for the purpose of preaching and expounding God's Holy Word and for the performance of other acts of religious worship.'

Right: The Old Methodist Chapel, now converted into a private dwelling.

The chapel was duly completed at a cost of £164 and opened on Good Friday 1829. In the absence of an organ, frowned upon by Methodists in those days, the singing was accompanied by violins. The sermon in the afternoon was preached by the Reverend James Ogers of Bideford from the text 'And I make them, and the places round about my hill, a blessing'. Local preacher Reverend Robert Bond led the evening sermon, from the text 'Who hath despised the day of small things'. At the opening it was written:

> There worshipped Philip Rock with joy beaming in his countenance and his cheeks bedowed with tears, while he contemplated the completion of a work in which he was permitted to take a foremost part; his pious kinsman, John Lamprey, true yoke fellow, who well sustained the burthen and heat of the day patriarchal Joshua Gould of Hole, swelling the anthem of praise.
>
> Source: NDRO B513/103.

In 1872 it was proposed that a new chapel[1] should be built and a suitable piece of ground was purchased from John Alford for £36. Conveniently, Alexander Lauder, appointed architect, was also a renowned lay preacher in North Devon. He was an influential man, not only an architect but noted artist and proprietor of the North Devon Pottery and brick works.

The Charity Commissioner's Report specified that in October 1872, a further agreement was made between landowner John Alford, Reverend Benjamin Browne, Joseph Irwin and fourteen charity trustees, in relation to two closes of land of half an acre known as

---

[1] In the fifty years between the building of the first chapel and the second, the congregation grew from fourteen to thirty-nine but averaged about thirty.

Lower Cawsey, Marwood. The land was granted in trust to Joseph Irwin and others for the purpose of erecting a new chapel in lieu of the former building and the rest was to be used as a graveyard. With the site for the new chapel agreed, William Kellaway was appointed builder and work began with the ceremonial placing of the foundation stone (*pictured below*) by John Alford who had bestowed a significant financial contribution to the building costs.

Charities

In her will made in 1858, Mary Ann Tamlyn of Prixford, bequeathed to trustees, John Crang and George Corney, the sum of one hundred pounds to be invested, and the dividends used for the benefit of the (former) Wesleyan Chapel and Sunday school.

By will, dated November 1873, John Alford bequeathed one hundred and fifty pounds to the trustees of the old and new chapels, with instructions to use the interest for 'keeping the fence of the old burying ground, together with his tomb, in order and sufficient repair, and, subject thereto, to pay and apply the interest, if any, towards warming of the new chapel'.

The plan for the new chapel incorporated an auditorium, with two-bay north and south transepts with galleries with wrought iron fronts (*pictured right*). Multilateral stair towers were located in the western angles of the transepts, with porches on the north and south sides of the stair towers. It was designed to seat two hundred and forty worshippers, which shows the great confidence the trustees had in their growing congregation.

Arrangements were made in September 1873 for the fast-approaching opening of the new chapel. It was proposed that the back seats be let for one shilling and sixpence per sitting per quarter, the two next at one shilling and the next two at ninepence per quarter. Instructions were given for the engagement of a 'competent caretaker' to tend the chapel, at a wage of one pound per quarter. Interment charges were noted as twelve shillings for a 'common grave' (four shillings apiece for the ground, sexton and Minister). For a 'wall' grave the cost was twenty shillings (twelve shillings for the ground and four shillings apiece for the sexton and the Minister). It was also proposed that no new graves be made in the old ground adjacent to the former chapel, but permission was granted to allow burials in the vaults below. The chapel was not registered for solemnizing marriages until May 15 1875, when a notification was published in *The London Gazette* confirming the details.

The opening services were scheduled for Thursday October 9 1874, exactly one year after the foundation stone was laid. A luncheon was planned and contributions were requested from the congregation. Mrs Irwin offered a rib of beef, Mrs Carder a ham, Mrs Hayward a round of beef, Mrs Corney two tongues and a couple of fowl and Mrs Chammings a goose. To assist with transportation of important guests, Mr Carder sent two traps to Barnstaple, Mr Rudd sent one to Pilton to meet the preachers, and Mr Brailey and Mr Irwin sent traps to Ilfracombe. The Reverend Hargreaves preached at the morning service which was followed by a fine luncheon in the old chapel. The afternoon service was led by the Reverend R Newton Young and the evening meeting was presided over by Mr Thomas May, Mayor of Barnstaple; Mr S D Waddy, Q.C, the parliamentary candidate for the Borough; the Reverend J Cooke of Bideford; the Reverend R W Pordige of Ilfracombe and the Reverend Benjamin Browne, Superintendent of the Barnstaple Circuit. The collections taken on that day combined with the generous gifts donated by the congregation, covered the costs of all the works undertaken without any debt, a remarkable achievement.

Above: The Methodist Church – located on the Ilfracombe road, between Prixford and Guineaford.

Following the opening of the new chapel, the decision was taken to convert the old chapel into a day school for local children. Opened in spring 1874, the school was popular locally but only remained open for two years. A brief history of the school is noted in Chapter Five. Afterwards, the old chapel was used regularly for Sunday school and for public teas during parish celebrations, for example the silver jubilee of King George V in May 1935.

More than seventy years after opening, it was proposed that the new chapel be renovated and a new central heating system installed. Work was carried out in 1946 at a cost of four hundred and thirty pounds which enabled the chapel to be painted, a new communion rail erected, piped hot water central heating to be installed and calor gas to replace the old oil lighting. Another notable change was the relocation of the pulpit behind the Communion table. It had been a common arrangement in Methodist churches to position the pulpit in front of the table, emphasising that preaching of the Word was to take precedence above all else. Practically however it had caused difficulties during services particularly during weddings, which led to it being repositioned.

On completion of the renovations, the chapel was reopened on June 12 1946 with services in the afternoon and evening being led by the Reverend William Proctor. The meetings were presided over by Lieutenant Commander Arthur Carder, a descendant of Thomas Carder of Whiddon who had been deeply involved with the building of the new chapel. Collections taken on the day and gifts from the congregation covered the costs of all the modernisation work completed without any debt, just as the congregation of 1874 had achieved when the chapel was first opened.

Harold Hopkins – Lay Preacher

In 1948, Harold Hopkins received his calling to become a lay preacher, receiving encouragement from the Reverend Harry Biggin and close family members. At first Harold wasn't sure he could do it, taking some time to think, although the Reverend persuaded him to at least try. After two years of studying and sitting a number of scriptural examinations, Harold qualified as a local preacher in 1950. His first service was held at Landkey, with a significant congregation of around one hundred people and Harold remembers that his sermon was linked to the cleansing of the ten lepers.

As a farmer, Harold was used to hard work, but an average Sunday began with an early start to milk the cows, then attending the morning service at Prixford Chapel, then home for dinner before cycling off to take the afternoon service at Langridge Ford. In those days the preaching circuit included Lynton, Barbrook and Parracombe Chapels, and Harold had all kinds of difficulties in reaching his destinations in the rural countryside. Sometimes he would get a lift with a friend on his motorbike, but other times he had relied on a pony, bicycle and eventually, a car, which made his journeys much easier.

In the summer of 2010, after many years on the circuit, Harold received a certificate in recognition of sixty years' preaching.

Above: The eastern end of the auditorium, with the communion rail
and table, and pulpit to the rear.

In 1958, Mrs Annie Gubb gave a stained glass window to the chapel (*pictured below*) in memory of her father, Mr John Smith who had been a preacher on the Ilfracombe circuit for over fifty years. Aptly, it depicts John Wesley, one of the founders of the Methodist movement.

Right: The beautiful stained glass window donated by Mrs Gubb.

Left: The dedication to John Wesley in the centre of the window.

Above: Marwood Methodist Church Youth Group circa mid 1950s.
Back row: Denzil Spear, Sidney HJ Gubb, Harold Hopkins, Doris Baker, Douglas Hamley,
Jill Joslin, David Pugsley, Beryl Pugsley, Fred Charley, unknown, unknown.
Front row: John Watts, Annie May Hopkins, Mary Stevens, Revd Harry Biggin,
Eileen Watts, Lottie Balment, Muriel Brailey, Terry Brailey.

Above: Marwood Liberal Fete.
Left to Right: Mary Chapple (standing), seated – Mary Chapple (senr), Ada Brailey,
Muriel Brailey, Christina Balment, Mildred Pugsley.

Above: Marwood Methodist Church, c.1955.
Back row: Dennis Spear, Graham White, Ron Tanton, Lou Spear.
Front row: John Watts, Harold Hopkins, Alan Brailey, Denzil Spear.

Above: Marwood Methodist Church, c.1955.

176

Muddiford United Reformed Church

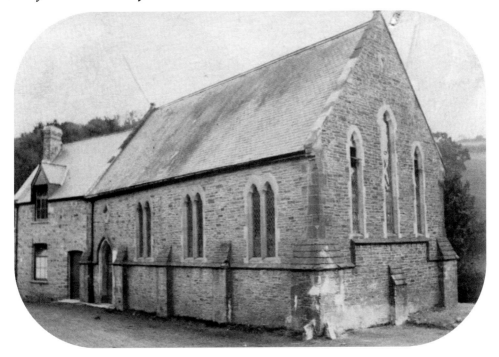

Above: Muddiford Congregational Church c.1930s, now
known as Muddiford United Reformed Church.

The first services known to have been held in Muddiford took place in around 1840, in a small chapel adjoining a cottage where carpenter William Curtis and his family resided. As the congregation grew, land was purchased to enable a larger stone chapel to be built in Lower Muddiford by the stream. In July 1845, the first foundation stone was laid there and following completion of the works, the official opening took place on September 9 1846[1]. Built in the early English style, it was initially known as the Independent Church.

A local benefactor Zechariah Carleton Stiff (b.1790, London), landowner of Newport, Barnstaple, generously paid for the solid oak front door and a magnificent pulpit of French Caen stone which is sadly no longer in situ. It seems that Zechariah was a strong supporter of the Independent movement, being a trustee for the Cross Street Independent Church schoolrooms in Barnstaple, although it is not known whether he had any particular connection with Muddiford, which would prompt such a generous donation.

Designed by architect Mr B D Gould of Barnstaple, the stone chapel was built of local Bath stone at a cost of two hundred and fifty pounds, which was almost entirely raised by members of the parish. It formed part of Barnstaple Village Churches circuit, which

---

[1] Former minister Reverend John Ticehurst and the late Ron Chapple undertook valuable research into the history of the church, and were able to determine the precise date of the official opening.

also included Bickington and Goodleigh, sharing one minister but remaining under the guidance of the Cross Street Church in Barnstaple. The inaugural service was held in the afternoon, conducted by the Reverend Henry Quick of Taunton. He referred to the text 'The glory of this present house will be greater than the glory of the former house, says the Lord Almighty' (Haggai, 2:9), perhaps a subtle reference to the capacity of the former wooden building. One hundred and ten people attended the opening service, which was followed by tea – the profits of which were added to the building funds. The evening service was led by the Reverend Robert Thomson of Ilfracombe, who drew upon the words of Isaiah 57:

> For this is what the high and lofty one says – He who lives forever, whose name is holy. I live in a high and holy place, but also with him who is contrite and lowly in spirit, to revive the spirit of the lowly and to revive the heart of the contrite.

The total offerings received on the opening day in 1846 amounted to eleven pounds, equivalent to almost six hundred pounds today, an amazing display of generosity in so humble a parish.

The Sunday school was led by John Prideaux, who held the position of Superintendent for thirty-six years. In July each year the church would celebrate the anniversary of the school with special services held in the morning, afternoon and evening, followed by a children's festival on the following Monday.

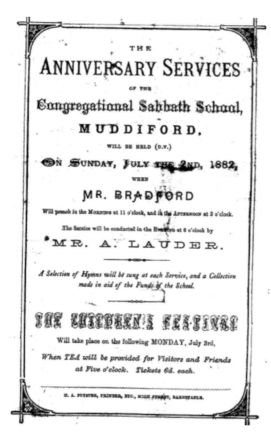

Above: John Prideaux, Superintendent of the Muddiford Sabbath School 1864 – 1900.

Left: The front cover of the hymn sheet used at the 1882 Anniversary service.

It is interesting to note that Alexander Lauder is officiating at the evening service. He was the architect of the new Methodist Chapel and renowned lay reader in North Devon.

Each year, the North Devon Journal would print an account of the celebratory service, two such accounts are shown below:

July 1919
At the anniversary of the Congregational Sunday School there were large congregations, eloquent sermons being preached by Mrs Huett of Ilfracombe, who also delivered a beautiful address to the scholars in the afternoon. Bright hymns were nicely rendered, Miss Born presiding at the organ - On the following day the scholars were entertained at tea, after which they enjoyed games in a field lent by Mr C Pugsley. Later, the children, led by the Pastor (Rev JG Cording) marched to the Chapel, where they each received cake and a packet of sweets.

Source: North Devon Journal, July 17 1919.

July 1930
Congregational Church – On Wednesday last the successful annual tea and prize distribution of the Muddiford Congregational Sunday school took place in the Schoolroom. Tea was served by the teachers, assisted by friends, and following tea, everyone joined in games, etc, spending an enjoyable time. The prizes were distributed by the Rev. W. R. Hostler, and a vote of thanks to all the friends who had given towards the tea was proposed by Mr C Watts (Sunday school superintendent).

A largely attended meeting was held on Monday evening in the Schoolroom. Mr J W Cooke, of Barnstaple, presided. Recitations were given by children of the Sunday School – Fred Webber, Eva Down, Ernie Webber, Alan Brailey, Clara Somerfield, John Watts, Beatrice Webber, Molly Hickman, Queenie Webber and Ernie Watts. Solos were sung by Nancy Watts, Olive Down, Vera Brailey and Miss W Webber. A song rendered by the children was entitled "What has become of the birdies?" They also sang a hymn, "There came a little child to earth." The boys of the School also sang. A dialogue was given by the senior girls.

Source: North Devon Journal, July 1930.

The annual celebratory service still continues today on the first Sunday in July, a fine and long standing tradition.

In the early 1900s, the village churches became independent of the Barnstaple circuit, although they still shared one minister between them, a system which remained in place until the 1960s. In 1972, the majority of English Congregational churches merged with the Presbyterians, to form the United Reformed Church (URC), and they were joined later by the Churches of Christ. The URC is committed to theological and cultural diversity, and aims to work with all Christians of all traditions, embracing a wide variety of theological understandings.

Source: www.urc.org.uk.

Reproduced with kind permission of Mr S Knight, RL Knight Photographers.

How times change? RL Knight took the photograph of Muddiford Church above in the 1930s – compare it with the same scene pictured below taken by the author in 2011.

Above: Muddiford Congregational Church – Harvest Festival c.1930s.

Above: Muddiford Sunday school outing 1910.

Above: Reverend Lesley Fisher, Reverend Haggett, Reverend
Wheeler and Reverend Garlick outside the church c.1960s.

Above: Muddiford Church Ladies c.1930s, including
Mrs Beard and Miss Alford.

Middle Marwood Chapel

Middle Marwood Chapel was erected in 1841 on land let by James Rowe, for ten shillings per annum and a term of two thousand years. A single storey building of colour washed stone rubble, a slate roof with gabled ends, two gothic pointed arch windows and a central pointed arch doorway with studded gothic door.

The origins of the chapel are believed to stem from an attempt by missionaries to address the unruly behaviour of the local people; in fact keen historian, Christine Watts (nee Harris) explains that Middle Marwood was quite an inhospitable place in early Victorian times because of its poverty and unsociable behaviour, especially drunkenness. This explains the rationale for building a prison in the tiny hamlet, which was a simple building, with one large cell on the ground floor and accommodation above for the warden. Rather than being used for long-term sentences or serious criminals, the jail was a useful safe house to throw troublemakers temporarily, particularly until such time as they had sobered up. The prison went out of use early in the twentieth century and was demolished in the 1960s.

Above: The former Chapel
at Middle Marwood.

Kathleen Harris (nee Braunton) was brought up in the hamlet and remembers as a young girl she would be required to attend church four times every Sunday. In the morning there was the first Sunday school lesson, followed by a second lesson after lunch at 2pm. At 3pm there would be a family service and then an evening service from 6pm to 7pm. Kathleen remembers there were very strict rules surrounding behaviour on Sundays. Once Mr Welch told her off for gaily skipping as she left one of her Sunday school lessons, which was considered inappropriate and on another occasion, she was reprimanded for not wearing a hat on a Sunday, despite being nowhere near church at the time. Kathleen's mother was also politely informed that it was not appropriate to wear flesh coloured stockings to chapel, she should have been wearing black. Kathleen laughs as she recalls the time later in life, her husband Alan Harris was asked whether he went to church. His response was 'no, I paid so much attention as a child I haven't needed to go since!'

In the 1920s a concerted effort was made to raise funds to enlarge the chapel, because the congregation had grown and at the same time the roof needed to be replaced. Elders such as Kathleen's father, Tom Braunton and Gilbert Welch took responsibility for collecting funds, which was all meticulously recorded in a book. Following completion of the works in September 1926, a re-opening ceremony was held to mark the occasion. Miss Blackwell of Barnstaple had the honour of formally unlocking the door for the first time since the restoration, and the Reverend Gilbert Isaac of Morchard Bishop conducted the service. The North Devon Journal reported that a tea was served after the service, 'the ladies responsible for the arrangements being Mesdames Stanbury, Welch, Brailey, Fry, Dart, Down, Williams, Chapple, Miss Stanbury, Misses F, J and N Brailey'. At a later gathering in the evening, Mr JB Chamings of Braunton presided and the speakers were Reverend Zeal of Tavistock and G Isaac.

Over time – perhaps due to the remoteness of the location and the gradual decrease of the local population, the congregation had begun to dwindle. In 2005, with only four or five regular worshippers remaining, the decision was taken to close the church and it was sold and converted for private dwelling.

Marwood Christian Worship

Within this chapter there have been many stories of faithful, enduring worship to God in all the Marwood churches and it is evident that successive generations of families attended either their church or chapel each Sunday, in unwavering devotion. It is therefore not surprising that in 1937, the North Devon Journal wrote 'the great cause of religion has always been most worthily upheld in the Parish, being indeed, a widespread family tradition in many cases'. This worship and faith has been central in the Marwood community regardless of class or occupation.

In our times, congregations are in decline in many parts of Britain, and here in Marwood we have already seen one of our local churches close its doors as a direct consequence

of diminishing numbers. We might well ponder the words of the Reverend Pryke, who said 'Shall we not again see our ancient Church filled with reverent crowds, not on Harvest Festivals only and on special occasions, but whenever it is open for worship, and especially on Sunday mornings?' We trust that the three remaining churches in the parish will strengthen their congregations, to enable the faithful to continue the time-honoured 'family tradition'.

Above: Painting of St Michael & All Angels Parish Church. Courtesy of local artist, Kathryn Greenslade.

Chapter Five:
School Days

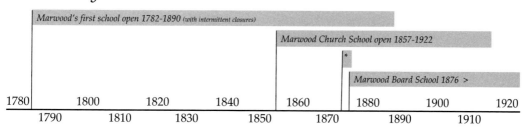

Above: The key timelines in Marwood's educational history.

The earliest mention of education in Marwood dates back to a bequest by the Reverend Richard Harding, the longest serving parish rector from 1714 until his death in 1782 at the impressive age of ninety-five years. Reverend Harding gave the sum of one hundred and fifty pounds to be invested, with the dividends used to pay a schoolmaster or mistress to teach five or six poor children of the parish to 'read the Bible, and to learn and repeat the Church Catechism distinctly and leisurely, and should instruct them in the principles of the Christian religion'. He specified that lessons should be for an hour or more, and to take place twice each week to 'examine, catechise and instruct them' at either the church or church-house (Charity Commission Enquiry, 1905).

In his will, Reverend Harding recommended that Rebecca Rock (b.1750) be appointed schoolmistress, describing her as his 'old and faithful servant'. In a codicil to his will, he later formally appointed Rebecca in the role 'for so long a time as she continued a resident in the parish, and behaved as she ought to do', affirming his belief that she was a woman of great probity and integrity. Rebecca gratefully accepted the post and continued teaching for as long as she was physically able, receiving payment of seven pounds and ten shillings per year.

Rebecca (nee Handcock) married Henry Rock at Marwood Parish Church in 1770. They had three children but sadly Henry died in 1778, leaving Rebecca to raise her young family alone. One of Rebecca's grandsons was William Frederick Rock (1802-1890), who is remembered as being Barnstaple's greatest benefactor. Amongst many contributions, William founded the North Devon Athenaeum in 1888 as a centre of learning and also donated the land known as Rock Park for the recreation of the people of Barnstaple.

At the time of Reverend Harding's bequest, the church-house was already in use, accommodating some of the poor families of Marwood, common practice in many parishes. To rectify this, the stables on the ground floor of the building were converted to living quarters, freeing the upper floor for the use of the school. This is evidenced by the 1823 Charity Commission Report, which describes pauper families living on the ground floor of the building with a schoolroom on the first floor.

Left: Marwood's first school was located in the church-house now known as the Lychgate Rooms.

In 1810, a second bequest was made in a will by William Westacott, a local agricultural labourer, who specified that the interest on an investment of one hundred pounds should be used to pay the same schoolteacher 'to teach two poor children writing and arithmetic and one poor child in reading'. Interestingly, William specified that preference be given to children of parents who had been exemplary in their good behaviour and attendance at church. This was an extraordinary sum to be left by a labourer, who had amassed a fortune of seven hundred pounds through a 'lifetime of conscientious saving' (Charity Commission Enquiry, 1905).

The Charity Commissioners Report reveals that dividends of the two bequests amounted to over eleven pounds each year and of this, seven pounds and ten shillings were paid to Rebecca Rock. By 1822, she had become too frail to continue in her role and made arrangements to pay another schoolmistress the sum of three pounds and eighteen shillings per annum to teach the children in her place. The report confirms that the new schoolmistress was instructing at the day school, '6 poor children in reading, and attending Sunday school where the same 6 children and other poor children of the parish were being taught'. The same schoolmistress received the dividends from the Westcott fund, for teaching the three poor children appointed by the Rector.

It is possible that the new teacher was Grace Warren of Guineaford (1793-1878), whose occupation was recorded as schoolmistress in the Marwood census of 1841 and 1851.

Above: One of the old dame schools was located beside *Alderhurst* in Middle Marwood c.1930.

During the early to mid nineteenth century, many women ran what became known as 'dame' schools from their homes. Locally, these were known to exist in Muddiford, Milltown and Middle Marwood, where each child was charged up to three pence per week for instruction in reading and writing.

The quality of education in these schools was variable. Some provided an acceptable standard but in other cases the dame's own literacy was inadequate, which meant the children were poorly instructed. Pamela Horn supports this view in her book *The Victorian and Edwardian Schoolchild* (1989), suggesting that many of the dame schools could be described as little more than child minders.

Vestry records show that in March 1833, John Smyth of Metcombe was teaching the boys separately, although he must have resigned by July 1842 as a later record mentions that the schoolroom was locked up until a new schoolmaster could be appointed. Thomas Jones of Prixford became schoolmaster in August 1842 and he remained in post until 1855. In December of that year, it was proposed at the Vestry meeting, that the church-house be repaired with a view to continuing a school there, this time under the instruction of John Gould, supported by voluntary contributions.

The first purpose-built school was erected in Marwood in 1857, after a long campaign by the Reverend Frederick William Portlock Collison. Not long after succeeding Reverend Riley as parish rector in 1853, he quickly concluded that the existing provisions for education were inadequate. The Reverend wrote to the Barnstaple Board of Education in October 1855 to state his case for a new school to be built.

Marwood Rectory
October 21st

My dear Sir

I wish to make application to the Board of Education for assistance towards building schoolrooms in this parish. The population exceeds 1000 and there is no building secured to the Church for such a purpose. At present the boys' school and the Sunday school are held at the church-house – but this building is in a dilapidated condition and is held by Feoffees whose power of conveying the site may be doubted. With such a population I think there ought to be schoolrooms capable of accommodating about 140 children (70 of each sex) and if sufficient funds can be raised I should wish to build also a master's house.

I am not yet prepared with any plan or estimate but of course I should not expect the Board to pay any grant that they may be disposed to make until I can satisfy them that the buildings are suitable and substantial and erected upon a site legally secured.

I remain my dear sir

Yours faithfully

F.W Collison

Source: NDRO B6Z/11/2/3.

Although no correspondence has been found giving approval for Reverend Collison's proposal, evidently he was given the go-ahead to continue with his plans. He went on to identify a suitable site for the new building and to seek the financial support of the local gentry to contribute towards the costs, keeping careful records of the donations received. Enclosing detailed plans, the Reverend wrote again to the Barnstaple Board of Education, on April 19 1856:

Marwood
April 19th 1856

My dear Sir,

I beg to submit to the Barnstaple Board of Education the plans and estimate for a National School at Marwood. My intention is to build it on a portion of the Glebe, which will be conveyed, to the Archdeacon as trustee according to a form of conveyance, by the cost of fencing and of additional internal fittings to (probably not less than) two hundred guineas. To meet this sum, I have received £89-14 from landowners, persons interested in the parish and private friends – including £20 from myself, and I hope to raise £40 more from similar sources.

I have applied to the National Society – their grant (judging by what they have done for other parishes) may be £30.

I have also applied to the committee of the council but without much hope of success as the small endowment connected with the school and my own opinions on the subject of education will prevent such management clauses as they usually insist upon. There is likely to be a considerable deficiency in consequence and I shall be truly glad of any assistance that the Board can give. I believe the circumstances of the parish are so numerous that I need say nothing of them.

Marwood National School

Builders' estimate	*£180*
Legal expenses, fencing, Stove + other fittings, about	*£30*
Received or promised	*£89-14s*
Expected from similar Private sources	*£40*
Expected from National Society	*£30*
	£159-14s
Deficiency	*£50 6d*

Source: NDRO B6Z/19/1.

The Reverend consulted local builder, Thomas Curtis of Barnstaple, who drew up plans for the new building *(pictured below)*:

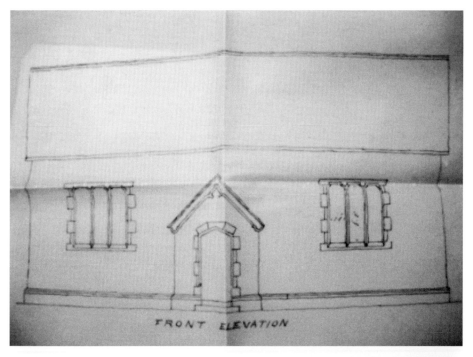

FRONT ELEVATION

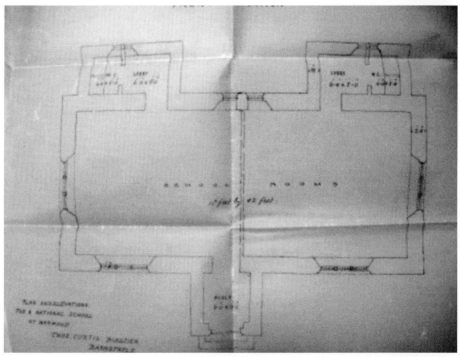

Source: NDRO B6Z/19/1.

Thomas Curtis also provided a handwritten specification of the works to be done, suggesting materials such as best Combe Down bath stone for the window frames and sills, quality Delabole slates for the roof and solid oak boards for the floor. He also designed a detachable partition wall that would run on rollers, and could be used to divide the schoolroom if required. An interesting observation is the proposal of internal water closets (W.C.) for each side of the partition. This was a forward thinking idea for this era, as the innovation of flushing waste without allowing any foul smell to escape was still relatively new, and was certainly far beyond the facilities that the vast majority of parishioners would have had in their own homes, indeed the Board school did not have W.C.s installed until 1901.

Following approval of the plans, a former orchard owned by the Marwood benefice was conveyed by the Archdeacon of Barnstaple in trust, for the purposes of a school and by deed dated February 28 1857. The school building was erected at a cost of two hundred pounds, positioned approximately halfway along the lane from Guineaford towards the parish church.

Above: The former Church school - it is now known as the Church Room and used by various groups as a centre for social gatherings, and 'Marwood Cream Teas' during the spring and summer months.

Once the new school was opened, it appears that some teaching did continue at the church-house. In the Charity Commission report of 1905, William Worth of Guineaford (1821-1908) reported that the building was used for both vestry meetings and school until 'relatively recently' and a paper written by R.R Sellman in 1964 also refers to a school at Marwood Hill, believed to have closed in 1891. This corresponds with the testimonies of some locals who believe their ancestors still attended lessons at the church-house in the 1880s. It is possible that the legacies left by Harding and Westacott continued to support the education of those who could not afford the few pence needed to attend the new school, until a change in the law in 1891 meant the attendance fees were no longer payable. The bequests then transferred to the National school funds, although a proportion of the funds were to be allocated to the Education Committee of Devon County Council.

The National School *(also known as the Church School)*
National schools, as they were so called, were an initiative of the Anglican National Society, which was established in 1811. Created to provide education for poor children, one of their aims was to ensure there was a school in every parish. Children were initially instructed in the three 'R's reading, writing and arithmetic, but also the fourth 'R' of religion, to provide for their moral and spiritual well being. Girls were also required to learn needlework, and a sewing mistress would be employed specifically to teach this subject.

They were funded by a combination of subscriptions from local people, pupil fees and government grants, which were made on a 'payment by results' methodology. Annual examinations were held in the four 'R's and it was those results together with a satisfactory attendance score which determined the amount of grant received. The amount of grant could also impact the amount of pay teachers received, so it was essential to ensure the children were fully prepared for these assessments.

The names of the earliest teachers at Marwood Church school can be identified through a combination of the Marwood census of 1861 and 1871, and Devonshire directories (White 1857; Kelly 1866 & Morris 1870). Here, the teaching was usually provided through a husband and wife partnership, the latter being responsible for teaching sewing to the girls, and most lived in the nearby hamlet of Guineaford.

The earliest records of some of the schoolmasters and mistresses are as follows:

1857	Mr John Gould Mrs Elizabeth Gould	**1875**	Mr John Mayne
1861	Mr Daniel Tolchard Mrs Mary Ann Tolchard	**1877**	Mr Wilfred Main *(held the position for 24 years)*
1870	Mr John Sutton		Miss Mary Jane Gore *(Succeeded Elizabeth Carpenter as schoolmistress from 1893 to 1895; left shortly before she married Noah Passmore)*
1871	Mr John Carpenter Mrs Elizabeth Carpenter *(Schoolmistress until 1893; remained after the death of her husband in 1875)*		

The best available source of information about the Church school's progress is *Marwood Church Monthly*, which includes reports about the school between the years of 1894 and 1901, when Mr Wilfred W. Main of *Byeways*, Guineaford, held the post of schoolmaster.

One of the earliest references is found in the April 1894 edition, which describes a recent inspection of the school by the Reverend RJE Boggis, Diocesan Inspector. With an attendance of forty-one pupils, the discipline and tone was considered to be good, while overall the school was classed as 'very fair'. There were criticisms regarding the younger pupils, specifically their aptitude for bible study and hymn singing requiring improvement, and a suggestion that overall an improvement in attendance would benefit all pupils. The article reinforces this suggestion by adding 'Perhaps parents can do most to improve it [the report] by sending their children regularly to school. No child should ever miss a possible attendance except under pressure of some unavoidable necessity of absence'.

Overall, the school met with the Inspector's approval, and he presented 'Diocesan Certificates' to pupils who passed their examination: Frederick Main; Hilda Main *[schoolmaster's children]*; Reuben Tamlyn; Mary Grace Pugsley; Charles Dennis and Lilian Tamlyn.

Reverend Pryke also gave prizes to Emily Jenkins; Edith Priscott and John Tamlyn of the middle group, and to Edith Rodd, Annie Manning and William Tamlyn of the infant class.

Several appeals were made to parents concerning their children's attendance throughout 1894, being 'earnestly requested not to keep their children from school for any reason whatever, when they are well enough to come. To do so is unfair to the children, unfair to the school and unfair to the Nation, which provides free education on the understanding that regular attendance is enforced' (*Marwood Church Monthly*, May 1894). Mr Main's appeal would also have been driven by the knowledge that poor attendance impacted the amount of financial aid granted to the school. Although by this time legislation had made attendance at school compulsory, it was still an ongoing challenge to ensure a steady turnout. All too frequently parents allowed their children to stay at home if they were needed to help out with chores, look after younger siblings or in particular, help out with major farming activities such as harvest and potato picking – a persistent problem in rural areas. In Marwood there was also a habit of regularly keeping children at home on Fridays when they were needed to help out on Barnstaple market day.

A final and solemn plea was made in the December 1894 edition of *Marwood Church Monthly*:

> We read, in an important Parish magazine, that the average number of absentees in Church Schools in England is 21 per cent of the number of pupils on the roll. This is the case in our own National School at Marwood. The attendance has greatly increased lately, in consequence, no doubt, of the improvements in the room; and the provision of two comfortable "shelters" in the playground, one for girls and one for boys, should attract more children to come to the school regularly. But the real remedy is in the hands of the parents. It is known that illness, and other unavoidable causes of absence do not affect more than ten per cent of the number on the roll. "No school, therefore, can be in a good condition which has 21 per cent of absentees". Parents should remember that, by even one hour's absence of a single pupil, the Teacher is reduced to the necessity of repeating that hour's work, which means the loss of an hour to the rest of the class, who are, consequently, in danger of becoming idle or inattentive. No such irregularity would be tolerated at work or in business. It is because the absence of children from School is a wrong and injury to others as well as to themselves, that the law of England already treats it as a crime, which may be punished. It is high time that the consciences of parents should be quickened and enlightened everywhere, so that they may see their duty in this matter, not only to their own children, but to the children of others as well.
>
> *Marwood Church Monthly*, December 1894.

An incentive scheme was introduced in April 1895 which aimed to reward good attendance each quarter for all children who had either never missed an attendance, or those who had never missed more than one attendance in a week.

In June 1895, the first prizes to be awarded for perfect attendance were presented to Lucy Lovering; Hilda Main; Mildred Main; Reginald T Main; Mary Grace Pugsley and Thomas Willis, and Arthur Carpenter[1] who had only been absent once. Once again Mr Main's own children set a good example, although it is likely that they had little choice in the matter!

In January 1898, the school received another visit from Her Majesty's Inspectors. On this occasion there was evidence of a notable improvement in the pupils. *Marwood Church Monthly* quoted the report findings, which stated 'the children are very well behaved and the instruction in elementary subjects is creditable. English is well taught and a pretty fair start has been made with geography. Singing from notes is promising. Needlework is on the whole good. Recitation should improve. The infants are well cared for'.

---

[1] Arthur's grandfather John Carpenter was schoolmaster in the early 1870s, and his mother Charity, also worked as a schoolmistress at the Church School in the 1890s. Arthur was tragically killed in the First World War and is remembered on the Memorial at the parish church.

The report also noted that Emily Jenkins (thirteen years) and George Manning (eleven years), both of Guineaford, had obtained Labour Certificates. These were presented to children who had demonstrated a satisfactory standard in reading, writing and arithmetic, enabling them to leave school and find work. During Victorian times, the earliest that children were able to obtain these certificates was at the age of eleven, but this was later extended to fourteen in the early twentieth century.

Further positive feedback was received following another inspection in August 1899:

> The Religious Instruction of the children in this admirably managed school receives careful and loving attention, and, although the answering is not, at times, so general as is desirable, yet it is evident that, as a rule, the children have well grasped the moral and spiritual lessons imparted to them in connection with the portions of Holy Scripture selected for the year's work". The following children deserve honourable mention, and have received prizes and certificates - Ethel Taylor, Ernest Taylor, Mary Manning, Ernest Willis, Edith Rodd, Nellie Yeo, Lucy Lovering, Arthur Carpenter, and Frank Dennis.

> *Marwood Church Monthly*, September 1899.

There are several mentions of improvements having been made at the Church school building, beginning with re-plastering and decoration of the walls, the addition of a wooden dado rail and hanging pictures which had been donated, including a map of the Holy Land, presented by the Reverend Edward Woodley Bowling. In June 1899, Mr Henry Collison presented a framed portrait, enlarged from a photograph of his father, the Reverend Frederick Collison, who founded the school in 1857.

In November 1899, the playground was enlarged by the removal of the stone boundary wall adjoining Quarry Close (which was previously part of the Marwood Hill estate). This made the passage between the wall and the school two feet wider than the old path, with the new boundary marked by a hedge.

One of the last references found about the school in June 1901, describes scholars who were said to be deserving of honourable mention. These included Ida Dobbs, Ernest Dobbs, Mary Manning, Annie Manning, Fred Herneman, Ethel Taylor, Annie Gammon, Reginald Main and Arthur Carpenter. It is interesting to see both Ida and Ernest Dobbs mentioned as being in attendance at the Church school, because shortly afterwards in April 1902, they were found on the admission register of the Board school in Whiddon, which by then had celebrated its twenty-fifth anniversary. More will be revealed about the Board school later in this chapter.

The Church school faced an ongoing battle to retain its pupils over the years. The numbers on the register fluctuated particularly on the opening of the school in Whiddon in 1876, with some pupils making an immediate transfer. The Carder family who lived in Whiddon were unsurprisingly some of the first to make the switch, transferring their five children on day one, and within one month, sixteen pupils from the Church school had transferred. There followed a few years of pupil ping-pong between both schools, as some parents were indecisive over which institution their offspring should attend. Several switched back to the Church school simply because of the distance, particularly for those walking from Prixford and Varley; including Ernest Kelly b.1865 and Mary Yeo b.1866, but there were other reasons including disagreements with the School Board.

For some years before and after the turn of the twentieth century, Church school numbers varied between forty and fifty. In 1910 there were just thirty-one, falling again to twenty-four pupils in 1914. After struggling with debt for a number of years exacerbated by the dwindling register, it was eventually closed in August 1922, at which time the thirteen remaining pupils on the register were transferred to the Board school at Whiddon. The church retained full responsibility for the upkeep of the building and renamed it the church room; it was then used for meetings, dances, elections and other events. In the 1940s renovations were undertaken including a new kitchen facility and cloakrooms, to enable social functions to take place there. Today it is still used by various groups as a centre for social gatherings, including the annual harvest celebration, and the delectable 'Marwood Cream Teas' are served there during the spring and summer months.

Above: A social event at the Church room in the early 1940s, including Bill Lock, Harold Hopkins, Flo Nicholls, Horatio and Lucy Lean, Charlie Fairchild, Ernest Harding, Margaret Lock, Gordon Lock, Amy Kelly, Noah and Mary Jane Passmore.

Above: Between 1965 and 1975, Marwood Women's Institute hosted an annual Christmas party for the 'Over 60s'. Held at the Church room each year, the parishioners were entertained by performers of Devon monologues and singing. Pictured here in 1965, (1) Vera Fairchild (facing group), (2) Ida Dobbs, (3) Bill Pengelly, (4) Fred Tucker, (5) Laura Hopkins, (6) Bill Lock, (7) Tom Hopkins, (8) Sidney Gubb, (9) WJ Price, (10) Fred Smith, (11) Arthur Tucker, (11) George Coats, (13) Richard Brooks, (14) Maud Brooks, (15) Ellen Carter, (16) Ellen Watts, (17) Mary Chapple, (18) Annie Gubb, (19) Ruth Herneman.

Education Act 1870

The Education Act of 1870 was introduced by the vice-president of the Department for Education, W.E Forster. Its fundamental aim was to make education available for all children regardless of their social class, with a qualified teacher in a suitable building. Existing schools across the country, including the Church school at Marwood, were given six months to ensure they could meet the necessary standards outlined in the act if they were to remain open. The parish was also required to investigate the possibility of erecting a new building to accommodate all of the children in the vicinity, which would be run by a school board of locally elected ratepayers.

A Vestry meeting was called on November 24 1870 to discuss the requirements of the Act, and how the parish would be affected. The immediate opinion of those in attendance was that there was insufficient accommodation for the education of all the children in the parish at that time. It was therefore proposed by John Alford and seconded by James Harris that a committee be appointed to make all necessary enquiries on the matter, in readiness for the next Vestry meeting on December 1 1870. The committee found that there were two hundred and forty children between the ages of six and thirteen within the district; a strong case for seeking additional accommodation for a school. It was recommended that voluntary contributions from local landowners should be encouraged to raise funds, and a board should be formed to communicate with the Department for Education on the erection of a new building.

The board members proposed were essentially a 'Who's who of Marwood farmers', a collection of men who had considerable influence in the parish. This included John Crang Esq. of Prixford *(farmer of 120 acres)*; Joseph Irwin of Metcombe *(farmer of 370 acres)*; Thomas Carder of Whiddon *(farmer of 130 acres)*; Thomas Hayward of Hartnoll Barton *(farmer of 280 acres)*; James Harris of Collacott *(farmer of 167 acres)*; John Westren of Whitefield Barton *(farmer of 375 acres)*; John Alford of Hewish Barton *(farmer of 480 acres)* and John Rudd of *Kennacott (farmer of 114 acres)*.

At the meeting, Thomas Hayward proposed Milltown as a possible site for erecting the school, and by amendment, James Day of Townridden, proposed No Man's Land at Wigley Cross. Further to this, John Crang proposed that the decision regarding the site should be left to the Department for Education. A ballot was held, resulting in a very close outcome with no clear majority however the motion proposing Milltown as a potential site was carried forward.

Vestry notes are scarce beyond this point, with no records to explain how the matter progressed between 1871 and 1873, except that minutes of the next meeting in November 1873 reported the need to rescind the motion to erect the school at Milltown. It was noted that the suggestion of a school in Milltown was 'now deemed by a great many of the inhabitants of this parish to be the wrong site for the general accommodation of the parish'.

The Department for Education began to add pressure by posting a notice on the Church door, requesting a decision on the site to be made imminently, because the time had come that 'a school must be built'. Vestry notes were cautious, warning that as the building will come 'at a great cost to the parish, it is desirable that the most suitable site should be selected'.

It would seem that a shift in thinking occurred between 1871 and 1873, from debating the site for a new school to be built, to acquiring an existing building (at a vastly reduced cost). The committee decided that a petition should be sent by the rate payers of Marwood to the Department for Education, to oppose a plan to accommodate children from other parishes. The reason given was that it would generate a greater number of children in the new school than had previously been accounted for. There was little desire to accept children from neighbouring Bittadon and Shirwell if it meant that Marwood had to bear the building costs, and it was requested that the Department 'kindly release us from providing for so large a number'.

In January 1874 the Department issued a negative response but Marwood was not ready to back down yet. A further letter was written to ask the Department to rescind their order, proposing that the new school should be accommodated at the old Methodist Chapel between Prixford and Guineaford rather than a new building at Milltown. Such was the determination to prevent the parish bearing the costs of building, an unlikely alliance between the Church of England and Wesleyan movement was formed

The Methodist Day School
The new Methodist Chapel was formally opened in October 1873, as discussed in Chapter Three. Mindful of the urgent need to provide a school for the parish, Thomas Hayward proposed that a new committee be elected to establish a school at the old chapel as soon as possible in a final attempt to satisfy the Department for Education.

At a chapel meeting held on January 6 1874, it was proposed by Mr Samuel Born and seconded by Mr William Geen, that 'there be established in the old Chapel premises, a Wesleyan day school; open to all children of the parish and neighbourhood'. Unanimously agreed by all in attendance, the committee was quickly formed to make the arrangements.

At one of the first committee meetings on January 26 1874, arrangements were swiftly made to appoint Mr Elliott as schoolmaster and for the purchase of desks. It was proposed and seconded that school fees for labourers' children should be two to three pence per week, tradesmen's children three to four pence per week and farmers' children four to six pence per week, with the actual amount being left to the discretion of the teacher. The school hours were also agreed to commence at quarter past nine until twelve noon; reconvening after lunch at half past one, until lessons ended at four o'clock.

In February the committee agreed on two female teachers, initially appointing Mrs Elizabeth Hill of Guineaford who agreed to teach sewing to the girls on Monday, Wednesday and Thursday afternoons, for payment of five pounds per year. It was also proposed that twenty year old Miss Elizabeth Worth of Guineaford be offered the position of assistant teacher subject to her parents' consent, and if she agreed, four pounds payment would be offered in her first year. Mr Elliott had prepared a list of other items that he would require including books, blackboard and a desk for his own use.

Upon opening in March 1874, the school quickly became popular amongst parishioners and admission grew rapidly, drawing some children from the nearby Church school. The schoolmaster received a commendation from the school inspector, and based on his apparent satisfaction, further expenses were incurred to improve the facilities. Nevertheless, despite such a promising start the school was never formally registered. Less than six months later, its future was thrown into doubt.

Marwood Board School
In the first week of July 1874, an announcement from the Department for Education ordered the parish to build a new school at Milltown to supercede the Chapel school, which had already attracted one hundred pupils. This was met with shock and disbelief. An article published in the North Devon Journal on July 9 1874, was positively scathing about the Department's final decision, which had made parishioners 'greatly surprised and annoyed'. The article suggested that the new planned location of the school was less mindful of the necessities of the parish of Marwood, but more for the benefit of neighbouring Bittadon, East Down and outskirts of Shirwell, quoting some residents as angrily asking 'what have we to do with neighbouring parishes? If we provide for our own children, let them provide for theirs'. It also implied that the Department's rejection was based on the school's nonconformist origins, despite the increasingly large numbers of Wesleyan followers in Marwood.

On November 19 1874 a meeting was held at the church-house, chaired by the Reverend Frederick Collison, where a subdued and now obedient school committee discussed preparations to bring the Department's orders into force. It was agreed that the Church school would remain open, albeit with strict standards to be met, however the Chapel school would be incorporated into the new system, transferring its pupils to the new Board school. Aware that locals regarded Milltown as a deeply unpopular location, John Crang proposed and Thomas Joslin seconded that one central school should be built at No Man's Land. Exactly how the school came to be erected at Whiddon is not documented in Vestry records, though presumably, the land was made available at a good price.

On December 8 1874, the Marwood School Board was formed with the election of John Crang Esq. (chairman), Reverend Frederick Collison, John Westren, Thomas Hayward and Samuel Born, all of whom had invested time and money in support of the earlier parish schools. The land was formally purchased and construction commenced. During the autumn of 1875, it was decided that John Crang Esq, Henry Dene Esq. of *Lee House* and James Mayne of East Down, should call on local landowners to ascertain what financial contributions they would make towards the new building. Evidently their plea fell on deaf ears, obliging the parish to borrow the two hundred and fifty pounds that was to be handed over to the new School Board to allow the building works to be finalised.

Construction was completed early in 1876 at the eventual cost of five hundred pounds. Shortly afterwards, the Marwood Board school welcomed its first pupils on March 6 1876.

Right:
Marwood School in 2011
(formerly known as the Board school).

We are fortunate that the history of the Board school is particularly well documented due to the existence of the old log books, which were kept since the school first opened its doors. It was a mandatory requirement for the schoolmasters in all Board schools to keep the book updated with all matters relating to the management of the school. Entries had to be made at least weekly, and were to record school progress, visits of managers, cautions and illnesses. Log books give an amazing insight into the way of life, not just at school but also of local customs, social activities and national events.

Left: The first Marwood school log book.
Source: NDRO 2315c/EFL 1.

The first schoolmaster to take up the post was Barumite, Frank Palmer, who was aged just twenty-one years when he took the job in 1876, in a period when the headship of schools was open to newly certified teachers. In his first week, he recorded the admission of just eight pupils, noting in the log book that they were 'backward' by his standards.

Week two brought ten new admissions although Frank was still unable to form a timetable with such small numbers. One pupil had left by March 14 due to parents being unable to pay the fees (three pence per week). The first absences due to sickness occurred, and the following week attendance was low again which was attributed to corn sowing.

The admission of new pupils began to grow steadily each week, attracting some children who had never been to any school before. By April 24 1876, just seven weeks after opening, sixteen pupils had transferred from the Church school, and others came from Shirwell and as far as Barnstaple.

Frank received frequent visits from members of the School Board in the first few weeks, and in April, James Mayne of East Down, clerk to the Board, carried out his first inspection. He recorded:

> The premises are very nice; the children are in good order and fairly taught. This promises to be a useful and efficient school. Object and alphabet cards are wanted, some elementary reading books and maps of Scotland and Ireland.
>
> Source: NDRO 2315c/EFL 1.

Frank Palmer himself described progress as slow and steady in the basic elementary subjects, with attention being given to spelling, and arithmetic being particularly difficult to teach given the absence of a blackboard. At the discretion of the board, religious education was still a key part of the school timetable and there were various references to non-denominational lessons on the books of the Bible.

In November 1877 the school fees, known as school pence, were noted in the log book:

Farmers' children

Under five years of age	one penny per week
Above five and under eight years	two pence per week
Above eight years	threepence per week

Artisans' children

Under five years of age	one penny per week
Above five years	the first child to pay threepence per week; every other child from the same family attending school pay one penny per week

Labourers' children

Under five years of age	one penny per week
Above five years	the first child to pay two pence per week; every other child from the same family attending school pay one penny per week

Source: NDRO 2315c/EFL 1.

R. R Sellman (1964) observed that while the schedule of fees were designed on a sliding scale relative to parental occupation, a farmer with one child aged between five and eight, would pay less than an a tradesman in a corresponding position each week.

By March 1877, only twelve months after opening, the school had enrolled one hundred and five pupils, with sixty of these transferring from the Church school. As mentioned earlier in this chapter, there had been much coming and going between the two schools, with many temporarily returning to the school at Guineaford, and later being readmitted at Whiddon, which meant that some pupils were counted twice. Seventeen children had also transferred from a dame school in Milltown, including William, Lizzie and Annie Hill and Thomas, Bessie, George and Bertie Bowden. William Hill was later described in the log book as an incorrigible truant! Another dame school in Muddiford appears to have continued running for several years in competition, but this closed in 1883 when the remaining pupils were transferred to the Board school:

Elizabeth Trump	Emma Willis	John Rudd
Hannah Balment	Elizabeth Willis	Thomas Rudd
Thomas Alford	William Lynch	Alice Quick
Annie Alford	Bessie Lynch	Polly Quick
Ada Brooks		

Source: NDRO 2315c/EFL 1.

Further transfers came from the dame school in Middle Marwood, last taught by Mrs Lake, and later from the church-house, as mentioned previously. By the 1890s, there was a regular attendance of sixty pupils on the register.

There was an obvious correlation between the weather and attendance, as the log book is littered with explanations for absences, for example *'attendance rather poor on Thursday on account of snowstorm'*, *'very stormy weather has made an appreciable difference in the attendance'* and *'if weather is fine, attendance stays up'*. In March 1877, Frank Palmer showed his concern about absenteeism by sending notes home to some parents asking that the children *'may be sent regularly to obviate the necessity of reporting them to the Board'*. Evidently there was little improvement because by the next month he notified the Board about the irregular attendance, and that this continued to be an ongoing problem, just as it had been at the Church school. In September 1877, notes were again sent to parents asking them to send their children for an examination. Some of the responses were quite indifferent and one parent stated that if their children wished to come to school they may, and if they did not, they may stay at home. Such a casual attitude towards attendance would not be tolerated within a few years when new legislation was introduced.

Excerpts from the Marwood School Log Book: 1870s

March 24 1876   *Average attendance low this week owing to corn sowing.*

Sept 29 1876   *Had to reprimand one boy for using profane language in the playground.*

April 20 1877   *Had occasion to inspect the shoes on Wednesday, many being very dirty. I found them cleaned and bright throughout the school on Thursday. Gave attention to faces and hands to ensure cleanliness.*

May 4 1877   *Had occasion to warn monitor against striking the children in his class, having frequently charged him not to do so.*

May 18 1877   *Had to reprove one boy for using bad language in school. Same boy has previously been guilty of the same offence.*

September 29 1877   *Had complaint of child's lunch being stolen. Have had many similar complaints before but cannot trace back to the offender.*

October 26 1877   *Wrote to the sewing mistress to request her not to continue her attendance at present on account of Typhoid fever being in her house.*

December 12 1877   *Had occasion to caution Prideaux about striking the smallest children committed to his care.*

March 22 1878   *Had a test examination in arithmetic on Friday. Satisfactory results but found in one or two cases such inefficiency that the children must have got their results previously by copying.*

June 28 1878   *Prideaux leaves today.*

August 9 1878   *Attendance unusually thin this week owing to hay harvest.*

September 23 1878   *Had complaint of three children running in standing corn.*

January 12 1879   *Many absentees this morning and more in the afternoon owing to harvest thanksgiving services at Prixford.*

April 10 1879   *Received intimation this (Thursday) morning that two of my scholars had been withdrawn to attend the National School because the clerk had written to their parents complaining of their irregular attendance here.*

Source: NDRO 2315c/EFA 1.

Above: Hay-making was a family affair – everyone had to lend a hand and
school attendance suffered. Rebecca Bartlett's Great-Gran and Great-Granfer
Spear pictured with family and friends at harvest time, c.1923.

Education Act 1880

The Education Act (1880) made schooling compulsory for the first time, initially for
five to ten year olds only. In rural areas such as Marwood, this was met with dismay
by some of the poorer families who were reliant upon the income previously gained
through the labour of their children. Not only would they lose wages, but also have
to pay school fees. The 'school pence' as it was known, had to be paid on Monday
mornings or the child was excluded for the rest of the week. As a result, some
labourers' children were duty-bound to attend lessons during the day and go to work
before and after school.

Before the new Act, if parents could not afford the fees they simply kept the child at
home. But from 1880 the School Boards were authorised to introduce attendance
by-laws, and the Marwood clerk James Mayne, was given the additional responsibility
of attendance officer. This involved visiting the parents of absent children to inform
them of their obligation to send them to school. In cases of extreme poverty, the officer
was able to apply discretion on the payment of fees in a concerted effort to ensure
attendance; otherwise the only acceptable reason for absence was sickness.

There are many references to quarrels about attendance either with obstinate parents
who still refused to send their children, or with children who were regularly playing
truant. This was extremely difficult to tackle, and threats of legal action still failed to

encourage compliance. In July 1881, an excerpt from the Marwood log book demonstrates an attempt to tackle absenteeism:

July 8 - Two children who frequently play truant were brought to me in the dinner hour by their mother, who requested me to keep them in school til dark. I confined them and went to tea. In an hour's time when I sent the monitor to unlock the door and release them, she found that they had both escaped by kicking out the windows in the two porches.

July 9 – The two children above referred to played truant again this morning.

July 21 – Punished five boys for playing truant, and warned the whole school against this evil.

Source: NDRO 2315c/EFA 1.

In Marwood as in many other rural parish schools, there were always challenges at certain times in the farming year where children were kept at home for a few days to help with potato picking and other duties. The log book entries acknowledge and reluctantly accept these absences - '*Commenced school this morning after three weeks of holiday. Good attendance but all the farmers' children absent without a single exception as harvest operations are not concluded*'. There are no attempts to contest this matter; maybe Frank realised he would be fighting a losing battle.

At this time there was an average of sixty pupils on the register, and Frank managed with the assistance of only the sewing mistress and an older pupil acting as monitor. This was clearly becoming unsustainable and probably led to Frank's decision to resign. In July 1882, twenty-three year old Charles Martin from Lincolnshire was employed and he received a visit from the inspector within just two months of taking the position. The subsequent report highlighted several areas for improvement that led to the School Board replacing the sewing mistress with an assistant teacher, who could take charge of the infants and enable Charles to concentrate on instruction. With the additional teaching support, the school began to receive significantly improved reports, being classed as 'Excellent' in 1885 and 1886.

In 1886, Charles married Emily Carder, daughter of influential yeoman, Thomas Carder of Whiddon, and the following year they left the parish as Charles went to teach in a school in South Devon. Within two years they had returned, and he was quickly reappointed schoolmaster at Marwood where he remained for a further five years until eventually resigning in 1894. The Martin family went on to live in Ilfracombe and run a guesthouse but Charles never returned to teaching.

Excerpts from the Marwood School Log Book: 1880s

May 3 1880   *Mangold sowing keeps home most of the boys.*

May 28 1880   *Small number present this morning. I find that many have gone to Barnstaple, the Yeomanry Cavalry being there this week.*

October 15 1880   *Several children suffering from measles. One boy was sent home ill, and one girl on Thursday, the latter having the spots plainly perceptible on her face. Several boys are detained at home by agricultural operations.*

January 25 1881   *Opened school again this morning having closed for a week owing to the roads being quite impassable on account of the snow.*

February 1 1881   *The library was opened today. £6 was raised through two concerts in the schoolroom.*

March 17 1881   *I obtained this morning the names of 15 children who are absent through sickness, chiefly through scarlet fever.*

March 24 1881   *Had a complaint lodged against a boy for using impertinent and abusive language to an elderly man in the public road. Cautioned him and caused him to write and learn one hundred words of spelling.*

November 11 1881   *Received complaints of stone-throwing and impertinence against four boys (Bowens and Coates) who were aiming at telegraph wires and clothes lines, the missiles falling into people's gardens by the turnpike road.*

December 15 1881   *Having found this week, many children coming to school unwashed, I have instituted a daily examination. On Thursday I supervised the thorough washing of six children at playtime, causing it to be done in two instances by their elder sisters.*

January 16 1882   *Received instruction from the Board to send home children arriving without their school pence.*

March 6 1882   *Punished a boy named William Trump, a scholar in the school for stealing dinners. The boy admitted the offence in the mother's presence. He was punished very reasonably yet he was shielded by his parents and withdrawn from the school.*

March 29 1882   *Had a report today of bad scarlet fever having broken out at Middle Marwood. Advised Downs' and Williams' children of the hamlet to return home and absent themselves for a while.*

October 2 1882   *Received authority from the Board to close school this week, finding that over twenty families are now infected with the measles.*

April 2 1883   *Admitted a new scholar aged ten, who did not know their letters.*

November 5 1886   *It will be necessary to withhold three boys from examination next year on account of deficiency of intellect and extreme dullness.*

October 4 1887   *Two boys will have to be placed on "exception" being of rather weak mental powers. I observed they were suffering from "diseased scalp" in an aggravated form I therefore advised their mother to keep them at home for a few days to prevent contagion.*

March 30 1889   *Received information that Joseph, Percy and Alice Brailey, Annie Alford and Alice Lynch, having the mumps are too ill to attend school*

Abolition of School Fees

A significant legislative change enacted in 1891 led to the abolition of school fees and increased the leaving age from ten to twelve. It had a positive impact on attendance, although it did not prevent children from poor families having to go out to work before and after school. This practice continued in some cases until the Education Act in 1918, which banned employment of children under twelve and imposed restrictions on employing those aged twelve years and older. It also specified that children were not to be employed in circumstances that might be 'prejudicial to his health or physical development, or to render him unfit to obtain the proper benefit from his education', and outlined penalties payable by employers found to be in breach of this legislation.

Other children may not have been in paid employment after school, but would certainly have been expected to do their fair share of chores in the house or on the land, especially those from farming families. Twentieth century Marwood was no exception - David Pugsley and Pauline Stentiford remember having to carry out chores such as milking the cows or collecting eggs before leaving for school in the morning. Colin Latham recalls having to milk three separate herds around Hartnoll and Bittadon before school!

Source: NDRO 2315c/EFA 1.

Following the resignation of Charles Martin in April 1894, Daniel D. Pill, the son of a coal miner from Gloucestershire took up the post of Schoolmaster. Before arriving at Marwood, Daniel had taught for three years at a school in Ilfracombe. He was to remain in the post for an astonishing thirty-five years, eventually taking his retirement in November 1929. He led the school through some notable historic events including two wars (Boer and the Great War) and the deaths of three monarchs (Victoria, Edward VII and George V).

Daniel had an excellent reputation and in December 1898, after only four years under his direction, the Marwood Board School was described by Her Majesty's Inspector as 'the best country school in North Devon' - quite an achievement.

Excerpts from the Marwood School Log Book: 1890s

Sept 26 1891	*Cautioned the boy Beer with reference to dirty hands and warned other children against such uncleanly habits.*
October 20 1891	*Received a complaint about children chasing sheep belonging to Mr Rudd. Punished the ringleader, an older boy, and warned the younger offenders.*
January 7 1892	*Recitation:* *Standards I: 'Good night and Good morning'* *Standards II & III: 'Keeping his word' & 'Hidden Treasure'* *Standards IV & above: 'The Last of the Flock' & 'England's Dead'*
March 25 1892	*Several children being kept home to assist with gardening and the planting of potatoes on the farms.*
July 3 1893	*Punished a big boy for striking a little girl on the nose, because she threw a little water at him. Gave a warning against such cowardly acts.*
September 20 1894	*No school tomorrow on account of the fair at Barnstaple.*
November 16 1894	*The excessive rains of the past week have prevented a large number of children from attending school.*
May 30 1895	*The operations connected with the building of a new classroom have now commenced. The infants are consequently being taught in the main room with the older scholars.*
September 9 1895	*The new classroom has just been completed and the infants are occupying it today for the first time.*
February 5 1896	*Heard today of a case of scarlet fever at Middle Marwood. Children from the infected family are consequently being kept at home.*
February 10 1896	*A case of scarlet fever is reported from Muddiford.*
April 13 1896	*A case of scarlet fever is reported at Prixford.*
August 14 1896	*Heard this morning of three cases of Diphtheria in a family at Metcombe.*
December 10 1896	*Ploughing match held at Metcombe today – only two boys present above Standard III.*
November 28 1897	*No school this afternoon on account of a "Band of Hope Tea" at Muddiford.*

| March 21 1898 | Five boys absent today are being employed in farm work. Not one possesses the required 'labour' certificate. |

| March 31 1898 | Have been trying to get a collection of useful objects to form a small museum. A good start has been made, and most of the specimens have been brought in by scholars. It is intended not so much to form a cabinet of curiosities as to make a collection of things, which will be useful for illustrations. |

| November 22 1898 | Seven boys are today being employed by Mr Conibear of Little Silver, brushing for a shooting party. Have written to the attendance officer. |

| November 24 1898 | Same seven boys employed by Mr Conibear again. Not one of the seven is legally exempt from school attendance. |

| July 26 1899 | The Rev WE Pryke, Chairman of the School Board has kindly presented the school with four fine oak framed pictures - Joan of Arc, by Sir J E Millais; Harlech Castle by J Ward, R; Queen Elizabeth by a contemporary artist; Oliver Cromwell by Robert Walker. |

| December 9 1899 | Twenty three children have earned prizes for perfect attendance during the quarter ended at Michaelmas viz; Walter Down, John Worth, Frederick Jenkins, Thomas Darch, Florence Norman, Ethel Down, Thomas Gammon, Edith Norman, Hannah Harris, Ellen Lewis, Alice Petters, Emily Jenkins, Evelyn Mitchell, William Down and William Gammon. Infants - Christopher Brooks, Herbert Jenkins, Thomas Gould, Thomas Turner, John Squire, Emma Tucker, Ada Dummett, Kate Gould. |

Source: NDRO 2315c/EFA 1.

Marwood School in the Twentieth Century

In September 1900, the school was inspected by James Mayne who observed that under the headship of Daniel Pill, the standard of teaching was exceptional. Within his report he summarised:

> *Mixed school: A remarkably well conducted and intelligently taught school.*

> *Infants' class: The infants are taught with much zeal and very creditable success.*

In January 1901, the log book reports the death of Queen Victoria. Daniel seized the opportunity to ensure the children were well informed of the significance of the event:

> *Her Majesty Queen Victoria died yesterday, Tuesday evening, at 6.30. Shall take every opportunity in the next few days of drawing the children's attention to facts connected with the late Queen's life, and also to state arrangements as to the change of Sovereign.*

On February 1 he noted:

> *Her late Majesty, Queen Victoria, is to be taken from Osborne to Windsor tomorrow. Services will be held tomorrow in most Parish Churches throughout the land, but the internment at Frogmore does not take place for a few days.*

In June of the same year, Assistant Teacher Miss Florence Thomas resigned from her post at the Board school to take up the more senior role of Head of the Church school in Guineaford. *Marwood Church Monthly* reported her appointment, mentioning that Miss Thomas was well known because of her connection with Whiddon and as such she 'enters her duties not as a stranger and we shall be prepared to give her a hearty welcome' (June 1901). Her replacement at Whiddon was Miss Emily Parkhouse, who initially took lodgings with local miller, Hayman Brailey and his family in Milltown. Emily was to remain in post for an astonishing forty-four years, retiring in 1945.

There was a challenging start to the following year as a major outbreak of measles overtook the parish. On April 16 1902, Daniel was notified of a case of measles, and as usual, requested the other children from the same family to remain at home. On May 14, he received information of cases of measles in five different families and over the next two days four more cases were reported. By May 24, attendance at school had fallen off badly as new cases were still being detected, and an epidemic was declared. At this time there were one hundred names on the register yet only thirty-five children were in attendance by the end of the month. On May 29 the Medical Office of Health ordered that the school be closed for a fortnight on account of the epidemic. When the school reopened there was still an attendance of only fifty and it wasn't until the beginning of July that normal attendance was restored.

The introduction of the Education Act, 1902 brought the abolition of School Boards, which were to be replaced by the Local Education Authorities (LEAs) and this brought a change in name to Marwood Council School. With effect from October 1 1903, the LEA took control of the employment of teachers, their pay and qualifications, and ensured the provision of books and equipment.

Illness and Epidemics

Like many schools in Victorian and Edwardian times, Marwood had its fair share of illnesses and epidemics which resulted in a surprisingly high number of temporary school closures. Scarlet fever, diphtheria, whooping cough, measles, mumps and influenza were frequent menaces, although the school log book indicates that remarkably only a few cases resulted in the death of their pupils since the school began in 1876.

One particularly heartbreaking case was the double tragedy that befell the Balment family of Whiddon in 1912. George and Bessie Balment lived at Whiddon Farmhouse with their six children, Robert, Mervyn, Thomas, Winnie, William and Henry. In December, their only daughter Winnie succumbed to diphtheria and laryngitis and she deteriorated very quickly. She died on December 3, aged just five years and eleven months, and the family and parish deeply mourned the loss of the little girl. The log book records that the school received official notification of Winnie's death on December 5, and that her three older brothers were kept home from school. After Winnie was laid to rest on December 7 at Marwood Parish Church, George and Bessie returned home after the funeral only to find that their youngest son William had been taken unwell. Again, the illness took hold with frightening speed and when William died on December 9 aged only four years, his parents were beside themselves with grief. He was laid to rest on December 12 alongside Winnie, and the touching inscription on their small headstone read:

Jesus called two little children
E'er sin could blight or sorrow fade
Death came with friendly care
The opening buds to heaven conveyed
And bade them blossom there

Above: Winnie (left) & William Balment c.1910.

As the news spread of the tragic events, the school's attendance halved as frightened parents refused to send their children to school in Whiddon. On hearing the news about the second death, the Ministry of Health declared that the school should be closed immediately, and remain so until December 20 1912.

One can only hope that the later birth of their daughter Kathleen in 1913 and son John in 1914 brought some comfort to bereaved parents, George and Bessie and their family.

Above: Marwood Board School Timetable March 1902 source: NDRO 2315C.
Reproduced with kind permission of North Devon Record Office.

A Marwood school timetable dated 1902 is retained at the North Devon Record Office, giving a real insight into a school day. Each day began at 9.15am with thirty minutes of prayer and religious instruction and after a short registration, there were lessons from 9.55am through to 11.05am in the three Rs, Reading, Writing and Arithmetic. A short recreational break of ten minutes was followed by another forty-five minutes in the three Rs. School closed for lunch break at noon when all the children went home for lunch, and reconvened at 1.30pm. Afternoon lessons offered more variety with the inclusion of History, Geography, Music, English, Spelling and Drawing until 2.30pm, and after a short ten minute break, the whole school spent twenty minutes partaking in physical exercise, known as 'drill'. This might have involved marching, jogging and stretching. The final lessons of the day included Elementary Science for the older children and more of the three Rs for the younger class, after which the school gathered for prayer and dismissal at 3.35pm.

"Memories of my part of North Devon" by William Lynch (1905-1996)

William Lynch wrote memoirs of his early years in Marwood, hoping that if they were published they *'could be of interest to those live at and love North Devon'*. Though never formally published, his manuscript is held in the North Devon Athenaeum and provides a valuable insight to life in Muddiford in the early twentieth century. William wrote fondly about his school years between 1906 and 1919, the most memorable being his first day. Having been used to the typical earth closet privy in use in most homes at that time, William was cautious to find flushing water closets were installed at the school. His father was employed there to make sure the rainwater was collected from the roofs to fill up the big tank enabling the flushing system to operate. On William's first visit to the toilet, he pulled the chain and watched with horror as the water rushed into the pan, and ran for dear life because he thought he had flooded the place! There was no drinking water at the school so each day the older children would take it in turns to fetch a two-gallon can of water from Joseph Brailey's farm nearby. The well was located close to the farmyard, which made the water slightly yellow in colour, much to the disgust of the children! He recalled there were no outdoor games or sports in those days, but lots of recitations such as "twelve inches, one foot, three feet, one yard" and so on, or "four gills, one pint, two pints, one quart" which they had to repeat as they marched out of school. William felt that Mr Pill was a fair schoolmaster – he had a cane of hazel wood, about two foot long but hated to use it unless it was absolutely necessary. If the misdemeanour did prompt such a punishment, the unfortunate child would be struck so hard on their palm that it would leave a red wheal.

Extracts from North Devon Athenaeum reference MSS-B08-92 D.

Above: Marwood Council School, Group II 1908, with Schoolmaster Daniel D. Pill (back left) and Assistant Teacher Miss Emily Parkhouse (back right). Includes Richard Brooks (centre, back row – Norman Brooks' father), Stanley Gammon (3rd from left, middle row – Peter Gammon's father).

214

Excerpts from the Marwood School Log Book: Early 1900s

April 15 1901	*The sanitary alterations have now been completed, the work having been commenced on January 21st. Water closets have been provided in place of the former cesspit arrangement.*
October 7 1901	*Miss Mabel Drew, late of St Saviour's National School, Bath, has been appointed to teach the Infants and the needlework of the older scholars.*
October 14 1901	*Mr and Mrs Arthur have very kindly invited all the children of Marwood to tea at Marwood Hill this afternoon. The school will be closed on this account.*
December 4 1901	*The Election of Marwood School Board took place yesterday. Out of eight candidates the following gentlemen were elected, Messrs T Joslin, J Lynch, J Rudd, W Worth and F Parkhouse.*
June 18 1902	*To enable some of the scholars to witness a lifeboat launch at Barnstaple at 4.30pm the school will assemble at 10.00am today and dismiss at 3.05pm.*
June 19 1902	*Am today sending a detailed report of the progress of each child in the higher divisions of the school to the parents, hoping it will tend to induce the latter to take greater interest in the school life of their children.*
June 20 1905	*School closed today on account of "Marwood Band of Hope" outing to Saunton Sands.*
September 21 1907	*Have been holding the final examination for the year during the past few days. Standard I appears to be not quite up to the usual standard of efficiency but the rest of the school is in a very satisfactory state.*
April 3 1908	*The flushing apparatus has been repaired today, having been out of order since March 31st. The flushing has in the meantime been carried out by hand.*
September 14 1908	*Received information concerning a case of scarlet fever in a home (Brooks) at Bittadon. Five children are absent from this cause.*
February 17 1909	*Received notice that the School Medical Officer will attend on the 19th at 9.45 for the purpose of seeing and examining scholars aged 12 yrs and over, and also children only recently admitted.*
August 23 1909	*The playground has been cleared of rough stones and the surface has had a coat of tar spread over it.*
November 5 1909	*Distributed the certificates for "Perfect" (14) and "Regular" (28) attendance.*
May 6 1910	*His Majesty King Edward VII died just before Midnight.*

September 9 1910	At a competitive examination for free places at the Barnstaple Grammar school, Stanley G Buckingham was placed among the successful candidates.
September 14 1910	Report on Religious Instructions – Rev W J Lewis: "The following children have struck me as exceptionally well taught: James Gammon, Leonard Carder, Elsie Chapple, Leslie Symons, Maggie Watts, Dorothy Symonds, Viola Morgan, Annie Chapple, Jane Mitchell, Alice Smyth, Stanley Buckingham, Reginald Jenkins, Phoebe Welch, William Conibear, Ernest Shaxton and Dorothy Tucker.
October 28 1910	Distributed the attendance certificates for year ending September 30th 1910. Reginald Jenkins, Fred Smyth and John Spear have made perfect attendance for five consecutive years.
January 12 1911	Ernest Shaxton accidentally broke a window pane in the boys' lobby. The managers have been informed.
October 1 1911	A case of spotted fever is reported from Milltown. The Medical Officer immediately requests the closure of the school for three weeks. The little boy, Walter Scott died October 1st.
November 23 1911	Dr Gould visited the school and examined a number of scholars. Two boys were sent home due to suffering from a skin disease.

Source: NDRO 2315c/EFA 1.

The school continued to receive excellent reports over the following few years, with special mention given to the teaching of writing, composition and arithmetic, and excellent order being 'quietly and pleasantly contained'. In June 1913, it was reported:

The very high level of efficiency reached at this school reflects great credit upon the Headmaster and his staff. The children are responsive and alert and show a creditable interest in their studies: this is especially noticeable in the first class where the attainments of the scholars, are in all respects, exceedingly good.

Kathleen Harris (nee Braunton) attended the school in the 1920s. She recalls that Mr Pill was awfully strict but concedes that whilst he made the children work hard, they achieved good results, especially in maths. In 1929, Daniel Pill took his well-earned retirement and was succeeded by Frank Chadder.

Above: Marwood school pupils photographed with Miss James at *Marwood Hill House*,
prior to a visit to the seaside, many are clutching buckets and spades (c.1925).
Marlow the dog is in the foreground!

Marwood School c.1930 - Left to Right.
Back row: Elsie Squire, Eva Down, Joan Quick, Gwen Babb, Molly Squire,
Phyllis Karslake, Katy Ridd.

3rd row: Mr Chadder, Walter Pugsley, Ernie Webber, _ White, Mary Manning,
Joan Ridd, Bert Squires, Harold Hopkins, Ernie Ashton.

2nd row: Bill Gammon, George Pugsley, May Pugsley, Barbara Spear, Gwen Webber,
Mary Crocombe, George Huxtable, Henry Coats.

Front row: Arthur Tucker, Roy Cook, Fred Jenkins, Jack Watts, Harry Quick,
Ern Watts, Jack Braunton, Wilton Pugsley.

Marwood School c.1931 - Left to Right.
Back row: R. Gammon, G. Lock, F. Karslake, A. Coats, M. Down,
K. Spear, Miss Symons (teacher).
2nd row: M. Herneman, M. Pugsley, L. Leverton, M. Coats, B. Bowden,
M. Perrin, M. Crocombe, F. Couch.
Front row: K. Gammon, J. Balment, N. Babb, C. Thorne, G. Karslake,
E. Jenkins, A. Smith, E. Quick, E. Jenkins, ___.

Edie Jenkins (*pictured above, fifth from the right, front row*) remembers her school days quite clearly, and names almost every pupil with ease in the Marwood class photos of the 1930s to the 1940s. In the back row of the same photograph above, (*pictured second from the left, next to Miss Symons*) was Edie's husband to be, Kenneth Spear, and they married in 1947.

In hot weather, Edie remembers the long walk home from school could be thirsty work. Once she had got as far as Milltown Farm, she would often take a drink by cupping her hands under the running water from the pump above the cattle trough.

The new schoolmaster Frank Chadder was born in Ilfracombe in 1895, the son of a tailor, and educated at the Shebbear United Methodist College, along with his brother Leslie. His younger brother Harvey was a promising footballer with amateur side Corinthians, who played in the third round of the FA Cup in 1927 against Newcastle United. Frank was also a keen footballer, and he went on to encourage the sport at Marwood and the first ever school football team was formed.

Above: Marwood School Football Team c.1932. It is unfortunately damaged but there are
some familiar faces including Jack Watts *(right end of the middle row)*.

Frank Chadder remained at Marwood for six years until 1935, when he was succeeded
by Mr Chugg. He had the responsibility of leading the school through the early years
of the Second World War; a time that many locals still remember clearly as described
further in Chapter Seven.

Of the many Marwood parishioners who attended the school during the 1940s and
1950s, most have mixed memories of fondness and fear about schoolmaster Mr William
Price. He had a reputation for being rather strict, being a frequent user of the cane and
was also inclined to have his favourites. Everyone knew they had to clear the lane after
school before he left the building, or risk a stern telling off.

Lou Spear remembers one occasion when Mr Price had given John Sanders the cane
for misbehaving. The next day John's mother, Mrs Sanders marched into the
schoolroom, straight to the map cupboard where the cane was kept. She got hold of
the cane and in front of the class she snapped it into pieces, presumably to the great
amusement of the pupils! David Fairchild remembers another occasion when Mr Price
sat down on a glass bottle and ended up with his assistant having to carefully remove
splinters of glass from his bottom!

Every Wednesday afternoon the pupils would undertake various activities including
gardening or woodwork in the purpose built workshop. John Sanders, Lou Spear and
his brother Denzil once found a football stud whilst gardening by the rockery. They
jokingly said that they should put it under 'Pricey's' car tyre, but Lou said he wouldn't
do it. However, one of the boys went ahead with the prank. Lou was off sick the

following Monday and when he came back to school the next day, he received the cane from a very annoyed Mr Price who mistakenly believed Lou had been the culprit!

David Fairchild and Lou Spear were among the many who had to take the long trek to and from school each day. They had a long walk from Whiddon to Prixford and to break up the monotony of their journey, sometimes they would find new routes home, crossing fields and crawling under hedges into orchards to scrump an apple or two on the way. Lou particularly remembers snacking on the occasional raw swede as they crossed the fields of No Man's land, and would carry a small penknife with him for that purpose! Often they would make a pit stop at the sweet shop in Guineaford if they had enough pennies, and head home across Chapel Field.

In September 1949 the new school kitchen was officially opened and was already serving over fifty pupils within its first week. At the same time Miss Kathleen Balment was appointed as cook, and for many years after, the pupils were extremely well fed – possibly the only children ever to actually enjoy school dinners!

Above: Back - Kath Balment & Mrs Jenkins; Front – Mr Price, c.1950.

Above: Marwood School c.1953, with Mr Price.

Above: Marwood School c.1954, with Mr Price.

Now in its 135th year, Marwood School continues to educate the children of the parish and those from further afield. One thing is for sure, Messrs Palmer, Pill, Price et al, would have taken great pride in the outcome of recent inspections under the headship of Mr Dobson and his team, which have been repeatedly outstanding. Perhaps the real testimony is in the multiple generations of families which have attended the school since its doors first opened in March 1876 and no doubt there will be many more to come.

Above: Marwood School c.1956, with Mr Rochester.

Chapter Six:
Diary of a Devonshire Farmer

Marwood farmer Fred Kelly (b.1865) has been mentioned frequently in earlier chapters, in connection with his life in the parish.

As the youngest and, by the turn of the twentieth century, only surviving son of yeoman Thomas Morrish Kelly, Fred would have begun to learn how to 'work the land' from an early age. He initially started undertaking bespoke jobs for people in the community, sometimes farm based but also transporting people or goods in his horse and cart. He also became a postman during the First World War when former 'postie' Arthur Carpenter went off to fight at the front. But Fred's first love was farming and the best part of his life was spent lambing, rearing, tilling, ploughing and harvesting.

After the death of his father in August 1908, Fred inherited some cottages in Kings Heanton which he let for approximately four pounds per year, supplementing his income and enabling him to purchase land of his own. He appears to have been a diligent landlord, ensuring regular maintenance and updating the fixtures and fittings.

Fred took a disciplined approach to managing his work, recording details such as sheep breeding dates and markings, poultry management, hay making, varieties of fruits and vegetables grown and sales of produce. All the entries were neatly recorded in a series of journals, bought from Sydney Harper & Sons Stationers, Barnstaple, and were also scattered with a wealth of information about family matters, property improvements, changes in land ownership and recipes for home remedies.

Such is the level of detail that it is impossible to examine it in its entirety within this volume. Instead, a selection of themed entries have been collated to give the reader an insight into the life of a Marwood farmer in the early twentieth century.

Left: Fred with a faithful friend, c.1930s.

Farming

Over three quarters of the entries in Fred's journal relate to farming and gardening and the pages are crammed with references to his activities throughout the seasons.

Fred also wrote down a number of detailed calculations which he considered to be standard practice for certain farming measurements. These formulae may have been the rule of thumb in Fred's day however to a layman, they would have been challenging to determine!

Rule for measuring a rick of hay:
Measure the length, breadth, (and height to eaves), add to this last one 1/3 or 1/2 according to pitch of roof. Multiply length by breadth by height in feet, divide this by 27 to find the cubic yards. Multiply these by the number of stones of 22lbs. New hay will average 6 stones old hay from 8 to 9 stones. Thus in a stack 22ft long, 12 ft wide, 9ft high to eaves and 3ft being 1/2 of roof. There will be 22 multiplied by 12, multiplied by 12, which equals 3168 cubic ft, these divided by 27 gives 117 and one third cubic yards each of 6 stones of 22lbs.

Rule for measuring threshed corn:
Rule level the grain; ascertain the space it occupies in cubic feet; multiply the number of cubic feet by 8, and point off one place to the left. Example – A box full of grain 20 ft long, 10 ft wide and 5 ft deep. How many bushels does the box contain? Answer: 800. Process – 20 multiplied by 10, multiplied by 5, equals 1000. 20 multiplied by 8, divided by 10 equals 800. Note: Exactness requires the addition to every 300 bushels of 1 extra bushel.

Rule for measuring live cattle:
Multiply girth by length and then multiply total by 23 which will give the weight in pounds then divide by 20. 23lbs is the superficial foot of less than 7 and more than 5 feet in girth. Example – a bullock measuring 6ft 6 in girth and 5ft 6 in length, equals 36 ¼ ft. These multiplied by 23 equals 833 ¾ lbs. These divided by 20 equals 41 score 13 ¾ lbs. When the animal measures less than 9 and more than 7ft in girth, 31 is the number of lbs to be estimated for each superficial foot.

Egg Laying:
A good plan is to set hens on her eggs about the 2nd week in April so that the chicks would be saleable in August for Ilfracombe.

'Udder ill' in sheep:
Make a paste in equal proportions of mustard and flour and well rub it on twice or three times at the same time it opens bowels, with sulphur and salts.

A typical selection of Fred's entries are shown below, with references to local farmers, labour costs and livestock prices, as well as the farming systems employed during this period:

October 25 1905	*Bought a ram from Mr Richard Dobbs £1 10s.*
February 18 1907	*Started ploughing lower half of Piley Park which has been out 4 years.*
March 19 1907	*Placed 6 hogs, 1 ewe and 1 ram = 8, to keep with Mr Philip Hopkins, Whitehall. Took same away April 14th, paid for same time 3 ½ s each per week.*
March 22 1907	*Sold William Lovering a load of dung 2 s 3.*
January 8 1908	*Agreed to exchange ½ ton of hay for 3 ton of mangolds with Mr G Hopkins.*
February 22 1908	*Number of moles caught:* *Primey Park IIII* *Piley Park II* *Wigley IIII*
March 3 1908	*Chain harrowing Little Meadow and Little Adderwell for Mr Arthur 4s 6.*
June 17 1908	*Self and horse, haymaking 10s at Marwood Hill House.*
October 7 1908	*Irwin ewe & cheviot, served Oct 7th, due to lamb March 3rd.*
December 18 1908	*Carried mow to Townridden to thresh the produce from 2 acres. 6 loads - William H Geen is helping.*
February 3 1909	*Began ploughing ley in Piley Park on Feb 1st, 2 ¼ acres higher side. Finished Feb 3rd. Rolled it same date, self and horse.*
March 24 1909	*Let Mr William Alford have 18 bundles of straw in exchange for mangolds.*
July 31 1909	*Haymaking, my field and Chapel Field. R Fishleigh, A Spear, G Cutcliffe, WH Geen, N Passmore, G Down and W Parkin - 7 men threshing @ 2s 6 each.*
October 22 1909	*Put the 6 rams that took the ram first with Henry Yeo's ram. No ram having been with them since Sep 30th.*
April 11 1910	*Tailed the 15 ewes myself.*
June 14 1911	*Finished shearing sheep. 21 ewes and 20 lambs, kept back 5 unsheared.*
September 9 1911	*Drenched lambs for husk with Turpentine and milk.*
February 27 1912	*Stocked Wigley clover with 6 ewes and 6 lambs.*

April 3 1912	Dosed all lambs with Coopers' tablets.
January 7 1913	George Worth cut down the oak pollard that used to grow in the round fence of Chapel Field for a hanging post to the big gate by the Old Chapel.
January 19 1914	Sold George Hopkins my stone roller, double draft, head chain, set of drafts and chains, cast iron and head collar for £1-10s but agreed to take 5 load and 3 ton of mangolds in lieu of the money.
March 24 1914	Sat hen on 13 J Herneman's and 1 hen on own eggs. 7 alive from Herneman's and 2 of my own.
August 26 1914	Harvesting for F Parkhouse from 12pm-8pm.
September 3 1914	Harvest for Alfred Kelly.
July 31 1916	Dipped 16 ewes and 16 lambs at Townridden. 1s 6, paid same time.
February 14 1917	Sat hen on 15 eggs for Noah Passmore – March 7th, 13 chicks hatched, 2 addle eggs.
September 12 1917	Harvesting for Mr Bater - 16 ½ hours.
February 5 1918	Rabbit skins worth 3s each.
April 8 1918	Mr Fairchild harrowed corn in Wigley to kill charlock.
October 23 1920	Mr William Geen put his 4 lambs with my ram.
December 11 1922	Pounded and filled my pipe cask with cider and it took about 15 bags of apples.
August 29 1923	J Joslin paid me for work done - £3 3s.
June 4 1925	Tommy Hopkins started shearing.
December 10 1925	Killed 2nd pig – sold to Mr S Ayres @ 15s per score.
January 23 1926	Pruned apple trees and now is the time to do currants & gooseberries.
February 20 1926	Bought pig 5 months old from Alfred @ £2 5s.
January 3 1927	Mr Fairchild paid for my work to date (£1 4s 6d).
May 12 1927	Sat 2 hens - 1 brood from Townridden, 1 brood from Mrs Wensley.
November 1 1927	Threshing for Mr Avery (paid 5s 6).
February 21 1928	Tilled shallots and broad beans.
February 24 1928	Memo of yeaning: Black foot 1 male. Close wool Hewish 1 male, 1 female.
May 8 1929	Sold Mr Lock one fat ewe £2-19s.
January 31 1931	Sold Mr C Isaac 26 hogs @ 42s each; £54 12s.
December 5 1931	Sold E Manning ½ ton hay @ £2-10s.

August 5 1932	Paid R Hopkins for cutting Nobles Park grass and 2 ½ acres in Chapel Field, also for help making and carting £2 2s.
December 24 1932	Sold 23 hogs @ 25s 6d each to Mr F Holland, £29-6s 6d.
January 18 1933	Sold 3 heifers @ £39 10s to Mr F Holland.
January 28 1933	Took in to graze 34 hogs @ 3d per head per week.
October 11 1933	Fetched 9 bags apples from Landkey, gave 25s for same. 12th October pounded same - about 72 gallons of cider.
June 22 1941	Bought a 9 weeks pig from Mr Watts @ £1 15s.

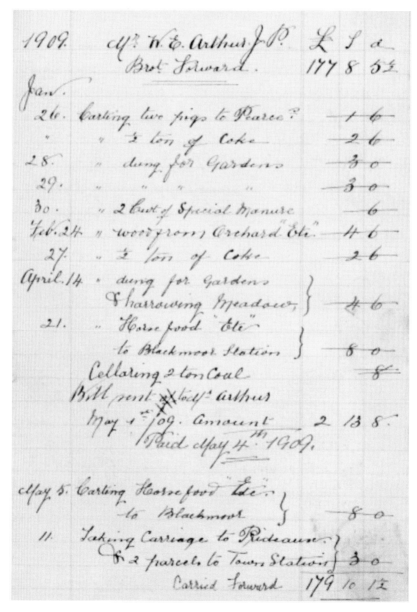

Above: An extract from Fred's journal - *Marwood Hill House* Account.

Family Matters

Fred married Eliza relatively late in life in Spring 1906, at the age of forty. They wasted no time in starting a family and Elizabeth, known as Lizzie, was born in August that year. In the book *From Cradle to Grave 1900-1919*, it was recorded that she was born in a cottage hospital in Barnstaple, where younger sister Elsie was also born the following year. In those days the majority of births usually took place in the home, which suggests that Eliza may have suffered some complications for which she required hospital care. Amongst the many farming related entries in Fred's journals, there is the occasional brief personal note, usually commemorating a milestone in one of his daughters' lives, such as her first step or starting school. In 1910 the Kelly family welcomed another new arrival when youngest child Amy was born, prompting more fond observations. Interestingly, Fred makes few references to Eliza in his journals with the exception of one or two entries such as 'Bought Mrs some boots'. He makes no mention of their wedding in 1906 or her untimely death in 1926 at the age of fifty-two, although it would be reasonable to assume that he considered such sentiments to be too private to disclose in this manner. Examples of the references to family members are shown below:

April 5 1907	*Lizzie walked away by herself the first time.*
August 28 1908	*Funeral expense at the death of Father - Spirits 3s 3; Beer 4s 6; Bread 7s 12; Cheese 1s 3; Tea & Sugar 1s 6; Cake 1s 10; Milk 2s; Butter 1s 5; Hat & Collar 4s 6; Gloves 4s 6; Coat & Shirt £2-5s; Hat & blouse making £1; Mrs Skinner 1s 5; Mr Johnson 6s 8; Mason 8s 3; Sexton 3s; Coffin £2-5s = Total £9 5s 9d.*
September 6 1908	*"The night is far spent, the day is at hand" was the text used on the Sunday morning after Father's burial, by the Rev JWJ Sowerbutts, curate at St Mary Magdalene, Barnstaple.*
September 8 1908	*Lizzie had new boots, being her first pair.*
July 4 1910	*Amy had sop for the first time.*
October 15 1910	*Lizzie dressed Elsie first time.*
June 7 1911	*Lizzie started school on Wednesday June 7th 1911 being then 4 years and 10 months old.*
January 27 1912	*Amy finished with the bottle.*
June 5 1912	*Elsie went to day school first time.*
June 15 1915	*Amy goes to day school and Sunday school in the afternoons.*
December 7 1915	*Lizzie and Elsie goes to school and church Sunday mornings for the first time December 7th 1915.*
October 12 1924	*Lizzie commenced to learn music from Miss W Lean at 10s 6 per quarter, twice weekly.*
October 7 1942	*Alfred Kelly died Oct 7th age 79 years, buried October 10th.*

Left: Fred's daughters,
Elsie (seated) and
Lizzie Kelly c.1908.

Right: Lizzie, Elsie and
Amy, pictured at school
c.1915.

Property

Fred took a keen interest in the sale of property in Marwood, exemplified in his journal by the many references to local auctions, with brief descriptions of the property, vendor, purchaser and the price paid. As the owner of several cottages in Kings Heanton, Fred was often busy agreeing letting arrangements and in some cases he would lease property to local farmers, who would then sublet the dwelling to one of their labourers. Fred appears to have been an attentive landlord, regularly arranging maintenance work, which was normally undertaken by carpenter George Worth or mason, Arthur Skinner. He sold the cottages in 1920.

One of his biggest projects was the purchase of a run down cottage and land in Guineaford in 1910. The journal notes suggest that it was in need of significant renovation work including replacing the thatched roof with tiles and the erection of several additional rooms to include a pantry and wash-house. All of this work was carefully contracted out to a number of local labourers with specific instructions. This came at considerable cost, demonstrating that Fred was a man of means having been the sole heir to his father's estate in 1908, including several cottages and over four hundred pounds. The restoration work was completed over the following two years and in November 1912, Fred and his family moved to what is now known as *Kellys' Cottage*, Guineaford. He mentions this event in his journal, perhaps feeling a little emotional after having lived in Kings Heanton for over forty years.

July 31 1908	*Arthur Skinner - two days whitewashing back parts of cottages and repairing garden walls.*
May 11 1909	*Saw Mr Lock in reference to the land @ Marwood Hill, when he said he would make a note of my application.*
June 30 1909	*George Worth repairing doors of the cottage and painting the same right through.*
February 25 1910	*I bought @ auction at Kings Arms Barnstaple, the Chapel Field with cottage adjoining at the price of £205. To take possession Ladyday 1910.*
February 15 1911	*Arthur Skinner colouring and whitewashing the Lower House.*
March 4 1910	*Cutcliffe's property at Guineaford (part) occupied by Summerfield, and field by owners, sold at the Kings Arms @ the price of £160, one of the joint owners being the purchaser "viz" Mr C Cutcliffe of Pilton.*
April 10 1910	*Arthur Skinner building wall in long shed (used 4 bags of lime).*
June 20 1911	*Arthur Skinner whitewashing and colouring kitchen of own house and William Down house.*

November 1 1912	Carting of furniture from Kings Heanton to Guineaford. I left Kings Heanton to live at my house at Guineaford after living at the first named village for a period of about 42 or 43 years.
March 31 1913	Agreed to let the Lower House at Kings Heanton to Miss Gatensbury @ £4 5s per year. Agreed to let Middle house and garden at Kings Heanton to R Fishleigh @ £6 per year.
July 25 1913	Stepps Farm at Middle Marwood 51 acres, sold for £1850 to G Chapple.
September 29 1915	Arthur Skinner building pillars for front gate.
November 23 1916	The North Devon Inn sold at £140 to Mr R Hopkins, buyer.
March 1 1918	Varley Farm sold by Mr Smale at auction to Alfred Kelly (tenant farmer) £2,675; 92 acres.
July 25 1919	Four fields being part of Marwood Glebe were sold by auction at the following prices: Wigley - 3 acres arable £150 to J Cutcliffe. Adderwell - 4 acres arable £180 to W Manning. Primey Park - 1 acre pasture £75 to N Passmore. No mans' land - 9 acres pasture £560 to W H Fairchild.
October 31 1919	A Skinner put two new fire bricks to the oven side of our Bodley.
July 30 1920	Sold my field at Mid-Marwood by auction for £170 to Mr T Braunton. Sold the Higher house, garden and stable to Mr Sinclair for £100.
October 23 1920	Sold Lower house, garden and premises to Mr Smith for £105.
October 23 1920	Sold Kings Heanton house to Mrs Webber for £175.
October 10 1924	A cottage, garden etc and field occupied by Miss Summerfield and owned by Mr W Cutcliffe was sold for £190 to Mr R Main.
March 5 1937	Agreed to let my 3 fields of grass to Mr W B Dallyn on same conditions as 2 previous years.
March 20 1943	Received from Mr W Dallyn rent for Chapel Field and Little Field due 1st March £6-10s. Also rent of meadow £3-15s due 25th March.
August 24 1943	Sold Mr W H Gubb, Guineaford, my two fields "viz" Chapel Field and Guineaford Close for £340. Possession to be taken March 2nd 1944. The empty Linhay included with the fields.

Shopping

Fred managed his finances carefully, noting down all the items he purchased and their respective costs.   For example, he lists basic grocery items such as butter and meat which he would purchase from local farms, household necessities including kettles and copper pans as well as numerous accounts of boots bought for all members of the family. Some of the store names may be familiar, such as Timothy White's and the Army & Navy store, but most were sole traders or market stall holders that have long disappeared from the streets of Barnstaple, even Woolworths.

February 18 1907   *New pair of boots from John Cutcliffe 15s.*

December 20 1909   *Bought turkey from Mrs Emily Alford 7¼ lb @ 1 1s per lb.*

March 1 1912   *Bought Lizzie pair of button boots (size 10) @ Arthurs' for 3s 11.*

January 2 1913   *Bought pair of weekday leggings @ Hoads in Market, @ 5s 6.*

August 11 1914   *Bought 2 undershirts @ 3s 11; pair of trousers 6s 11, umbrella 3s 6 at Mr Richards, Joy Street.*

May 11 1915   *Used enamelled kettle for first time - cost 1s 6.*

January 7 1916   *Bought Elsie pair of school boots at Dartmoor Co (size 13) @ 5s 11 (those being too small for Elsie, Lizzie took them).*

April 1 1916   *Bought a boot shining brush @ Barrows stall in the market for 1s 6.*

May 26 1917   *Bought 2 cotton shirts. Collar no 5, 17 inches @ 2s 11.*

January 26 1918   *Bought Mrs some boots (size 6).*

October 20 1922   *Bought oil well (glass) at Hunts for hand lamp at 3s also Globe for table lamp @ 8s.*

December 31 1925   *At Woolworth's, bought firepan and 5 pudding basins. Bought hot water bottle (rubber) at Timothy White's.*

July 5 1926   *Bought Iron bed £2-5s; wire mattress £2-5s; wool mattress £2-5s.*

October 31 1927   *Had 4 lbs butter in pot from Mrs Joslin @ 1s 10d per lb.*

December 7 1928   *Bought mac at Army & Navy store £1-17s 6.*

July 11 1931   *Went to Wrafton after 6 nitches of reed for self and 6 for R Hopkins.*

December 1 1931   *Bought 2 hams from W Lock.*

March 2 1934   *Bought 2 flannelette shirts at Lyles @5s 9 each, also 2 soft collars @ 1s 6.*

November 20 1935   *Bought cap at Lyles' 2s 6d.*

Weather

As a farmer it was natural for Fred to keep a close watch on all matters relating to the weather because his livelihood was dependent upon careful forecasting. In his journal, Fred describes occasions of extreme weather conditions which caused terrible damage to crops, including especially severe hail and late frosts.

May 21 1905	*On the night of 21st May 1905 we had a very severe frost, damaging the potatoes badly, Noah Passmore's in particular.*
August 15 1905	*Had a very severe thunderstorm with very vivid lightning and torrential rain, also hails as large as wrens' eggs.*
October 16 1905	*Sharp frost as thick as a 2s piece.*
Feb 29 1907	*Very stormy day quite a blizzard, snow for about an hour, bitterly cold.*
April 24 1908	*Very stormy snow and hail also sharp frost doing considerable damage to potatoes etc.*
Sept 11 1908	*Very stormy with showers of hail and a lot of corn still uncarried.*
Dec 27 1908	*We had a fall of snow covering the land generally to the depth of 2 or 3 inches very cold at the same time, the weather previous to this had been exceptionally mild ever since the latter end of August and the first week in September when we had a very rough and wet time.*
March 17 1909	*The month of February was practically dry with some sharp frost. 1st March the same, followed by snow on the 2nd up to the 5th and very sharp with frost and snow up to 17th.*
May 15 1909	*Had sharp frost on Saturday night May 15th 1909, which cut the potatoes very badly.*
June 22 1909	*Had some very heavy showers of rain, also hail, hard on peas.*
May 17 1935	*In the afternoon we had a very heavy fall of snow… 6 and 8 inches deep in places … sharp frost doing untold damage to young growing crops.*
June 22 1910	*Very heavy hail storm, hail as large as marbles.*
July 4 1915	*About 1.15pm we had an awful storm of hailstones with lightning and thunder. Some of the stones were 5 ½ inches in circumference and six of them weighed 8 ounces. All the crops being in the leafy state suffered disaster. Wheat in particular being practically worthless while other corn suffered accordingly. Windows were in some instances a complete wreck with panes being smashed while the slates on the roofs suffered terribly, some of them being holed as with a punch. The garden things were practically spoilt being literally cut to pieces. It lasted about ten minutes and its width was from Longpiece to Metcombe (extreme), coming in a south-westerly direction.*

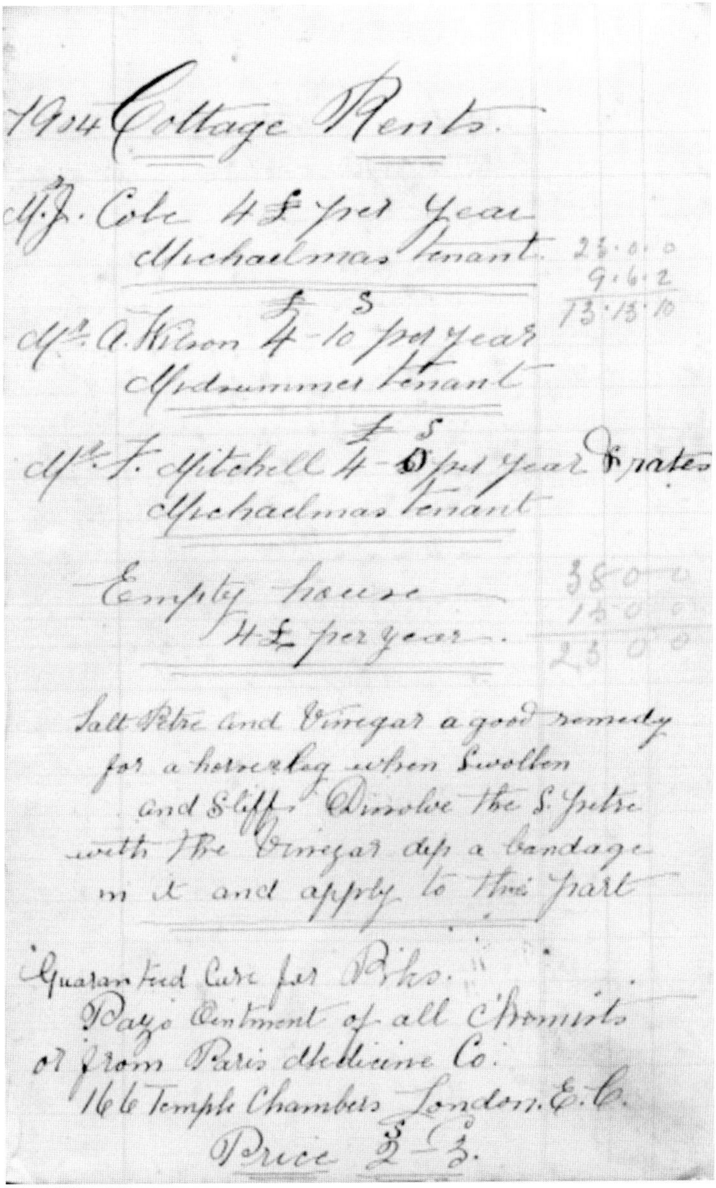

1904 Cottage Rents.

Mr J. Cole 4£ per Year
    Michaelmas tenant   23.0.0
                     9.6.2

Mrs A. Wilson 4-10 per year   13.13.10
    Midsummer tenant

Mr F. Mitchell 4-5 per Year & rates
    Michaelmas tenant

    Empty house   38.0.0
         4£ per year.   15.0.0
                      23.0.0

Salt Petre and Vinegar a good remedy
for a horses leg when swollen
    and stiff. Dissolve the S. Petre
with the Vinegar dip a bandage
in it and apply to the part

Guaranteed Cure for Piles.
    Day's Ointment of all Chemists
or from Paris Medicine Co.
  16 Temple Chambers London. E.C.
         Price 2-3.

Above: Extract from Fred's journal: Cottage rents and some remedies.

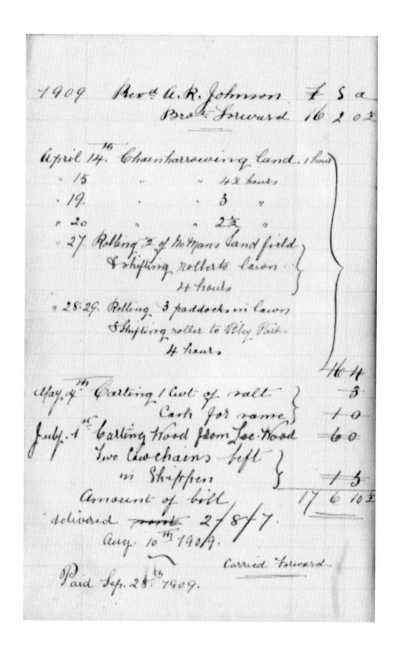

Above: Extract from Fred's journal: Reverend Alfred Johnson's account.

Health

In November 1911 Fred made a long list of patent medicines which he had purchased for the family, at some considerable expense, to remedy various ailments. These included Dinneford's magnesia, Stedman's teething powder, Mother Seigel's curative syrup 'for biliousness, wind and constipation', together with tamarind syrup 'for lung troubles, bronchitis, coughs and colds', lozenges, cough mixture, charcoal biscuits and dill water.

> 1911 Expenses in patent medicine ... Bovril for Elsie 1s 9; Charcoal biscuits 9d; Stedman's powders 4d; Hypophosphite salts 2s 10; Cascara pills 8d; Lozenges and powders 7d; Dill water 2d; Dinneford's Magnesia 11d.

As a farmer it would have been essential for Fred to remain physically fit, to enable him to continue working for as long as possible. Working outside in often wet and cold conditions would have put him at risk of suffering from ailments such as rheumatism and bronchitis, so he would have needed to treat any symptoms of ill health swiftly to reduce the need to take time away from his work. When Fred's wife Eliza died aged fifty-two years in 1926, their three daughters aged twenty, nineteen and sixteen, were still at home and reliant upon him, so it was essential that Fred was fit and well.

In his journal, Fred notes down what appear to be his personal recommendations for treating a range of conditions, and some of these are listed here.

> 1904 Chlorodyne - a good remedy for coughs and colds.

Chlorodyne was originally invented as a treatment for cholera, but was later sold by the pharmacist for many conditions including diarrhoea, insomnia and migraines. The ingredients of Chlorodyne were a mixture of laudanum, an alcoholic solution of opium, tincture of cannabis and chloroform. Unsurprisingly, it gave marvellous pain relief! Although it was effective, the combination of ingredients made it highly addictive and caused deaths from overdoses. Later in the twentieth century the cannabis and opiates were removed making it a far safer medicine for the family.

Perhaps through fear of the consequences of treating coughs and colds with chlorodyne, Fred noted down an alternative homemade cure which the family may have used. Old remedies such as these were often used to avoid the expense of regular visits from the doctor.

> 1911 Recipe for a cough or cold: 1 peppermint, 1 paregolic, 1 essence liquorice; 1 Ipecacuanha wine [wine of iron] and 1/2 lb treacle.

Fred also noted down his own remedy for measles, which no doubt would raise a few eyebrows today!

> 1910   *Measles in children: Give them about 1/2 a teacupful of warm beer and put them direct to bed.*

In 1912 at the age of forty-seven, Fred appeared to be struggling with aches and pains from rheumatism. He wrote out the following instructions on taking brimstone, otherwise known as sulphur and commonly taken with treacle. This was a popular remedy during Victorian times and was thought to be very beneficial to health. It was often given to children.

> 1912   *One teaspoonful of brimstone taken 3 times weekly is a very good medicine for rheumatism, or throat and chest. To be taken first thing in the morning in a little milk or water.*

Fred also believed in a mixture of essential oils – juniper in particular is known for its value in relieving pains from rheumatism and arthritis.

> 1913   *Oil of amber and oil of juniper are good for a lame back.*

In the long list of patent medicines purchased by Fred in November 1911, there are several treatments for indigestion. Possibly these medicines provided insufficient relief because in 1913 he noted down a new homemade remedy. Notice again the presence of opium based ingredients amongst others.

> 1913   *Recipe for Indigestion: 1 worth of Laudanum [opium based painkiller], 1 worth of paregoric [opium based, used to stop diarrhoea], 1 worth of aniseed, 1 worth of peppermint and 1 worth of syrup or treacle. Dissolve the syrup or treacle with one quart of boiling water and when cold, add the other ingredients and take a wineglassful after dinner.*

Evidently one member of the family suffered from asthma and Fred noted that he had to obtain the medicine from a chemist in Okehampton named Seth Harry. This was one illness that Fred was not going to leave to chance with a home remedy, paying one shilling and four pence for the medicine that Mr Harry would send in the post.

Fred suffered from one condition which was not so easy to fix with home remedies or patent medicines. In 1926, aged sixty-one, Fred was suffering from serious problems with his teeth, prompting a number of visits to the dentist. During two consecutive appointments on March 5 and 12, he had a total of fourteen teeth removed! Worse still, his journal reveals that his new false teeth were not fitted until December of that year by Mr Shapland of Barnstaple, at the cost of twelve guineas.

Left: Fred smiling for the camera on horseback.

Right: Amy Kelly, pictured at Guineaford Bridge c.1922, holding a young Harold Hopkins in her arms!

Above: Lizzie Kelly outside the family cottage, c.1930.

Local Interest

This sample of entries gives us a feel for Fred's awareness of his environment as he records observations that today, we might blink and miss. It is likely that some notes such as the arrival of the swallows or picking primroses in January were significant to Fred as they signified the changing seasons and expected temperatures. For example, the early arrival of the swallows tends to indicate a warm Spring.

Some of Fred's other entries reveal his interest and involvement in parish matters. On several occasions he cared enough about the results of the parish council election to list the number of votes received by each candidate. He also made note of momentous occasions such as the departure of the Reverend Mattinson, who had been incumbent in the parish for nineteen years. The entries below include just a few of those observations.

October 1 1904	*Picked ripe strawberries in Mare Lane.*
January 3 1905	*Picked primroses in Beara Charter Lane.*
March 23 1905	*A motor car owned and driven by Dr Ware passed through Kingsheanton today. The first that was ever in the village.*
April 29 1908	*First time I heard a cuckoo for the year.*
April 7 1909	*Saw some swallows today, first time for season.*
April 16 1910	*First time I saw a swallow for the season.*
May 7 1910	*Heard the cuckoo first time.*
August 10 1914	*Started post office round.*
June 29 1921	*Choir treat to Ilfracombe.*
April 2 1928	*Results of Parish Council Election: PJ Brailey 220 votes; J Ellis 196 votes; R Harris 193; J Pugsley 192; F Parkhouse 187; Reverend Mattinson 184; GH Balment 182; A Gammon 169; W Pengelly 169 – all elected.*
April 16 1929	*Saw a swallow.*
April 29 1929	*Heard a cuckoo.*
May 12 1937	*Coronation Day and in the night I went up to the Varley Park, stood on the hedge between it and Mr Dobbs' Home Tongues and counted 15 bonfires lighted.*
September 27 1937	*Reverend Mattinson preached his two farewell sermons on leaving the Rectory. The morning text: Ruth 2, ch 4 and the evening text: Corinthians 6, ch 1.*

Fred's journal entries began to dwindle by the 1940s as he approached his eightieth birthday. The pages were no longer crammed full with entries, in fact they became increasingly sporadic as his workload wound down to occasional apple picking or binding wood. He gradually let and then sold his land and his last entry was made in July 1948, concerning a visit from the Pension Officer.

Fred Kelly died in January 1949, at the age of eighty-three years. Thanks to his disciplined attention to detail in recording day to day farming and family life in Marwood one hundred years ago, his legacy is an invaluable archive that will endure for many years to come.

Left: Fred pictured by his front gate in 1937, aged seventy-two. One of his unique journal entries was:

"Fortune is fickle and ever a lover but friendship is friendship the whole world over"

Chapter Seven
Soldiers' Sacrifices

For hundreds of years the men of Marwood have courageously stepped forward when the nation was called to arms. Farm labourers, carpenters, masons and boot makers alike joined up with their brothers and friends, leaving behind their rural existence. They were trained for warfare and posted like parcels to distant lands to fight for monarch and country.

Some survived to tell the tale. Many did not. This chapter is written in tribute to the brave men of Marwood who fought in conflicts between 1899 and 1945. Many years have now passed since peace was declared so lest their courage be forgotten, the stories of many of the Marwood men who fought for their country are told here.

Local military historian, Brian Barrow, has researched the journeys of many soldiers from North Devon parishes who fought during the Great War 1914 -1918. I am deeply grateful for his assistance through sharing his findings and confirming the various regiments and locations of the Marwood men.

Above: Marwood War Memorial, St Michael & All Angels Parish Church.

Boer War 1899-1902

Throughout Queen Victoria's reign, there were ongoing military campaigns to continue the expansion and protection of the British Empire, sending Her Majesty's armies far and wide to Afghanistan, Egypt, South Africa, India and Russia.

The last conflict to occur during Victoria's reign was the second Boer war, which arose when Dutch settlers attempted to oust British rule. In November 1899 it was reported:

> The President of the Transvaal Republic in South Africa sent a defiant ultimatum to the British Government on Tuesday October 10, which amounted to a declaration of war. Hostilities have been carried on ever since in the British colony of Natal, with varying success. Serious losses have been sustained by our troops, amounting so far to about 1500 killed or wounded. The Rector will give a lecture on the war in the National School, on Thursday November 16 at 7.30pm and a collection will be made afterwards. No greater responsibility rests on Englishmen and Englishwomen than the care of the wives and families of their soldiers and sailors, who have made England the greatest nation in the world.

> Source: *Marwood Church Monthly*, November 1899.

National and local newspapers had reported the build up of the unrest in South Africa over the preceding years, so the outbreak of war came as little surprise to the nation. Those already serving in the army were the first to make the long voyage overseas. Amongst the first of the Marwood men to be posted was Thomas Read de Guerin of Muddiford, who was engaged in fighting at the front almost immediately.

In February 1900 *Marwood Church Monthly* told of special services of intercession that were held at Marwood Parish Church and Muddiford Mission Church, on behalf of the soldiers and sailors serving in South Africa. A total of twenty-three pounds was raised within the parish and names of those who made donations were printed in the newsletter.

In the next edition an account was given of some of the first battles in South Africa. On February 16 1899, news was received of the relief of Kimberley by Lords Roberts and Kitchener and General French, following the surrender of Boer General Cronje, together with four thousand prisoners. On February 28, news arrived of the relief of Ladysmith after a four-month siege, which led to great rejoicing in Marwood:

> The flag upon the Church tower announced both the victories, and the bells rang out joyfully in the evenings. Those who have prayed for relief and victory, and they are many, must not forget to give thanks. The thanksgiving after a victory in the *Forms of prayer to be used at Sea* which may be found at the end of the Book of Common Prayer, will be used in our churches, and is suggested for private use at home.

> Source: *Marwood Church Monthly*, March 1900.

It was reported that Thomas Read de Guerin was involved in the fighting at Ladysmith and that another Marwood man, Lawrence Heyworth had left for South Africa. Lawrence, a graduate of Trinity College, Cambridge, was the only son of Colonel and Mrs Heyworth of Whitefield Barton. He sailed from Dublin on the *S.S. Cheshire* with his regiment, the 3rd South Wales Borderers.

Sergeant Thomas Read de Guerin

Thomas was born in Bournemouth in 1878, the son of Guernsey born Thomas and Mary de Guerin, who lived in *Lee House* in 1889 and *The Dell*, Muddiford in 1891. His family were regular worshippers at Marwood Parish Church where his father was a churchwarden, his mother was often involved in decorating the church with flowers and his sister played the organ. He signed up to join the army at the age of eighteen in February 1895 and was initially drafted into the 2nd Dragoons 'of the Line'. His papers noted that he was five foot nine with a fresh complexion, blue eyes and red hair. By August 1897, Thomas was appointed Lance Corporal and transferred to the Royal Scots Greys. Shortly before departing for South Africa in August 1899 he was promoted to Corporal, and later promoted to Sergeant in April 1901.

While Thomas was in active service he wrote regularly to his mother in Muddiford and in the interest of the parish, she arranged for Reverend Pryke to publish the letters in *Marwood Church Monthly*. Two of the letters are transcribed below, giving a personal and unique account of early twentieth century warfare:

> *Koodowran Camp - March 8 1900*
> *We, that is, the whole British Army Corps here, are waiting for our convoy and transport to arrive, so as to be able to march to Bloemfontein. We have been having a very rough time since we left Kimberley – short rations, no tents and heavy rains. For two nights the rain has come down in torrents and forced us to walk about till daylight ...... I never knew the meaning of hunger before, but, when you are living on half rations, viz: two and a half biscuits and a bit of fresh meat for your mid-day meal, when you could eat a horse, you know what hunger is. The air of the veldt is a great producer of appetite ...... Cecil Rhodes is giving everyone who relieved Kimberley some kind of memento – either a watch and chain with an inscription or a silver medal with a gold centre.*
>
> *We had a skirmish with the Boers the other day. My regiment and the carabineers, with a battery of artillery, went to reconnoitre the Boer position on a high kopje about four miles from here, and we were received by a heavy shellfire. The shells shrieked over our heads and fell around us. They also treated us to a heavy rifle and hotchkiss[1] fire. Three of our gunners were wounded. We retired after about one hour's artillery duel having gained our object and unmasked their position ...... The present idea is that my column (General French's) is going to push on*

---
[1] An early hand-operated machine gun, mounted on horse drawn carriages.

to Bloemfontein, while Lord Roberts tackles the Boer position with his infantry and artillery, we are not going near the place, but moving rapidly as we did with Kimberley ...... All our kits were left at the Modder Camp, before we started on this flying column.

Bloemfontein Camp - March 15 1900
We are occupying Bloemfontein camp, which our column reached after some fatiguing days' marching and fighting ...... We left camp on the afternoon of March 8th, and marched to another camp a few miles farther on, where we bivouacked[1] till midnight. After saddling our horses in the dark, we moved off to begin our flanking movement on the Boers' position, which was about five miles from the Koodowran camp.

We marched in silence till daybreak, when the Boers perceived us, and opened a heavy artillery fire on our left flank. This soon resulted in a general engagement, but we had fairly flanked them, and, our artillery playing on them in rear, and Lord Roberts' heavy guns shelling them in front, they began to come out of the kopjes and streamed across the plain. They treated us to some shelling as they retreated towards Bloemfontein. After a hard day's fighting, we encamped at a place on the Modder, only about nine miles from where we started, but we had gone round between twenty and thirty miles to do the flanking movement. We kept on the march day after day, encountering heavier opposition and severer fighting on some days than on others and I had one or two very narrow escapes. One day I was acting signaller to Colonel Porter, our Brigadier and had just been told to bring my helio to signal from a kopje. When I reached the top the bullets were whistling all around me, so I lay down near some others, who were up there, having to abandon the idea of signalling.

You hardly seem to realise the danger you are in, until you see your comrades fall around you. One bullet, which grazed my helmet sounded like hitting a piece of wood. Another hit the ground close in front of me, sending the sand flying up in my eyes. A third hit and glanced off an anthill, which I had got behind ...... We arrived about twenty-four miles from Bloemfontein on the 12th ...... When we reached the vicinity of Bloemfontein, the Boers had never dreamed that we (the Calvary Division) were working around and flanking them. They first saw us about five o'clock in the afternoon and opened a terrific rifle fire on our advance squadrons. Fortunately for us, the range was rather too far, but four of our horses were shot and one bullet hit the ground just in front of my horse's nose. C Squadron charged some Boers, who were raking us with a severe fire, and they fled on close quarters being reached. There were no casualties although the range was short – only a few hundred yards.

---

[1] A temporary camp, often in an open or unsheltered area.

We bivouacked that night, lying beside our horses, with the reins tied to our arms and legs, ready to turn out at a moment's notice. No alarm occurred, and in the morning we advanced. Lord Roberts gave the people of Bloemfontein until 4pm (24 hours) to surrender, and after shelling a number of Boers who were in the neighbourhood, we marched in and took possession. My regiment is now encamped a few hundred yards outside the town, and we hear that we are stopping here for three weeks at least to rest.

We are getting plenty of food now …… My cheeks are hollow and sunk in, and cheek bones sticking out, but I am thankful to say my health is good. It is now nearly two months since we slept in a tent. Lord Roberts gave an address, which was read out in orders this morning, praising us all for our endurance, soldierly spirit and courage, and saying our march from Modder river to Bloemfontein was a feat of which any army might be proud.

Source: *Marwood Church Monthly*, May 1900.

On March 14 1900, Lord Roberts declared that Bloemfontein had been taken, stating 'By the help of God, and by the bravery of Her Majesty's soldiers, the troops under my command have taken possession of Bloemfontein'. Those words, the Reverend Pryke foretold, would 'move the whole nation, and influence the whole civilised world'.

Back at Marwood, Mr and Mrs de Guerin themselves faced a perilous situation. They had been riding their horse and cart near Blatchford in June 1900, when the horse suddenly took fright and bolted. After several frantic minutes the horse eventually fell over, throwing them both out of the cart. Fortunately neither received serious injuries, but they suffered from severe shock.

Every Tuesday a weekly working party was held at the rectory, led by Mrs Pryke. Almost twenty ladies worked diligently to support the men overseas, knitting socks and other items. By April 1900, twenty-five knitted pairs of woollen socks and two flannel shirts had been made and sent to the soldiers at the front. These items were gratefully received and shortly afterwards, Lieutenant Colonel Batson, commander of the 2nd Devonshire Regiment wrote to Reverend Pryke, expressing his sincere gratitude for the items and asking him to thank the ladies of the parish. He wrote 'the men much appreciate their kind thought. The parcel arrived rather dilapidated but the contents were in capital order, not a bit damaged and I very much thank you for forwarding it. The weather here is intensely cold at night ….. The men are well and standing the cold weather all right, but I am glad we have our tents again. We were without them from the 7th May until the 18th June' – a situation that must have deeply dismayed the mothers of Marwood.

A church service was held at the parish church as a thanksgiving for the relief of Ladysmith and other victories by the British armies in South Africa, including Lord

Roberts' recent entry into Bloemfontein, the capital of the Orange Free State. A letter was received by a member of the Church Army who had regularly spent time in Marwood preaching in each of the hamlets. Corporal Daniels was on active service and he spoke of his grief at the loss of men in his regiment, praying that they had all been as ready to die, as they had been to fight. He told the story of a fellow Christian soldier who had received severe head wounds. When offered a drink of water he replied, 'No, give it to my chums. I have tasted of the water of life' upon which he quietly passed away.

In April 1900, *Marwood Church Monthly* reported that besides Thomas de Guerin and Lawrence Heyworth, several other Marwood men had joined them on active service in South Africa:

Gunner James Gubb, Royal Artillery
Private W Gubb, Royal Marines
Private Joseph Richards, 3rd Grenadier Guards
Private E White, 2nd Devonshire Regiment
Sergeant Charles Worth, 2nd Devonshire Regiment
Lance-Corporal Thomas Worth, 2nd Devonshire Regiment
Corporal Walter Worth, Military Foot Police

Charles, Thomas and Walter were brothers, sons of Mr John Worth, former gamekeeper of Kings Heanton and later a resident of Longpiece.

Sergeant Charles Worth

Born in Eggesford in 1875, Charles Worth started his working life as a gardener and later signed up to the Devonshire Regiment in February 1892 at the age of seventeen. His records show that he was five foot seven with a fresh complexion, blue eyes and dark brown hair. During his initial service in Britain he was quickly appointed to the rank of Lance Corporal by August 1892 and Sergeant by 1899. Charles was transferred to the army reserves early in 1899 but recalled to service by October under special army order, as the outbreak of war was imminent. He was posted to the 2nd Devonshire Regiment on October 9 1899 and departed for South Africa on October 20. Within just four months of active service he was wounded at Ladysmith in February 1900.

Charles wrote to his mother in Marwood, who also gave permission for it to be printed in *Marwood Church Monthly*:

> *Military Hospital, Pietermaritzburg - March 22 1900.*
> *I am pleased to say that my wound is mending slowly, although the bullet is still in my right thigh and they have not yet decided upon an operation … On our way out we encountered a gale mid-Atlantic and the ship's engines broke down. On entering Durban harbour we ran aground. I said, "The captain of this boat must be in league with 'old Kruger'!" We landed on 19th November and since then I have taken part in all the fighting done by General Buller's army in Natal – at*

Mooi River, Colenso, Spion Kop, Vaal Kranz, Monte Cristo and at Pietersdown – to the 24th February when I caught this Mauser bullet. I was bagged by a stray shot at a distance of about a mile a half, and that too, only four days before the actual relief of Ladysmith. It was very annoying. I was conveyed here on the following day in an ambulance train and am very comfortable. Tommy, I have just heard from, he is enjoying good health. Walter, I saw a couple of days ago; he is looking well and getting like an elephant! I trust now that Ladysmith and Kimberley are relieved, Cronje and his army prisoners, and Bloemfontein taken, that the war will soon be over, and then, if all be well, when we get home again, we shall have a few tales to tell, which would take up too much room to write.

Source: *Marwood Church Monthly*, May 1900.

Charles returned home in July 1900 and was later discharged as medically unfit in June 1902. After over ten years service, during which he received the Queen's South Africa War Medal with clasps for the relief of Tugela Heights and Ladysmith, Charles' military career ended as a Chelsea pensioner[1].

Sergeant Walter Worth

Charles younger brother Walter began working as a labourer before he joined up in May 1894 at the age of eighteen, two years after Charles. He had previously served in the 4th Devonshire Militia, who discharged him with permission to enlist in the regular forces. His army records show that he joined the 2nd Devonshire Regiment and was six feet tall with fresh complexion, blue eyes and brown hair. Walter was appointed Lance Corporal in April 1895 and remained home based until November 24 1899 when he embarked for South Africa. He fought there until March 26 1901 and was home based for the rest of the war, later receiving the Queen's South Africa War Medal with clasps for Cape Colony, Transvaal, Tugela Heights, Ladysmith and Laing's Nek.

Remaining in the forces until November 1912, by which time he had been promoted to Sergeant, Walter requested to be discharged with good conduct following eighteen years service. Like Charles, he became a Chelsea pensioner, and upon his discharge at the age of thirty-seven, he gave the intended address of no. 7 Raleigh, Barnstaple.

Corporal Thomas Worth *d. October 2 1900.*

The youngest of the three brothers, Thomas was a member of the 2nd Devonshire Regiment. Whilst on active service in South Africa in October 1900 he died of pneumonia at the British Garrison in Standerton. Unfortunately, most of the service records of men who perished in the Boer war were destroyed in the 1920s, leaving limited information, although Thomas is honourably mentioned on a war memorial at Exeter Cathedral.

---

[1] The Chelsea pension was awarded to all former soldiers who had been injured in service, or who had served for more than 20 years.

Private William H Trump

William was born in Marwood in 1877, the son of George and Sarah of Muddiford. Like his father he began life as a farm labourer and belonged to the 4th Devonshire Militia. He signed up to the regular forces in February 1897 at the age of nineteen, and his army records show that upon enlistment to the Princess of Wales' 18th Hussars, he was five feet eight inches tall with a fresh complexion, grey eyes and brown hair. William served at home from February 1897 to October 1899 and left for South Africa on October 20 1899, where he remained until May 1903. Whilst on active service he was convicted of disobeying a lawful command, resulting in his pay being forfeited and imprisonment for one month in May 1902. In respect of his otherwise dedicated service, William received the Queen's South Africa War Medal with clasps for the relief of Ladysmith, Tugela Heights, Laings' Nek, Orange Free State and Transvaal, remaining in the army until his eventual discharge in February 1909 after twelve years' service. He settled in Ilfracombe with his wife Martha and three children, working as a delivery man for a local baker.

Private George H Down

A bricklayer by trade, George enlisted in December 1898 but was stricken with scarlet fever in the summer of 1899. He was unable to set sail for South Africa until October 1900 and remained there until April 1901, receiving the Queen's South Africa War Medal with clasps for Transvaal, Orange Free State, SA 1901 and SA 1902. George was later called up to fight in the First World War where sadly he was killed in action.

Private Henry McMahon

Henry was born in Stirling in 1882, the second son of Marwood born Eliza (nee Hill) who had relocated to Scotland when she was married. Eliza returned to Marwood with Henry and her oldest son John in the early 1890s, to live with her brother Thomas in Little Silver. *Marwood Church Monthly* recorded that Henry did not embark for South Africa until March 1901 along with the Sharpshooters Corps, 18th Imperial Yeomanry. He received the Queen's South Africa War Medal with clasps for Cape Colony, Orange Free State, SA 1901 and SA 1902. Henry was later called up to fight in the First World War.

Trooper Frederick Willis *d. 30 September 1901.*

In February 1901, Trooper Frederick Willis set sail for South Africa. He was twenty-five years old, the second eldest son of William and Mary Willis, born and raised in Higher Muddiford. William was a former army Sergeant in the Royal North Devon Hussars for twenty-six years and after his discharge, he became the gardener at *Muddiford House*. Like his father Frederick joined the Barnstaple squadron of the Royal North Devon Hussars, later transferring to the 27th Devon Imperial Yeomanry.

He saw heavy fighting as soon as he arrived and in July 1901 his horse was shot under him at Viakfontient, where he was taken prisoner but released shortly afterwards.

In November 1901, *Marwood Church Monthly* reported that Frederick had been killed in action on September 30, during an engagement at Moedwell in which Colonel Kebewich's force was attacked by General De La Rey. Although De La Rey's attack was unsuccessful the British lost four officers and forty-five men, with many more wounded. The South Africans took even heavier losses.

Having only left England seven months before, there was deep sadness when the news was received in the parish and *Marwood Church Monthly* reflected 'the reality of war has been brought home to us very closely by the death of Trooper Willis'. Reverend Barlow proposed that once the war was over, a suitable memorial should be placed in the church to commemorate Trooper Willis and also Corporal Thomas Worth of Kings Heanton, who had lost his life in South Africa almost exactly one year earlier.

At Peace
Peace terms were eventually concluded with the Boers on June 2 1902. On hearing the news, the pupils of Marwood school were led by their Headmaster Mr Pill, to the top of the hill behind the school where they stopped and sang the National Anthem.

Two years later in August 1904, a service was held at Marwood Parish Church to unveil a white marble tablet in memory of the late Frederick Willis. The church was overflowing, attended not only by parishioners but also thirty members of the North Devon Royal Imperial Yeomanry, led by Captain-Adjutant Paterson and three Sergeant Majors.

Marwood Church Monthly reported that Sir Bourchier Wrey unveiled the memorial, handing over the guardianship to the Reverend Alfred Johnson and his churchwardens, to its new position on the south wall. As well as a record of admiration and esteem for their fallen comrade, the memorial was described as an expression of sympathy for the Willis family, who through Frederick's father William, had been closely linked with the regiment for over quarter of a century. The Reverend gratefully accepted it and assured the regiment it would be cherished as a symbol of a Marwood man who 'in the hour of the Empire's need, had volunteered to serve her and had laid down his life in defence of his country'.

Reverend Wrey, rector of Tawstock and Chaplain to the Regiment, then spoke of his hope that the tablet would inspire the young men of Marwood with the same thought of their country in its distress as that which had inspired Trooper Willis. He encouraged them to join one of the auxiliary forces, to learn to be able to come forward in times of need to help their country, prophetically preaching 'God alone knew when another crisis would come upon this country'.

First World War

The Great War of 1914-1918 was the first truly global conflict. It commenced on July 28 1914 in mainland Europe and within weeks, countries around the world became embroiled. Britain joined the conflict on August 4 1914 after declaring war on Germany. The King's army mobilised immediately with many battalions leaving within days. Amongst the hundreds of thousands of British men called to arms were many brave men of Marwood, who found themselves up to their knees in mud in trenches in France and Belgium, while others found themselves further afield in places such as Mesopotamia (Iraq), India or the beaches of Gallipoli.

The first serious battle was at Mons on the French-Belgian border, where the British Expeditionary Force was unable to hold back the advancing Germans. At home, this prompted a great surge in recruitment with thousands of volunteers enlisting throughout the nation.

On September 10 1914 the parish council assembled to discuss a letter from Colonel Radcliffe, requesting them to stimulate army recruitment. Several Marwood men were already on active service and others had volunteered, so those present at the meeting decided no action should be taken at that stage. Attendees were Samuel Born, William Willis, John Alford, Richard Dobbs, George Balment, William Isaac, Fred Parkhouse and Thomas Joslin. In October a more serious letter was received from the Lord Lieutenant of Devon, requiring the council to confirm the specific number of men already serving in His Majesty's Forces at the outbreak of war and the number who had enlisted by October 1914. Since the chairman of the parish council, and former Mayor of Barnstaple, Major George W.F Brown had been posted with his regiment, it was agreed that Fred Parkhouse should deputise for him in the interim. Fred agreed to obtain the full list of names of those serving and forward it to Exeter by the required date of October 31.

Captain Herbert Whipple *d. November 24 1914.*

The first Marwood man to lose his life in the Great War was Captain Herbert Connell Whipple (b.1879). He was the oldest son of Dr Connell and Harriet Whipple, newcomers to the parish in 1912 and resident at *Muddiford House* until 1935.

Originally from Plymouth, Herbert was a career soldier and by the age of twenty he had been appointed 2nd Lieutenant in the 1st Devonshire Regiment. He served in the Boer War and West Africa (1909-1910) and on August 21 1914, his regiment embarked for France on the *S.S. Reindeer*. They were soon in action in the trenches of Messines, Belgium, facing heavy losses of both officers and men which probably hastened Herbert's promotion to the rank of Captain on November 4 1914. Tragically, less than three weeks later, he was fatally wounded on November 20 1914, and died from his injuries on November 24. Herbert was laid to rest at the Bailleul Communal Cemetery in France, close to the border with Belgium and is commemorated on the Marwood War Memorial and he was posthumously awarded the Victory, British War and 1914 'Mons' Star medals.

North Devon Journal - April 29 1915.
Major GWF Brown of the 1/6 Devons, stationed in India, has been attached to the 1st Sussex Regiment, is taking a detachment to Peshawar, near the Khyber Pass, on the North West front. The spot is 14,000ft above the sea level. The detachment includes three Marwood men, Messrs Worth, Smith and Jenkins. Major Brown is the coroner for North Devon.

Private Reuben Tamlyn *d. July 3 1915.*

Reuben Tamlyn was born in 1881 in Guineaford, and soon after moved with his family to *Broom Cottage*, Middle Marwood, where they lived for many years. His father James was a farm labourer and Reuben followed in his footsteps, initially working for William and Emily Alford in Kings Heanton. At the time of joining the army in September 1914, he was working for Thomas Joslin at Westcott Barton. Reuben set sail for Lahore as a member of the 6th Devonshire Regiment, where he was to experience the most extreme conditions he had ever known. Camped on the plains of Punjab in June 1915, the heat was stifling with temperatures reaching up to 118 degrees in the shade and averaging 100 degrees over a twenty four hour period. Unused to these conditions, many soldiers succumbed to severe heatstroke, and unfortunately in Reuben's case, this condition proved to be fatal as he died on July 3 1915 at the age of thirty-four years. His name is honoured on the Karachi 1914-1918 War Memorial and Marwood War Memorial, and he was posthumously awarded the British War Medal.

Reuben's death was deeply mourned by the parishioners of Marwood. He had been a friend to many and was well known for his success in the local ploughing matches, winning prizes for thatching, spear making, rope making and ploughing.

The enlistment of volunteers had been high in the first few months of the war, helped by Lord Kitchener's compelling poster campaign, however by spring 1915 numbers were dwindling. At a parish council meeting on October 12 1915, a letter was read out from Colonel Alexander, once again raising the issue of recruitment in the parish. He requested the formal appointment of local influential men to encourage volunteers; yet somewhat uncooperatively the council responded that it would be useless for a local to recruit for the army. At a follow-up meeting a month later, a letter was read out from the Secretary of the Parliamentary Recruiting Committee, to which there could be no refusal. It called for the council to appoint canvassers, under the Lord Derby voluntary recruiting scheme which specified that if men signed up they would only be called up for service when absolutely necessary. It was resolved that Messieurs Thomas Joslin, William Willis, George Balment, Fred Parkhouse and William Worth should be appointed to act in this capacity.

Despite the various efforts by the Government and Lord Derby to avoid the politically unpopular idea of conscription, it was perhaps inevitably introduced in January 1916. Initially conscription affected only unmarried men between the ages of eighteen and forty, however as the numbers of recruits still failed to meet demand, from July 1916 it also applied to married men.

Captain Heyworth Potter Lawrence Heyworth *d. August 6 1915.*

Lawrence was the only son of Colonel Heyworth, Commander of the 3rd Welsh Regiment and Mrs Rosina Heyworth, owners of Whitefield Barton in Marwood. Although they did not live there permanently, there is mention of their involvement in the parish, such as allowing land to be used for ploughing competitions and hosting a tea for the children of Muddiford and Milltown.

A career soldier, educated at Harrow and Trinity College Cambridge, Lawrence first saw action in South Africa in the Boer War where he earned the Queen's South Africa War Medal with clasps for Cape Colony, Transvaal and Orange Free State. Perhaps in tribute to his son, Colonel Heyworth later named areas of his woods at Whitefield after battles in the Boer War, including Spion Kop and Tugela Woods.

Lawrence and his regiment arrived in the Dardanelles in June 1915, where two months later at the age of thirty-eight, he was killed in action near Sari Bair on August 6. Heyworth was laid to rest at the Shrapnel Valley Cemetery in Turkey and posthumously awarded the Victory, British War and 1914-1915 Star medals, also gaining a mention in De Ruvigny's Roll of Honour 1914-1924. He is not mentioned on the Marwood War Memorial, though a stained glass window was later erected in his memory in the Lady Chapel of the Marwood Parish Church (see Chapter Four).

Lance-Corporal Ernest Dobbs *d. Nov 10 1915.*

Born in 1894 in Queensland, Australia, Ernest Dobbs was the only son of Richard and Kate, and younger brother of Ida. The family left Australia in 1897 and settled in Kings Heanton, purchasing the farm known as Herders' Tenement. After attending both the Church school in Guineaford and the Board school in Whiddon, Ernest worked with his father on the farm. He was a keen participant in local ploughing matches, often winning prizes for sheep shearing.

A keen horseman, Ernest joined the Royal North Devon Hussars and each summer he went off to camp for a fortnight to learn military skills. In July 1913 he sent a postcard to Ida from Salisbury Plain where he was on exercise:

Dear Ida.
Just a line to let you know we are A1. We have been out yesterday in the saddles, at work from 3am until past ten o'clock in the night. Love Ern.

Source: NDRO B900.

When the war broke out in August 1914, the Royal North Devon Yeomanry and Hussars were amongst the first men to be called up and they spent the winter on the east coast of Britain, guarding against an invasion that never came. The following year in September 1915, the men were dismounted in preparation for service as infantry and departed on the *S.S. Olympic* for Gallipoli. The Devons spent much of their time in the trenches where they were constantly in danger from Turkish snipers. It was here that many of the regiment lost their lives, not through bullets or shells but disease. Ernest succumbed to dysentery and like many of his comrades he was evacuated to a hospital in Malta. Sadly he died on November 10 1915 at the age of twenty-one, and he now rests at the Pieta Military Cemetery. Ernest was posthumously awarded the Victory, British War and 1914-1915 Star medals and is commemorated on the Marwood War Memorial.

North Devon Journal - December 2 1915.
Among the gifts received at the Guildhall, Exeter, on behalf of the fund being raised for the Red Cross Society, was the sum of 13s 6d, contributed by the members and friends of Muddiford Congregational Church.

North Devon Journal - December 9 1915.
Sgt G Worth (Marwood) of the 1/6th Devons, now at Lahore, has passed an examination in physical training, which includes horizontal bar work, parallel bars, fencing, bayonet fighting, hand balancing and a general knowledge of anatomy. Out of over 40 competitors three only obtained
1st class certificates, Sgt Worth being one of them.

North Devon Journal - December 22 1915.
Sgt H McMahon of the 1st London Yeomanry, son of Mrs McMahon of Little Silver, Marwood is now in service in the Mediterranean. In a letter to his mother he says he saw the Royal North Devon Yeomanry when he was in the Dardanelles. The Turkish trenches he said were not very far from his trench, and in the day kept up a sharp fusillade, but one thing they were all glad of was that the Turks rarely disturbed them at night. The Turkish guns are now in the hills covered with bushes and it is very hard for our artillery to locate them.

Private William Jenkins *d. February 29 1916.*

Born May 18 1896, William was the son of Samuel and Susannah Jenkins. He grew up in Kings Heanton with his five brothers Samuel, Ernest, Fred, Herbert and Henry, and four sisters Ann, Edith, Grace and Lily. On leaving school at the age of fourteen, William found work as a farm servant with Richard and Bessie Rudd at Bradiford. As a member of the 6th Devonshire Regiment he was sent to Basra, Mesopotamia (Iraq) in January 1916, where he was immediately involved in the relief of Kut, which was under siege by the Turkish army. The men had to undertake four hard weeks of marching and just as the battalion arrived in the province of Senna in February 1916, William was reported missing, as detailed in the 6th Devonshire Regiment book which stated: 'Jenkins, W, Pte D Coy. No.2482 missing off the river boat T2, on the Tigris river, Mesopotamia, believed drowned'. William's body was never recovered and his official date of death was recorded as February 29 1916, aged nineteen. His name is included on the Basra memorial, along with the names of over forty thousand soldiers from the commonwealth who lost their lives in Mesopotamia, and on the Marwood War Memorial. William was posthumously awarded the Victory and British War medals.

North Devon Journal - April 6 1916.
It has been officially reported that three Marwood men in the Devons were wounded during recent fighting. They are Sergt. George Worth, son of Mr and Mrs Worth of Muddiford, Pte Thomas Dummett of Milltown, and Pte Frank Dowdle, son of Mrs L Dowdle, Milltown. They are all fine types of soldier, and a speedy recovery is wished them by their many friends at Marwood.

Private Albert Manning *d. April 21 1916.*

Albert was born in 1895, the youngest son of William and Sarah Manning of *Bridge House*, Guineaford. After attending the Church school, just a hundred yards from his home, Albert worked as a horseman for John Pengelly at Upcott Farm, Shirwell, and later for James Pugsley in South Wooley. Albert was engaged to Alice Watts, daughter of Charles and Hannah of Muddiford Post Office.

Albert joined the 4th Grenadier Guards in August 1915 and standing at over six feet tall, he was described as a splendid soldier. Less than a year after enlisting, he died from gunshot wounds on April 21 1916, aged twenty-one. William Lynch of Muddiford wrote that on hearing the news, Albert's fiancée Alice was so distraught she dressed in black and cried for months. Albert was laid to rest at Lijssenthoek Military Cemetery in Poperinge, Belgium and later awarded the Star, Victory and British Service medals. On May 14 1916, an article in the North Devon Journal reported that Reverend Palmer led a memorial service the previous Sunday at Marwood Methodist Church and the hymns 'Peace, perfect peace' and 'Forever with the Lord' were sung. The mourners included Albert's parents, brothers Harry, John, Evan, Fred and George, Mr and Mrs Prance (aunt and uncle) and Mr and Mrs Yeo, Ebberly Arms, Barnstaple.

Albert's name is commemorated on the Marwood War Memorial and he was posthumously awarded the Victory, British War and 1914-1915 Star medals.

North Devon Journal - April 27 1916.
Pte R Harris, A.O.C has visited his home in Marwood on brief leave.

Private Ernest Jenkins *d. May 1 1916.*

Samuel and Susannah Jenkins had three sons fighting in the war, namely Ernest (b.1887), Fred (b.1890) and William (b.1896, mentioned previously). Before William was born, the family had lived at Kennacott, where Samuel was working as a farm labourer. In November 1895 *Marwood Church Monthly* reported that a fire had broken out in the cottages occupied by the Jenkins and Ley families, resulting in the loss of much of their furniture and belongings. Reverend Pryke issued an appeal to the parish and a collection raised ten pounds for the two stricken families.

Further difficult times were to follow for Samuel and Susannah when William died in Mesopotamia in February 1916. Tragically less than three months later, they received news that Ernest, a member of the 6th Devonshire Regiment had died in the same country on May 1. In an article in the North Devon Journal on May 18 1916, entitled 'Marwood Soldier Succumbs to Fever' it was written: 'The deceased who was 28 years of age had previously been in the employ of J.M Montague Esq. of Broomhill. By a mournful coincidence, Mrs Jenkins received a postcard from her son by the same post, saying he was in perfect health. He also said he had met his brother Fred of the Welsh Fusiliers. Much sympathy is extended to the bereaved family in their second loss'.

Ernest is commemorated on the Amara War Memorial in Iraq and Marwood War Memorial, and was posthumously awarded the Victory and British War medals.

North Devon Journal – May 11 1916.
Dispatch rider A. Lean of Guineaford, who has been in France for the last twelve months, has visited his home on brief furlough.

North Devon Journal – May 18 1916.
Pte R Harris, A.O.C of Marwood, has been appointed Lance-Corporal.

Above: Robert Harris of Varley.

North Devon Journal – June 22 1916.
Pte F. Yeo of Prixford, Marwood has been home on brief leave.

By late 1916 the state of agricultural operations had become of increasing concern to the Government due to a combination of poor crop and potato harvests, labour shortages and loss of imports from abroad. Most imports came from America and Canada and the journey across the Atlantic Ocean had become increasingly perilous as German submarines were frequently sinking ships. In Marwood, William Lynch recalled in his memoirs that 1916 was a terribly wet summer and the hay and corn rotted in the fields. The school was closed at harvest time to enable the older boys to assist the farmers in saving what they could. He mentioned that things were getting serious, food was becoming scarce and substitute foods such as margarine tasted awfully nutty.

As food shortages became more evident, the Government commenced the rationing of some food types and launched a national campaign to encourage food production. At one point it was reported that Britain had only six weeks' worth of wheat left and consequently, bread was one of the first items to be rationed. As a result of these developments, food prices escalated, a fact that was noted by Fred Kelly in Guineaford. In one of his journals he wrote out the typical items you might expect to find on a shopping list or for sale at a cattle market, comparing the cost before and after the war commenced:

	Before the war	After war started
Flour	9lb for 1s	5lb for 1s
Lump Sugar	2s per lb	6s per lb
Tea	1s 6 per lb	1s 10 per lb
Beer	2s per pint	3s per pint
Maize	15s per sack	30s per sack
Oats	2s 6 per bushell	4s per bushell
Calves	£3	£5
Fat Ewes	£2 5s	£3
Sucking Pigs	£1	£2

At a parish council meeting on May 8 1916, a letter from the Board of Agriculture was read out, requesting the chairman provide a statement of produce in hand on the various farms in the parish. It was resolved to inform the Board of Agriculture that only sufficient crops remained in hand to supply the needs of the parish until the harvest.

Private Ernest Smith *d. June 18 1916.*

Born in Kings Heanton in 1894, Ernest was the son of Charles and Mary Smith. In the early 1900s the family moved to Milltown where Charles, a carpenter, worked as an agricultural implement maker and machinist. Ernest joined up immediately following the outbreak of war and was enlisted into the 6th Devonshire Regiment alongside William Jenkins of Kings Heanton. The North Devon Journal reported Ernest's story in February 1919:

'During the past week, Mr C Smith of Milltown has received information regarding his son, Ernest Smith, whom nothing has been heard of since the fall of Kut. A young man of splendid physique and gentle disposition he joined up at the commencement of the hostility and went to India with the 6th Devons. He was almost the first volunteer for service in Mesopotamia. The communication from the Red Cross Society states that he died of dysentery in Samara Hospital on June 18th 1916, two months after being taken prisoner.

The information has been obtained through a repatriated prisoner of war. Much sympathy has been expressed with the family with the suspense and the bereavement'.

Ernest is honourably mentioned on the Basra Memorial, the Marwood War Memorial and posthumously awarded the Victory and British War medals.

Private Frank Dowdle *d. July 1 1916.*

Frank was born in Arlington Beccott in 1898, the youngest of five children. After the death of his father William in 1906, Frank and his mother Lucy went to live with his grandparents in Milltown. He left Marwood to join the 6th Devonshire Regiment, like so many of the young men in the parish and was sent to Mesopotamia. During action at Es Sinn in March 1916, Frank was wounded and later died in hospital at Basra of diphtheria on July 1. Lucy received official news of his death on July 13. Her oldest son George (b.1888) was already serving in the South Wales Borderers, and younger sons Albert (b.1890) and Fred (b.1892) were both serving on *HMS Highflyer*, so it must have been a time of deep anxiety for her.

Frank was just nineteen years old when he was laid to rest at the Basra War Cemetery and is honourably mentioned on the Marwood War Memorial. He was posthumously awarded the Victory and British War medals.

Private Arthur 'Ernest' Ashton *d. July 7 1916.*

Born in 1893 in Berrynarbor, Ernest was one of seven children of William and Elizabeth Ann Ashton of Westgate, Muddiford. Although he spent his early years in Marwood working for Mr Beard at Plaistow Mill, Ernest had moved to Cardiff in the years preceding the war. He was amongst the first to sign up in November 1914, at the age of twenty-one.

As a sniper with the 16th Welsh Regiment, Ernest saw action at the Battle of the Somme, where he was involved in an offensive to capture the village of Thiepval on July 1 1916. The allies were met with strong resistance by the Germans, resulting in heavy losses and it was during this offensive that Ernest lost his life on July 7 1916. Ironically, the day before his mother was notified of his death, she had received a postcard from him, assuring her he was keeping well. Ernest was described by his regiment as a clever shot, much respected by his comrades.

Ernest's name is commemorated on the Thiepval Memorial, also known as 'The Missing of the Somme', which was established in memory of over seventy thousand men who died with no known grave, and also the War Memorial at East Down. Tragically, his father William who was serving with the Royal Engineers was killed in action in February 1918.

Private George Dowdle *d. August 16 1916.*

The news that Lucy Dowdle must have been dreading came just a few weeks after she had learned of the death of her youngest son, Frank. George, her oldest son was officially reported missing in August 1916 and here follows a tale of undeniable courage. After growing up in North Devon, George moved to Cardiff where he initially lived with his uncle, working as a haulier for a building firm.

Initially accepted by the South Wales Borderers, George was posted to France where he fought until February 1915, earning him the 1914-1915 Star Medal. His battalion was then posted to the Dardanelles as part of the Mediterranean Expeditionary Force where in May 1915, he received a gun shot wound to his right upper arm. At the same time two shells exploded nearby, concussing him and causing some deafness. George was transferred to a hospital in Cairo and shortly afterwards, departed Port Said on board His Majesty's transport ship, the *S.S. Marquette,* arriving in England in July 1915.

George spent some time recuperating at the Devonport Military hospital and during a medical inspection he was deemed to have a permanent disability, rendering him fit for home service only. His left ear had a perforated drum with partial hearing and his right hear was damaged, causing complete deafness. George evidently pleaded that he was able to continue in active service and the Medical Officer wrote: 'In fairly good health, apart from his ear trouble. Will gladly work for his country in any capacity for which he is qualified. This mental capacity will make him successful in whatever work he finds suitable'.

By March 1916, George managed to gain a transfer to the Royal Welsh Fusiliers, and was immediately sent to join his new regiment. He left Devonport with his new regiment on His Majesty's Troopship *S.S. Minnewaska,* arriving in Alexandria on March 16 1916, later departing on the *S.S. Border* to rejoin the fighting at the Somme in July. As a member of the 10th Battalion, George was involved in the attack on Delville Wood. This was an attempt to break through the German line following the bloodbath that had happened during the first two weeks of the Battle of the Somme. It was near here that Private George Dowdle was officially declared missing and later confirmed as dead on August 16 1916.

His name does not appear on the Marwood War Memorial alongside his brother Frank, but is commemorated on the East Down Memorial, the parish of his birth. He was posthumously awarded the Victory, British War and 1914-1915 Star medals.

North Devon Journal- August 17 1916.

Sgt H McMahon (Marwood) of the 1st County of London Yeomanry, has been promoted to commissioned rank; having been granted a Second-Lieutenancy in the 8th Cornwall Regiment. He has seen active service in Egypt, from whence he proceeded to Salonika. Lieut. McMahon is a well-known North Devon Athlete.

North Devon Journal - September 21 1916.

Pte J McMahon (Devons) of Little Silver, Marwood, has been recently wounded in France. His brother, Lieut. Harry McMahon (D.C.L.I) is on active service.

Private Arthur Carpenter *d. October 6 1916.*

Arthur was born in Guineaford in 1892, the only child of Charity Carpenter, and grandson of two former schoolteachers, John and Elizabeth Carpenter. As a pupil at the Church school at the turn of the twentieth century, Arthur received frequent honourable mention for his religious knowledge and near perfect attendance.

Arthur was local scoutmaster for the troop set up by Mrs Montague of *Lee House*. After leaving school, his occupation was initially recorded as boot repairer/postman, though he was later in the employment of Garnish & Lemon, agricultural implement makers of Milltown. Upon enlistment to the army, Arthur was a drummer with the Royal North Devon Hussars, though he was soon transferred to the 2nd Devonshire Regiment.

Arthur was involved in fighting in Northern France and after receiving serious injuries, he was invalided home in the Spring of 1916; returning to the front after his recovery in September that year. Sadly only a month after his return, Arthur died of wounds on October 6 1916, aged twenty-five. He was laid to rest at the Philosophe British Cemetery in the small town of Mazingarbe, and his name is commemorated on the Marwood War Memorial. Arthur was posthumously awarded the Victory, British War and 1914-1915 Star medals.

Lance-Corporal William Dummett *d. November 24 1916.*

Born in 1895 and raised at Crockers, Milltown, William was the youngest of the three sons of Henry and Annie Dummett. After leaving school he worked as a horseman at Lower Churchill Farm in East Down and later found employment as a labourer for Barnstaple builder, James Hill. Like Ernest Dobbs, William initially joined the Royal North Devon Hussars, enlisting in November 1914 and was later transferred to the 5th Dorsetshire Regiment in September 1916. He was killed in action on November 24 1916, aged twenty-one, less than a week after the Battle of the Somme had ended. William's name is commemorated on the Thiepval Memorial, along with another Marwood comrade, Ernest Ashton, and also on the Marwood War Memorial. He was posthumously awarded the Victory and British War medals.

Private Richard Brooks

Richard Brooks *(pictured right)* was born in Bittadon in 1898 and after attending Marwood school, he was engaged in farm work until the war broke out. He was quick to volunteer for the Devonshire Regiment and was among the many thousands of young men sent out to fight in France. On the first day of the Battle of the Somme, when so many British soldiers lost their lives, Richard received a serious gunshot wound to his shoulder and was lucky to survive. He was invalided home to a Military Hospital in Reading where it became apparent that the injuries he received were of such a serious and disabling nature that they led to his honourable discharge in February 1917, as shown by the certificate below.

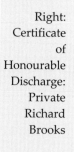

Richard later married Maud Latham and they lived at *Rose Cottage*, Kings Heanton, where their two sons Norman and Bernard were born.

Left: Richard Brooks' Silver War Badge "FOR KING AND EMPIRE – SERVICES RENDERED"; awarded to military personnel medically discharged as a result of wounds or sickness received during WWI.

Right: Certificate of Honourable Discharge: Private Richard Brooks

Gunner Ernest G Spear *d. March 16 1917.*

Born in Kings Heanton in September 1895, and baptised in February 1896 with his sister Bessie at Marwood Parish Church, Ernest was the oldest son of Alfred and Bessie Spear. Prior to the outbreak of the war, he was employed by local farmer, James Herneman of Whitehall.

Ernest joined the Royal Field Artillery in January 1915 and was already in action by April 1915 in the second Battle of Ypres where poisonous gas was used for the first time in battle. He was reported as receiving bullet wounds to his hand and side in June 1916 and was brought back to England, where sadly he died of his injuries at Sutton Hospital, on March 16 1917. Since his death occurred in his home country, Ernest is the only Marwood casualty of the First World War who could be laid to rest in his home parish, and is buried in the parish churchyard. An article in the North Devon Journal on March 29 1917 reported that his funeral took place on March 20, with his close family and many parishioners in attendance. Ernest's name is honoured on the Marwood War Memorial and he was posthumously awarded the Victory, British War and 1914-1915 Star medals.

North Devon Journal - February 15 1917.
Pte Bernard Muir Bridger has spent brief leave from France at his home at Muddiford. Although not yet twenty years of age, he served through the Gallipoli campaign and he was in the great push on the Somme last July.

North Devon Journal - March 22 1917.
Pte Preston Welch (Devons) has been home on leave at Marwood. Pte Ernest Prance (Welsh Regiment), son of Mr J Prance of Marwood, has been wounded in action and is now in Worcester hospital.

Private Reginald Gammon *d. April 4 1917.*

Reginald (b.1895) was brought up in Milltown, the son of William, a former soldier in the Royal Garrison Regiment, and Emma Gammon. After leaving school he initially worked as a farm servant for Edwin Chamings of Coxleigh, but later followed in his father's footsteps, joining up when the war broke out.

Reginald initially joined the 8th Devonshire Regiment, later transferring to the 6th Duke of Cornwall's Light Infantry but was killed in action in Arras, Northern France on April 4 1917, aged twenty-two. Just five months later his mother Emma died aged fifty-two and both are commemorated on a gravestone together in the parish churchyard. Reginald's name is also honoured on the Marwood War Memorial and he was posthumously awarded the Victory, British War and 1914-1915 Star medals.

North Devon Journal- May 24 1917.
Pte E.H Shaxton of the Royal North Devon Hussars, attached to the 1st Devons, of Westgate, Muddiford, has been admitted to a London Hospital suffering from bullet wounds in the neck. His many friends will be glad to hear he is progressing favourably.

Private Stanley Willis *d. July 31 1917.*

Stanley (b.1897) was the nephew of Trooper Frederick Willis who perished in the Boer War. Frederick's parents William and Mary had four sons serving in the First World War, namely Sergeant William Willis, Army Veterinary Corps; Corporal George Willis, Army Mounted Police; Private Samuel Willis, Royal North Devon Hussars and Thomas Willis, Army Service Corps, as well as their grandson Stanley.

After leaving school Stanley worked for Jack Chapple of Muddiford as a horseman, but later in 1916 he enlisted and became a member of the 4th King's Own Royal Lancaster Regiment. Stanley's active service in France began in December 1916 and less than a year later on July 31 1917, he was reported missing at Ypres. Stanley's body was never recovered and like many of his comrades, his name is commemorated on the Menin Gate memorial to the missing at Ypres (now Ieper) in Belgium, and Marwood War Memorial.

Stoker Albert Dowdle *d. August 9 1917.*

By August 1916, Lucy Dowdle of Milltown had received the sad news that two of her four sons had lost their lives in the war. Her remaining sons Albert and Fred were both serving with the Royal Navy, on board *HMS Highflyer*.

Albert was born in December 1889 at Arlington Beccott. After leaving school in 1904 he worked as a milkman before joining the Navy on March 10 1909. It is likely that his reasons for joining were motivated by his younger brother Frederick's decision to enlist in January 30 1909. Having served their initial five year engagement, both brothers were transferred to the Royal Fleet Reserve in the Spring of 1914 but with the outbreak of war in August that year, both were recalled to action and set sail on the cruiser *HMS Highflyer*. Their first major action was the capture of the 14,000 ton Dutch liner *Tubantia*, carrying a valuable bounty of German reservists and gold which was safely escorted to Britain. This was followed by the hunt for the German commerce raider *Kaiser Wilhelm der Grosse*, which was sunk after the short but fierce battle of Rio de Oro. *Highflyer* remained in West Africa until the spring of 1917, at which point Albert was transferred to *HMS Vivid II*, Royal Naval barracks at Devonport for three months and following this he boarded the destroyer *HMS Recruit* on July 17 1917. Frederick transferred to the armoured cruiser *HMS Devonshire*.

In what must have been devastating news for Lucy Dowdle in August 1917, it was confirmed that *HMS Recruit* had been torpedoed by a German submarine and sunk in the North Sea. Albert Dowdle, then aged twenty-seven, and fifty-two sailors on board lost their lives. On August 16 1917, the North Devon Journal printed the following update:

'Stoker A.W Dowdle, who has lost his life through the sinking of one of HM Ships, was the second son of Mrs L Dowdle of Milltown, Marwood. This is the third son of Mrs Dowdle to make the supreme sacrifice. At Marwood profound sympathy is felt for the bereaved mother who is a widow'.

Albert's name is commemorated on the Plymouth Naval Memorial and Marwood War Memorial. Lucy's only remaining son Frederick remained onboard *HMS Devonshire* and thankfully survived the war, finally being demobilised in June 1921.

North Devon Journal - September 3 1917.

Pte Harry Jenkins (A.O.C) youngest son of the late Mr John Jenkins of Patsford, Marwood, and whose wife resides at Bear Street, Barnstaple, has been promoted to full Corporal. He has been in France over two years.

North Devon Journal - September 13 1917.

Pte Gilbert Down (Dorsets, formerly R.N.D.H) has been awarded the Military Medal for bravery in the field. Pte Down is a son of Mrs Down of Corser Cottage, Vicarage Street, Barnstaple, formerly of Marwood. Mrs Down has another son in France, Pte Wm H Down.

North Devon Journal - September 29 1917.

News has been received from the War Office that Pte G Pugsley is in hospital in France suffering from a fever. Pte Pugsley was formerly in the employ of Mr F Blackwell of Snapper, and is a son-in-law of Mr and Mrs J Tamlyn of Middle Marwood. His many friends wish him a speedy recovery.

Private Fred Corney *d. October 4 1917.*

Fred was born in the middle cottage at Longpiece in 1880, the eldest son of George and Emily Corney who ran the post office at nearby Ashford. At the turn of the century Fred was a gardener at Comyn Hill in Ilfracombe, but later moved with his wife Jane to Bexhill-on-Sea in Sussex to work as a nurseryman and florist. He initially joined the East Kent Regiment in 1917, later transferring to the Royal Warwickshires. On his arrival in France he was immediately involved in heavy fighting in the Battle of Passchendaele (Third Battle of Ypres), and was last seen wounded, walking to a dressing station. At first Fred was reported as missing in action but news of his death was later confirmed, much to the distress of his relatives. He was laid to rest at the Tyne Cot Memorial, near Zonnebeke, Belgium.

Corporal Harry Jenkins *d. February 3 1918.*

Harry was born in 1875 at Patsford Cottages, the youngest son of John and Susan Jenkins. After marrying Frances Garland in 1893 he had several occupations including groom/coachman at Crediton Hall and labourer at Raleigh Cabinet Works. He joined the Army Ordnance Corps but in February 1918 he died in a tragic accident in France. He had gone for a walk with a friend and by the time they made their way back it was dark. Their return journey involved crossing a small bridge over a canal and it was presumed that one fell in the water while the other tried to save him, as both died from drowning. It must have come as a great shock to Frances and their three sons, who had only just received a cheery later from him, describing the weather as very hot but they were all in good spirits, playing lots of football. Harry was laid to rest at Les Baraques Military Cemetery, Sangatte, near Calais and posthumously awarded the Victory and British War medals.

Pioneer William Ashton *d. February 16 1918.*

Born in Pilton in 1866, William was a gardener who joined up at the age of fifty, an act that was above and beyond the call of duty. He had been living in Muddiford in 1911 with his wife and his four youngest children and working at *Muddiford House.* Two of his eldest sons Ernest and Harry were in active service in France and Italy respectively, and maybe this was the reason he had felt compelled to volunteer. William was recruited as Pioneer in the Labour Corps, Royal Engineers, but sadly after just two years' service he died from wounds inflicted when a bomb exploded near him in February 1918, at the age of fifty-two years.

William was laid to rest at Ham Cemetery, Muille-Villette in France. His name is honoured on the East Down War Memorial and on a headstone in Marwood parish churchyard, together with Ernest.

Sergeant George H Down *d. April 24 1918.*

Born in November 1880, George's childhood years were spent in Milltown before he joined the army to fight in the Boer War in 1898. After demobilisation, he married Beatrice Nellie Clift of Witheridge in 1907 and became a bricklayer, though he remained in the army reserves. On August 5 1914, the day after Britain declared war, he was mobilised as a member of the 3rd Devonshire Regiment, leaving his wife and three young children in Chulmleigh. Interestingly, his army records show that in December 1915 he was discharged, his period of service having expired, however at a later date he joined the 2nd Devons and returned to the front in the Somme. He was reported missing in action on April 20 1918 and it was not until several months later that he was officially reported as killed in action on April 24 1918.

Private Herbert Geen *d. April 24 1918.*

Herbert was the son of John and Eliza Geen (nee Yeo) of Prixford. His father John was a labourer who died at the young age of thirty-nine, leaving Herbert at home with his mother who took on work as a sewer to make ends meet. Herbert signed up to join the army, enlisting with the 2nd Devonshire Regiment and was involved in the torrid battle that began in Spring 1918, when allied forces were driven back in large numbers across the former Somme battlefields. Herbert died on April 24 1918 aged nineteen, just a few months before the advance to victory. He is commemorated on the memorial at Pozieres and Marwood War Memorial, and posthumously awarded the Victory and British War medals.

North Devon Journal- May 30 1918
MARWOOD: The Rev G Cording, pastor of Muddiford Congregational Church is leaving for a few months duty in France.

North Devon Journal- June 13 1918
Private Ernest Shaxton awarded Military Medal for gallantry serving with the Hampshire Regiment, of Westgate, Muddiford.

In July 1918, the National War Aims Committee in London wrote to local councils requesting a telegram be sent to the President of the French Republic on the twelfth of the month, presumably to ensure its arrival by Bastille Day, 14 July. Marwood Parish Council duly obliged:

> *We members Marwood Council Devon. Send. Hearty. Congratulations. To. Our. Gallant. French. Allies. On. Magnificent. Resistance. Made. Against. Our. Common. Enemy. Vive. La. France.*

Source: Parish Council Records, NDRO B8A/1/1-5.

This was later acknowledged in October 1918 when a letter was received from the President, thanking the council for their good wishes. It was agreed that this letter should be framed and hung in the parish room.

Pte William Lynch *d. August 8 1918.*

William, born in 1884, was the youngest son of John and Lois Lynch of Muddiford, a family of generations of carpenters. In the early 1900s William took the brave decision to leave his family behind in Marwood and emigrate to Canada, where he worked as a miner. In January 1916, he enlisted with the Canadian Overseas Expeditionary Forces, perhaps following the lead of his older brother Thomas who had joined the 6th Devonshire Regiment in August 1914. At enlistment he was described as five feet six inches with a fair complexion, blue eyes and brown hair.

William later joined the 54th Canadian Central Ontario Regiment and was killed in action during the battle to recapture the village of Beaucourt from the Germans, specifically during an attack on a German machine gun. The village was successfully recaptured on August 8 1918 but with huge losses to the Central Ontario Regiment. William was laid to rest at the Beaucourt British Cemetery alongside forty-nine comrades, all of whom tragically perished with him on August 8 1918. He is commemorated on the Marwood War Memorial.

William's older brother Thomas was invalided home from the war in 1916 after becoming seriously ill with dysentery and malaria, and his son William (1905-1996) remembered that he had to attend hospital every week for the following twelve months until fully recovered. Having been discharged from the army, Thomas found employment in Barnstaple, building concrete ships at the quay near Shapland and Petter.

Thomas' son William was the author of *Memories of my part of North Devon* as referenced in Chapter Two. Like his uncle and several other family members, William junior emigrated to Canada in his late teens and fought with the Canadian army in the Second World War. Thankfully he survived and returned to Britain in 1956.

North Devon Journal- November 21 1918.

News of the cessation of hostilities was received in the parish with great delight, the juveniles especially celebrating the event with gusto. The fronts of the houses were soon ablaze with colour, and the good tidings were discussed with evident pleasure, mingled with regret for those who had made the supreme sacrifice. A thanksgiving service was held in the Parish Church, conducted by the Rector (Rev G F Mattinson) and there was a crowded attendance. Throughout the parish in various places of worship on Sunday last, special references were made to the event.

Marwood War Memorial

After the First World War ended, many parishioners gave donations towards the cost of a permanent memorial to the sixteen men of Marwood who made the supreme sacrifice for King and Country. The monument was sculpted in a form of a cross of Dartmoor granite by Messrs Bryant & Sons. It was eight feet in height with a heavy base mounted in cement, positioned to the west of the bell tower. It bore the inscription 'All honour give to those who, nobly striving, nobly fell that we may live'.

The arrangements had been made by a committee chaired by the Reverend Mattinson, with the assistance of Charles Watts and William Worth of Muddiford, Tom Ward of Middle Marwood, Joseph Brailey of Whiddon and others who collected subscriptions which amassed the sum of fifty pounds.

The North Devon Journal reported on June 23 1921, that prior to the official unveiling ceremony, a well attended church service was conducted by Reverend Mattinson who read the lesson from the Book of Revelations, with a sermon preached by Reverend

Johnson of Ilfracombe. After the service the congregation gathered around the memorial, with those mourning the loss of relatives and friends given places of honour. Ex-servicemen, led by Sergeant-Major George Worth, lined up to pay tribute to their fallen comrades.

The Reverend explained that there had been a slight delay in the completion of the memorial due to problems in procuring the necessary granite, but thanked all those parishioners who had made contributions and the committee for their hard work and perseverance. Mr WT Buckingham, Chairman of Barnstaple Board of Guardians then removed the Union Jack to reveal the cross, which met with a period of silence out of respect for the fallen. Mr Buckingham spoke of the cross as a symbol of sacrifice and salvation, which would remind those present, and many generations later, of the men who went forth to battle for them He then read out the list of names of those who left field and farm, warehouse and workshop for the sake of their country. The 'Last Post' was then sounded and all joined in to sing 'O God Our Help in Ages Past' as the ceremony ended.

Marwood War Memorial

Pte Arthur Carpenter
L.Cpl Ernest Dobbs
Pte Frank Dowdle
St^{kr} Albert Dowdle
L.Cpl William Dummett
Pte Reginald Gammon
Pte Herbert Geen
Pte Ernest Jenkins
Pte William Jenkins
Pte William Lynch
Pte Albert Manning
Pte Ernest Spear
Pte Ernest Smith
Pte Reuben Tamlyn
Capt Herbert Whipple
Pte Stanley Willis

And in tribute to those honoured on memorials in other parishes, who had lived in Marwood:

Pnr William Ashton	**Pte George Gammon**
Pte Ernest Ashton	**Pte Thomas Shaxton**
Cpl Harry Jenkins	**Pte George Dowdle**
Pte Fred Corney	**Capt Heyworth P L Heyworth**
Sgt George H Down	

Lest We Forget … Those Who Fought and Returned Home

The parish also honoured the many gallant Marwood men who fought for their country and survived, returning home to their families and friends as changed men. Many haunted by distressing memories of horrors seen, heard, smelt and felt, which they would fight to suppress yet would still disturb their dreams for many years.

Former Sergeant-Major George Worth who returned from the war to his trade as carpenter and builder, carved a beautiful oak tablet inscribed in gilt letters with the names of forty-nine men who returned from the war. It bore the dedication 'This tablet was erected by the Parish of Marwood, and contains the names of those who took part in the Great War 1914-1918, and returned alive' and was placed in Marwood school as part of the memorial honours.

At Muddiford United Reformed Church hangs a Roll of Honour dedicated to the former members of the Congregational Sunday School who fought in the war, including those who made the supreme sacrifice.

In recognition of those Marwood men who fought and returned home safely to their loved ones, the following list has been compiled with reference to available records. It is hoped but cannot be guaranteed to be a complete list.

Soldier's Name	Born	Places lived prior to enlistment	Pre-War Occupation
Charles Alford	Shirwell	Whiddon	Estate carpenter
Fred Alford	Marwood	Muddiford/Loxhore	Farm worker
William Alford	Marwood	Muddiford	Labourer
Harry Ashton	Berrynarbor	Muddiford	Cattle boy
Bernard Muir Bridger	London	Muddiford	Recent school leaver
Richard Brooks	Bittadon	Bittadon/Kings Heanton	Farm worker
Major George Brown	Pilton	Roborough House	Solicitor & coroner
Arthur (Tommy) Coats	Marwood	Collacott	Recent school leaver
George Henry Coats	Marwood	Prixford/Marine Camp	Royal Marine
Fred Dowdle	Shirwell	Shirwell	Labourer
Gilbert Down	Marwood	Stepps Farm/Guineaford	Gardener
Wallace Down	Marwood	Milltown	Recent school leaver
William H Down	Marwood	Stepps Farm/Kings Heanton	Quarryman
Charles Dummett	Marwood	Milltown	Unknown
Thomas Dummett	Marwood	Milltown	Horseman
William Gammon	Marwood	Crockers/Little Silver	Farm worker/Soldier
William Gammon	Marwood	Milltown/Goodleigh	Cattle boy
John Harris	Shirwell	Little Silver	Farm worker
Robert Harris	Swimbridge	Muddiford	Builder
Fred Holmes	Braunton	Milltown/Swansea	Carter
Charles Jenkins	Ilfracombe	Crockers/Hewish	Horseman
Fred Jenkins	Marwood	Kennacott, Kings Heanton	Farm worker
Herbert Jenkins	Marwood	Crockers/Lynton	Farm Servant
Reg Jenkins	Marwood	Crockers/Milltown	Clerk

Arthur Lean	St Minver	Prixford	Cycle Engineer
Thomas Lynch	Marwood	Muddiford	Carpenter
Albert Mitchell	Shirwell	Muddiford	Agricultural machinist
Jack Mitchell	Marwood	Muddiford	Agric machine maker
Richard Mitchell	Shirwell	Muddiford	Carriage painter
Henry P McMahon	Sterling	Little Silver	Soldier (Boer War)
John McMahon	Edinburgh	Little Silver	Railway Technician
William Norman	Marwood	Muddiford	Carter
Alfred Prance	West Down	Muddiford	Railway porter
Ernest Prance	West Down	Metcombe	Carter
Fred Pugsley	Marwood	Milltown	Horseman
George Pugsley	Barnstaple	Middle Marwood	Basket maker
John Pugsley	Marwood	Milltown	Farm worker
Joseph Pugsley	Marwood	Milltown	Farm worker
Charles Quick	Marwood	Milltown/Kings Heanton	Farm worker
Ernest Quick	Marwood	Milltown	Woodworker
Frank Quick	Marwood	Milltown	Steamroller driver
William Quick	Marwood	Milltown	Carter
William Scott	East Buckland	Milltown/Whiddon	Farm servant
Ernest Shaxton	Barnstaple	Westgate - Muddiford	Farm servant
John Spear	Marwood	Milltown/Shirwell Cross	Recent school leaver
Fred Smith	Marwood	Milltown	Recent school leaver
William Watts	Barnstaple	Guineaford	Farm worker
Preston Welch	Marwood	Middle Marwood	Farmer
George Willis	Marwood	Muddiford	Unknown
Samuel Willis	Marwood	Muddiford	Dairyman
Thomas Willis	Marwood	Muddiford/South Molton	Farm worker
William H Willis	Marwood	Muddiford	Coachman
Robert Worth	Marwood	Muddiford	Clerk
George Worth	Marwood	Muddiford	Carpenter & Joiner
Frederick Yeo	Marwood	Guineaford, Ashford	Horseman

Of those who returned safely, the soldiers mentioned below received special commendation for their gallantry on the battlefield:

Gilbert Down - Military Medal

Gilbert was born in Middle Marwood at *Stepps Farm* in 1893, and later lived in *Merrifield*, Guineaford. He had been working as an apprentice motor mechanic when the war broke out but chose to join up and serve with the Royal North Devon Hussars. His expertise in repairing engines however, probably led to his later posting as a motorcycle dispatch rider with the 5th Dorsetshire Regiment. Gilbert was awarded the Military Medal for bravery in the field.

Henry McMahon - Mentioned in Despatches

After serving with the Royal Imperial Yeomanry in the latter years of the Boer War, Henry was transferred to the army reserves. He returned to his mother and family at Little Silver in Marwood, where he worked as an agricultural labourer. A keen athlete, Henry won many trophies at local and county level and was renowned in the district.

At the outbreak of the First World War he was called up and by August 1916 he had been promoted to the commissioned rank of Second Lieutenant. Whilst in the Dardanelles with the 1st London Yeomanry, Henry wrote to his mother describing his trench which was close to the Turkish line, and the relentless shelling that took place all day long. At night he reported that it was rare to be under fire, because the flashing light of the gunfire would reveal the Turks' location, enabling warships out in the sea to quickly silence them. He saw considerable service overseas, including Egypt, Salonica and Serbia, and in August 1918, he was mentioned in despatches[1] for his 'hard and useful work'. After the war, Henry remained in Marwood, farming poultry.

Ernest Shaxton - Military Medal

Ernest was born in November 1897 in Barnstaple but raised by his grandparents in Westgate, Muddiford. He was one of the younger men to sign up, along with his classmates, Stanley Willis, William Scott and Wallace Down. Ernest joined the Royal North Devon Hussars and later served with the Hampshire Regiment, and it was while serving for the Hampshires that he received a bullet wound to the neck in May 1917, as he was retrieving the wounded during severe fighting. It was this immense bravery, which led to him being awarded the Military Medal for gallantry in June 1918. In September 1918 he was injured again, receiving shrapnel wounds to his head and leg, which caused him to be invalided home to a hospital in Sunderland, and eventually returning to Marwood.

Above: William Watts' Battalion of the Royal Garrison Artillery c.1914.

---

[1] Despatches - an official report written by a senior officer and sent to the high command, in which is described the soldier's gallant or meritorious action in the face of the enemy.

Second World War

News of Britain's declaration of war on Germany came on the morning of Sunday 3 September 1939, a moment that Harold Hopkins remembers clearly, having heard the announcement by Neville Chamberlain on the radio before going to church. Garfield Spear overheard the same broadcast whilst walking past an open window at *Prixford Cottages*.

Even before the outbreak of war, the British Government had done their best to prepare people for the difficulties ahead, supplying a series of 'Civil Defence Public Information' leaflets which explained their responsibilities should hostilities erupt. Entitled 'Some things you should know if war should come', they included very specific guidance on matters such as air raids, gas masks, tackling fires, evacuation, food rationing and restrictions on travel. In Marwood as early as 1938, an address was made at a parish council meeting on air raid precautions in the event of war. They were told that any part of the country could be attacked due to advances in aircraft technology, so even rural areas could not afford to be unprepared. Councillors were told of the different kind of gasses that would probably be used, their effects and how to treat them, which must have been a frightening thought.

The nation was given detailed instructions on lighting restrictions and advised that action should be taken immediately to black out all windows, sky lights and other openings with dark blinds or blankets. They were told that there would be no street lighting or any other outside lights permitted.

Shortly after the war broke out, road signs in the countryside were removed due to the threat of invasion. It is still debated whether this order was given primarily to confuse German spies or because the country needed to recycle scrap metal for weapons.

It is hard enough for tourists to find their way around some parts of North Devon even with sign posts and satellite navigation systems, so it is likely that the removal of signs and place names would have been most effective!

Above: The road sign which was removed at Guineaford.

The War and the Women's Institute

Marwood Women's Institute were quick to discuss the outbreak of war at a monthly meeting on September 5 1939, when chairwoman Miss Mattinson advised members not to listen to rumours which were likely to be spread over the coming days, but to await official announcements. They agreed on practical changes such as swapping evening meetings to the afternoons to enable members to get home before dark and inviting local speakers, as petrol rationing would prevent long distance travel.

Where possible, members of Bittadon WI were to be invited along to share speakers. At the October meeting, news was received from the National Federation of Women's Institutes, which gave advice on the nature of war work that could be carried out by branches throughout the country and Mr Prideaux of Trumps Ltd gave the first of many talks about growing vegetables in gardens. In November 1939, the WI offered to 'blackout' Marwood school, which would enable them to use it for fund-raising events, dances and other evening entertainments to raise spirits.

Members of the Institute volunteered to prepare parcels for all local men serving in the forces. A Parcel fund was organised and various activities such as knitting items for soldiers and regular fund-raising whist drives were arranged. At a meeting in December 1939, Miss Mattinson asked for helpers to pack the parcels to ensure they would be received before Christmas. The soldiers were very grateful for the supplies and each year they wrote to the Institute to express their thanks. The kind ladies also worked hard to make garments for evacuees who arrived in 1940, some of whom were short of clothing. They also arranged Christmas parties for them with entertainments and a special tea.

In March 1940, Mrs Winnie Born proposed that the WI funds should be put into war bonds, one of a number of Government managed National Savings schemes that were established during the First World War to raise capital to fund military operations. It was unanimously agreed and arranged by May 31 and by the end of February 1941, parish council minutes reveal that the WI had saved over one hundred and twenty pounds.

In almost every town in Britain, local savings weeks were held to encourage people to save money for the war effort, normally with specific themes designed to encourage patriotism and help civilians feel directly involved. Targets were set locally and every year, events were held including parades and military bands. In addition to the WI savings group were the Marwood school, New Inn and Parish savings groups in Marwood.

During 'War Weapons Week' in 1941, Marwood WI set a target of one hundred pounds to pay for a machine gun. The industrious ladies surpassed their goal, raising one hundred and twenty-eight pounds. In March 1942, they were busily preparing to raise money for 'Warships Week', planning a concert and other entertainments, eventually raising five hundred and twenty-five pounds. In March 1943, the ladies set the target of two hundred and fifty pounds for 'Wings for Victory' week, which aimed to raise money towards a Spitfire, Lancaster or Wellington bomber. By the end of that year they had achieved the incredible sum of over one thousand three hundred pounds, earning them a certificate of honour from the National Savings Campaign.

THIS

CERTIFICATE OF HONOUR

IS AWARDED TO

MARWOOD WOMENS INSTITUTE

SAVINGS GROUP

IN RECOGNITION OF SPECIAL ACHIEVEMENT

DURING THE

WINGS FOR VICTORY

NATIONAL SAVINGS CAMPAIGN 1943

I EXTEND MY THANKS TO ALL CONCERNED IN THIS IMPORTANT NATIONAL SERVICE.

Archibald Sinclair

SECRETARY OF STATE FOR AIR

Above: The WI worked tirelessly to raise funds to support the war effort.

North Devon Journal - September 26 1940.
Marwood Spitfire Effort

Thanks to the children of Kings Heanton, Marwood, the villagers of that hamlet, and of Prixford and Middle Marwood were entertained to a Carnival, and the Spitfire Fund was augmented by no less than 5 pounds. The procession was marshalled by Mrs Alford, and those taking part were Sally and Joseph Barr, Beryl and David Pugsley, Marjorie Manning, Nan Webber, Lilian and Arthur Leverton, Derek Webber, Graham and Laurie Wright, Doris Baker, Sheila Born, Norman and Bernard Brooks, E Squire, Albert Cook, Mrs W Coates, Mrs Leverton, John Leverton, Mrs Brooks and Margaret Delve. Music was provided by accordions and the whole effort will be repeated at Muddiford and Milltown today (Thursday).

In 1944 all the local parish savings groups merged to form the Marwood Savings Committee. Various events were held in aid of the 'Salute the Soldier' campaign, including whist drives, a fancy dress dance and a concert by the Marwood Home Guard, with refreshments provided by the WI. At a parish council meeting it was confirmed that overall, they had raised the astonishing amount of six and a half thousand pounds, far surpassing their target of five thousand pounds and again earning them a certificate which was framed and hung in the parish room by Hugh Westcott of Kings Heanton.

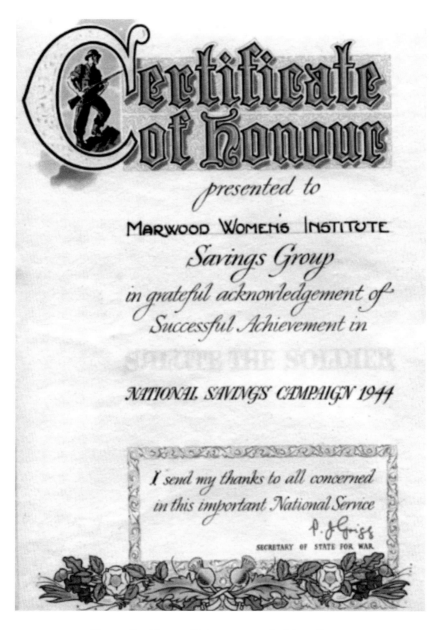

Above: Certificate of Honour awarded for efforts in
raising funds during the Savings Campaigns.

Over the war years, the parish council appealed to locals to grow as much fruit and vegetables as possible to supplement rations and Marwood WI invited speakers to attend their monthly meetings and share tips on managing households during shortages of food and clothing. In September 1940, Miss Smyth-Richards asked Marwood WI members to do all they could to preserve and save food and produce more winter vegetables, and in February 1941, Miss Lilton gave a talk on wartime cookery. In April, members decided to form a Fruit Preservation Centre, which involved gathering fruit grown in local gardens that would otherwise have been wasted and using it to make great quantities of jam or bottled fruit. This led to a three-day training programme to be set up for members to teach them how to make the most of the fruit they obtained. In August 1941 recipes were shared for making use of wild fruit or berries and several appeals were made for members to pick blackberries and rosehips, the latter being used for making syrup. Miss Coleman, a regular speaker from Devon County Council gave a demonstration on cheese making with small quantities of both fresh and sour milk, and talks on curing bacon and ham, which members found particularly helpful. In November 1942, the emphasis changed to coping with the recent introduction of clothing rations, with sewing classes arranged and demonstrations held on 'dress-making renovation' and 'make do and mend'.

Competitions were held to test members' thriftiness, setting challenges such as making a meal for three people at a cost of no more than sixpence; something new from something old; something made from oddments; a thrift garment; a meal made from potatoes and thrift Christmas presents. An independent visitor always judged entries, and regular winners were Kathleen Balment, Eva Mattinson and Florence Manning.

Above: During the war years the Marwood WI members were unable to continue with their annual outings due to petrol rationing, instead arranging picnics at nearby Pippacott. Mrs Blyth, Mrs Sadd and Miss Worth are amongst those pictured above.

Above: In July 1940 Marwood WI met at Townridden to celebrate with their oldest member, Mrs Ellison Worth and her husband William, on reaching their Diamond Wedding Anniversary. Mrs Worth later died in March 1945 aged ninety-one, sadly just a few months before the couple would have celebrated their 65th (Blue Sapphire) anniversary.

Above: Marwood WI often ran a stall selling homemade jams and chutneys, cakes, biscuits and home grown vegetables amongst other things. Mrs Batson and Mrs Vera Fairchild are pictured manning the stall at a Marwood fete in the 1950s.

The School Prepares for War

In the months before the war broke out, the parish council were asked to enrol in the proposed Government evacuation scheme. Councillors perused the electoral roll to identify suitable households in Marwood who could take evacuees if and when the need arose, and registration forms were sent to them. The council met to review the returned forms completed by householders, who gave particulars of the accommodation they could provide and various offers of cars to transport the children.

Britain officially entered the war in August 1939 during the school summer holidays, therefore the parish council instructed the headmaster to extend the closure of the school past the beginning of September, to enable preparation for the possible arrival of evacuees. In the first week of September, Mr Chugg, and his assistant teachers Miss Parkhouse and Mrs Ashton waited patiently for evacuees to arrive as part of 'Operation Pied Piper', a huge exercise that saw hundreds of thousands of children removed from British cities. Evidently this first wave of evacuees did not travel as far as North Devon, and on September 6 Mr Chugg was notified that now they should not expect any arrivals in the short term and that the school should reopen. On their first day back at school, the first job was to ensure the children knew how to wear their gas masks and much time was spent ensuring they fitted correctly. They also had plenty of practice in putting them on quickly although in the log book Mr Chugg noted his concerns that some children had not received their masks yet. Peter Gammon remembers being instructed to carry his gas mask with him at all times but when outside of school, most children left the hated masks at home.

In November 1939 Mrs Ada Brailey who farmed nearby, regrettably informed Mr Chugg that she could no longer allow the school to use one of her fields for outdoor games. As a farmer, the Government paid her an incentive for ploughing any grassland and fertilising it in preparation for crop planting, in order to maximise food returns. This was part of a scheme to steer the country to become more self-sufficient as quickly as possible, because at that time Britain had been reliant on imports for more than half of all its food.

On June 13 1940 Mr W Martin, Head Warden for Barnstaple Rural Areas, visited the school to ensure it was prepared for possible air raids. He suggested that 'windows should be cellophaned and porch windows reinforced with wire netting as the children would have to take shelter in the latter, seeing that we shall probably have no warning'. If they had time, the existing arrangement was to disperse the pupils along the lane, which Mr Martin thought was quite acceptable. The school set about making arrangements to net the windows but were only able to protect the glass in the porch and infants room initially due to a shortage of materials.

When the pupils broke up for their summer holidays at the end of July 1940, the teachers were instructed to keep the school open throughout, as this time evacuees would soon be expected. The teachers staggered their holidays so that there was always at least one member of staff present. Mr Chugg planned to take the first two weeks, however on August 8 his break was interrupted after he was notified that evacuees were on their way.

Home Guard

Anthony Eden, the Minister for War, initiated the Home Guard on May 14 1940. He appealed to the nation for men aged between seventeen and sixty-five to join a new force called the Local Defence Volunteers, 'who wish to do something for the defence of their country.' Many signed up straight away, including those who were too young or old to fight, in reserved occupations or deemed unfit to fight for medical reasons. Winston Churchill later renamed them the Home Guard, which he felt was a more fitting title.

At first what they lacked in equipment, they made up for in enthusiasm. The early patrols were carried out using pitchforks and broom handles, wearing simple armbands. After many months, they eventually received standard issue army uniforms and old rifles used in the First World War.

Above: Richard Brooks, c.1940.

Norman Brooks was living in Kings Heanton at the outbreak of the war, and remembers his father Richard joining the Home Guard. He was issued with a gun, which was a frighteningly unreliable weapon that could go off without the trigger being pulled! Having served in the First World War, Richard Brooks was keen to do his bit for the war effort and his main occupation between 1939 and 1945 was working as a steamroller driver on the construction of the 'American Road' from Vellator to Saunton Beach. This road was used by the American soldiers in rehearsal for the 'D-Day' landings.

Members of the Home Guard would train on Sunday mornings plus one evening per week, particularly focusing on how to use weapons. Captain Gladwell led the Bittadon and Muddiford men, who used the former Mission Church outside *Downlyn* as a base. Their rifle range was located in the field opposite *Sunnybank*, and on Sundays when they had shooting practice, it was often in front of an audience of excited boys including Peter Gammon and his friends. Lou Spear remembers the Prixford Home Guard used to have rifle practice at the old quarry behind the old Methodist Chapel, which he also loved to watch as a boy.

Harold Hopkins and Ernie Watts joined the Prixford and Guineaford Home Guard, led by Bob Harris of Varley, a veteran of the First World War.

An important role of the Marwood Home Guard was to man the searchlight battery in the field next to *Hillsview* in Guineaford. A number of nissen huts were erected in the upper end of the field to accommodate the British Artillery unit, but it was the responsibility of a Home Guard member to operate the searchlight each night, keeping watch for enemy planes overhead. If spotted, the guard had to focus the powerful beam of the searchlight onto the German plane to provide a target for the British fighter planes. Hilda Watts' parents Ellen and John Carter were living in *Hillsview* at that time, and they found their new neighbours to be very friendly and would often drop in for a cup of tea and a chat! Evidently the soldiers were also a hit with the Marwood Women's Institute as they were invited to join in their Christmas party in 1943!

Several locals remember one night the guard managed to successfully locate a German plane with the searchlight and the base came under fire. Bullets deflected off a nissen hut roof but fortunately no one was hurt. Afterwards it became a standing joke amongst the men that Marwood Home Guard had come under direct fire from the Germans! The next morning, Lou Spear's father found some empty bullet cartridges in his garden, which were believed to have come from the German plane.

Many parishioners can recall the drone of German planes heading for bombing raids on industrial areas of Swansea and other parts of South Wales, which meant the war never felt too far away. The hum of the planes served to remind locals of their duty to have black out curtains and if they allowed even a slither of light to show, they would receive a knock on the door from a member of the Home Guard.

Marwood Home Guard c.1940:
Back row: L-R includes Sam Braunton, Harry Perrin.
Front row: L-R Reuben Tamlyn, Capt Gladwell, Arthur Chapple, Mr Spear, Robert Harris.

Above: Reuben Tamlyn and
Jack Rashley, Muddiford.

Above: Sam Braunton,
Middle Marwood.

Right: When the Home
Guard was eventually
disbanded at the end of the
war, members were
awarded a certificate in
honour of their service.
Henry Balment of Milltown
was the proud recipient of
the certificate pictured right.

In the years when our Country
was in mortal danger

GEORGE HENRY BALMENT

who served from   May 1940 to 31st. Dec. 1944.
gave generously of his time and
powers to make himself ready
for her defence by force of arms
and with his life if need be.

George R.I.

THE HOME GUARD

Muddiford Home Guard 1940-1945
Back row L – R: F Tucker, C Kift, 2 instructors, W Gammon, A Tucker.
2nd from back row L – R: J Gould, T Balment, V Heal, A Smith, I Brailey.
3rd from back row L – R: A Gladwell, J Born, H Pugsley, H Couch, J Lethaby, H Perrin,
C Lethaby, Frank Smith, H Balment.
Front row L – R: W Karslake, F Spear, F Pugsley, J Rashley, R Tamlyn, F Smith,
W Blyth, K Spear, J Karslake.

*Marwood Home Guard members included: Henry Balment, Tom Balment, Alan Brailey,
Richard Brooks, Bill Blyth, John Born, Sam Braunton, Arthur Chapple, Arthur Coats, H
Couch, Walter Gammon, Captain Gladwell, J Gould, Bob Harris, Victor Heal, Harold Hopkins,
J Karslake, William Karslake, C Kift, James Lethaby, Charlie Lethaby, Harry Perrin, Fred
Pugsley, Herb Pugsley, Jack Rashley, Alan Smith, Frank Smith, Fred Smith, Frank Spear, Ken
Spear, Herb Tamlyn, Reuben Tamlyn, Arthur Tucker, Fred Tucker and Ernie Watts.*

Besides the Home Guard and Searchlight camp, the military was often present in and around Marwood. The army were regularly on manoeuvres around the parish and many locals can remember tanks passing up and down the once quiet lanes. Stella Money (nee Balment) was only a young child at the time and she was quite understandably petrified of the noisy vehicles. David Fairchild and Lou Spear remember the American GIs marching through Prixford and if they sat and held out their hands they'd be rewarded with a stick of chewing gum as the men passed by. David Pugsley recalled that sometimes his grandfather Charles would let passing soldiers rest on the hay in the rick yard and pick baskets of apples for them.

Evacuees

In July 1940, the first major bombing raids known as the Battle of Britain began, causing devastation in British cities. Although thousands of children had already been sent to the countryside, the raids prompted a new surge of evacuees, some of whom were scheduled to arrive in Marwood on August 8 1940. The school had been designated as an official receiving centre, so all teaching staff were required to be on hand to welcome the new arrivals and assist with their placements into homes around the parish. In return, the host families would receive a small allowance via the post office and the child's ration book. Forty-six evacuees were eventually allocated to local households in Muddiford, Milltown, Blakewell, Little Silver, Kings Heanton, Whiddon and Whitefield, but not before the Marwood Women's Institute had provided all the new arrivals with refreshments. In the months that followed, several hundred evacuees arrived and settled in Barnstaple and the surrounding parishes.

After scrutinising their new classmates, some of whom were just six years old, the Marwood children were interested to find they dressed differently and spoke with accents that they could barely understand. Pam Chapple (nee Balment) learned that her parents took in a nine year old girl named Betty who was evacuated from Willesden, North West London. Like many children, she had been put on a train with just a small suitcase and dispatched to an unfamiliar environment, which looked and sounded vastly different to the life she knew in the city.

Understandably, Betty found it extremely difficult to be parted from her family and it broke the heart of Pam's mother, Daisy Balment, who tried hard to comfort the young girl and help her to adjust to life in the country. Daisy told how she once found Betty at her bedroom window looking out into the night, saying that she could see her mother's face in the moon. Betty's mother wrote within a few days of her arrival in Milltown, evidently trying her best to reassure her young daughter, telling her that she was in a nice place, and keeping her in touch with day-to-day activities at home. Pam still has the letter, sent on August 13 1940 (shown overleaf).

Above:
Daisy Balment
c.1930s.

Sadly nothing could be done to comfort the poor child and within just one week of her arrival in the parish, it was agreed that Betty could return to her family. The trauma of separation was simply too much for her to cope with. An entry in the school log book showed that she returned home to be with her family in Willesden on August 16 1940, though it is frightening to think that the borough was heavily bombed during the years that followed.

Above: The touching letter written by Betty's mother in August 1940.

In addition to the unaccompanied children who were evacuated to Marwood, there were some entire families who fled the dangers of city life with some renting cottages in Kings Heanton. There were also eleven mothers who came with younger children. In January 1941 the parish were asked to give particulars of all properties, whether churches, chapels or large buildings, which could be used for temporary housing of people whose homes had been bombed, such was the need for accommodation.

Marwood School Adjusts to Wartime

The school opened for the autumn term on September 9 1940 and Mr Chugg was relieved to welcome London schoolmistress, Miss Woods, who was sent to help the staff at Marwood cope with the increase in pupils. Not long after arriving, Miss Woods received instructions from the County Education Office to report to Heathcoat School in Tiverton and two weeks later, replacement teacher Miss L. Rider arrived from London, and boarded with Mrs Born in Muddiford.

Due to the sheer number of evacuees in Marwood the school was unable to accommodate all the pupils in the existing building, so a temporary classroom was set up in Muddiford Congregational Church for the twenty-three pupils of Class Three, including both local and evacuee children. Mrs Ashton's infant class increased to thirty-nine pupils; Miss Parkhouse had twenty-seven pupils and Mr Chugg was responsible for the thirty-seven older pupils.

David Pugsley of Milltown was one of the pupils of Class Three who had to transfer to the church for his lessons. He remembered that Miss Rider would sneak to the kitchen area for a quick smoke when she thought no one was looking and if it was a nice day, she would take the class up the hill at lunchtime.

One group of evacuees were billeted at *Muddiford House* and David recalled that there was an outbreak of diphtheria there so they had to be isolated. To the dismay of the local children, all pupils had to be vaccinated as a precaution and the log book shows that this occurred in February 1941. Dr Harper of Barnstaple was called to administer the inoculations to over ninety children.

Older boys were allowed twenty-one half days off school each year to help the farmers with jobs like potato picking and harvesting during the war. They had to get the farmer to sign a blue card to prove they were working and not playing truant though! More often than not the farmers would need them for the whole day, and in return the boys would receive a good meal and a couple of shillings in wages.

In May 1942 the school was asked to investigate the possibility of introducing hot meals for the pupils. This had become a priority during the war as it was a means of ensuring the children received at least one nutritional meal each day, at a time when rations were thin. Arrangements were made to install the required fittings over the following months.

In August 1942 Mr Chugg left Marwood, after what he described as 'six happy years with the children of this district'. Mr Collier provided interim cover for a few months before new schoolmaster Mr Price began his duties in December 1942. By this time the number of pupils attending the school had fallen slightly from just over one hundred, to eighty-two pupils, as a result of a number of evacuees returning home. This meant the temporary classroom at Muddiford could be closed and all children brought back to the main school. As Christmas approached, the pupils were delighted to each receive a gift of a sixpenny war savings stamp and a festive card from Miss James of Marwood Hill, who also presented each member of staff with a new diary, a tradition that she was to continue for several years.

In January 1943 Mrs Jenkins was employed as a kitchen assistant as the plans for a new school canteen progressed. Mr Price was requested to calculate the number of pupils who were eligible to receive free school meals based upon certain income limits, and the canteen officially opened on January 18. Other children had to pay for their meals which meant for the first time they were required to bring money into school. Mr Price noted on January 29 that he had to perform 'a most unpleasant duty' to confront a young boy who had been stealing money from the children's coats in the cloakroom. He took him to the boy's mother, who managed to recover the eight shillings.

The War Draws to a Close
As the war years rolled by the school log book made fewer and fewer references to the impact of the war on the day-to-day life of the pupils. On June 6 1944, Mr Price recorded that on the occasion of D-Day, which marked the start of the allied invasion of Europe, he assembled the school together to hear the events broadcasted on the newly acquired school wireless and together they sang hymns and prayed for the armed forces. From this point onwards, the log book makes reference to various evacuees returning to their homes in Woking, Croydon, Deptford and other parts of London.

By May 1945, the war in Europe was finally over and the parish council was informed that expenditure could be incurred towards the cost of a celebration in Marwood. After a discussion, it was agreed that there was a stronger feeling of thanksgiving for the cessation of fighting rather than cause for celebration, until the war in Japan was over. A Peace Celebrations committee was elected, chaired by Reverend Rickett, which included Henry Balment, Vice-Chairman; Preston Pugsley, Treasurer; Samuel Lister James and John Born, Secretaries. The committee nominated collectors to ask parishioners to make a small contribution towards the cost of celebrations and the following were chosen to undertake this task: Bill Pengelly, Prixford/Longpiece and Blakewell; Harry Bourne, Guineaford and Kings Heanton; Frank Spear, Milltown and Muddiford; Fred Smith, Little Silver and Bill Lock, Muddiford.

The Committee agreed that as soon as the war with Japan had ceased and local men had been demobilised and returned home, a tea would be arranged for all the children in the parish and a day of thanksgiving and celebration for all parishioners would be held at a later date. They eventually raised funds in excess of one hundred pounds that went towards the celebrations and a Welcome Home fund for the returning soldiers of Marwood. The peace celebrations eventually took place on June 8 1946, attended by the parishioners of Marwood and Bittadon.

Certificate of Appreciation.

1939 ✿ 1945

ON behalf of the Victory Committee and the Parishioners of Marwood in the Rural District of Barnstaple, we hereby express to you

WILLIAM JOHN WATTS

our grateful appreciation of your patriotic service with the Allied Forces.

The achievements of those Forces under Divine Providence, have made possible the complete and glorious Victory in the Second World War for World Freedom and Liberty and the building of a New World, and we tender you our heartfelt thanks for assisting our Beloved King and Country in time of dire need.

W. Pengelly .... Chairman
Parish Council.

W. T. Rickett. .... Chairman
Victory Committee.

Dated 8 JUN 1945

S. J. Born. .... Secretary

Above: William John Watts (known as Jack) was one of the Marwood soldiers who were honoured with a 'Certificate of Appreciation' from the parish, for their patriotic service during the Second World War.

Marwood Men at War 1939-1945

All men aged between the ages of eighteen and thirty-nine were required to register their details with the Government, who decided whether they could best serve the country in the armed forces or by remaining in their current role. These became known as protected occupations and included farmers. In stark contrast to the First World War, this resulted in far fewer Marwood men being called up to fight. Amongst those who did sign up were Alan Harris, Jack Watts, John and Kenneth Gammon, Bill Lynch and Ernest Pratt. Other brave men who went to fight were Bill Lovering, Frederick Olive and John Balman but tragically, these three were killed close to the end of the war.

Service records of soldiers who served in the Second World War remain classified and retained by the Ministry of Defence. However, alternative sources of information have been compiled, including interviews with Marwood parishioners, North Devon Journal articles and some basic online records.

Driver Frederick W Olive *d. 14 June 1943, age 25.*

Frederick (b.1918) was raised by his father, Frank Olive ,because his mother Ann sadly died as a result of complications arising from his birth. Six years later, Frank married again and the family settled at no. 2 *Sunnybank*, Muddiford. Before the war, Frederick had been working for Mr P Ham, a furnisher based at the High Street in Barnstaple, and later signed up to join the Royal Army Service Corps. In August 1940, Frank received the disturbing news that his son had been made a prisoner of war in Germany. The ladies of Marwood WI forwarded parcels via the Red Cross to Frederick, but it was eventually learnt that he had died at his POW camp in North Poland in June 1943. He was laid to rest at Malbork Commonwealth War Cemetery and commemorated on the Marwood War Memorial.

Sapper William H Lovering *d. 29 October 1944, age 32.*

Bill was the son of James and Emily Lovering of *Lee Cottages*, Whitehall and had been working as a stonemason in Braunton before joining the Royal Engineers, 90th Field Company. Kathleen Harris remembers Bill came back to Marwood on brief furlough and when the time came for him to return, he asked if she would drive him to the railway station. She remembers that they were in the car and about to set off when Mr Dallyn stopped them. Knowing that Kathleen was heading into Barnstaple, he asked her to buy a pair of wellington boots for him - "size ten, size ten!" he said. Bill leaned over and said, "if Kath can't get size ten, will two size fives do?" That was the last time Kathleen saw Bill as he was killed in action on October 29 1944 in the province of Gelderland in the Netherlands. He was laid to rest in the Jonkerbos War Cemetery and commemorated on the Marwood War Memorial.

Sergeant John H Balman *d. 11 Dec 1944, age 19.*

John, the only son of John and Gertrude Balman, was an air gunner on a Lancaster Bomber (514 Squadron). Extracts from the Bomber Command war diary reveal that his crew left their base at RAF Waterbeach at 0833 on December 11 1944, heading for the Sterkrade-Holten oil plant, located within the heavily defended Ruhr Valley, Germany. After reaching their destination, they were hit by anti-aircraft flak and went down in a built up area of Sterkrade, destroying several houses. All seven crew members on board were killed: Pilot - Ellis Hill; Navigator - Reginald Cowles; Air Bomber - Frank Guest; Flight Engineer - Norman Readman; Flight Sgt - Cyril Atter; Air Gunners - Sgt John Balman and Sgt Alan Bowen. All were buried in the Reichswald Forest War Cemetery, close to the border with the Netherlands. John is also commemorated on the Marwood War Memorial.

Corporal Ernest Pratt

Several locals remember Ernest Pratt of Milltown (1912-2007) who used to have an engine repair shop in Muddiford some years ago, and later worked for British Gas in Barnstaple. Ernest was a member of the Royal Engineers during the Second World War, but in July 1940, his parents, Sidney and Mary Pratt received the distressing news that their son was missing in action. It may therefore, have come as some relief to hear a few months later that Ernest was alive although a prisoner of war, and on September 26 1940, the North Devon Journal reported that he was being held at a camp in Germany.

Just a few months later in January 1941 the Pratt family were struck by more devastating news. Whilst at work, Ernest's father had died as a result of a terrible accident, although exactly how he died remained something of a mystery due to media censorship. Today, locals disclose that Sidney was killed by a plane crash, yet due to Government imposed media censorship this could not be reported by the press at the time. Such censorship was part of an attempt to present a picture of life going on as normal in spite of the war, in order to preserve morale. After Sidney's death, an inquest was held and the proceedings were reported in the North Devon Journal. It was confirmed that he was employed as a road sweeper for Devon County Council and was working on the North Road near Westaway, Pilton, when the accident happened. The inquest recorded that there were no witnesses, although today, locals recall that Milltown man, Ernest Gammon had been talking to Sidney, just moments before the crash and was fortunate to have escaped injury himself. Help arrived on the scene quickly after the accident, and Sidney was taken to the North Devon Infirmary, where he died shortly afterwards. At the inquest, the cause of his death was given as 'severe head injuries and shock due to burns', which would under normal circumstances prompt a major investigation, however the verdict of 'accidental death' was given and the matter was drawn to a close.

Meanwhile, it was ascertained that Ernest was detained at a prisoner of war camp in Cieszyn, Poland (Stalag 8B) where he remained for the majority of the war, hopefully finding some comfort in the Red Cross parcels organised by the Marwood WI.

In January 1945, under German orders, Ernest was amongst hundreds of thousands of prisoners of war, who were force-marched across Europe, ahead of the advancing Russian army. He later told of the extreme hardship faced by the soldiers, many of whom died along the way, falling down at the roadside as they trudged along. Conditions were freezing and food was scarce as they were marched through Czechoslovakia to Bavaria. Fortunately Ernest survived the ordeal and shortly afterwards his camp was liberated by the Russians.

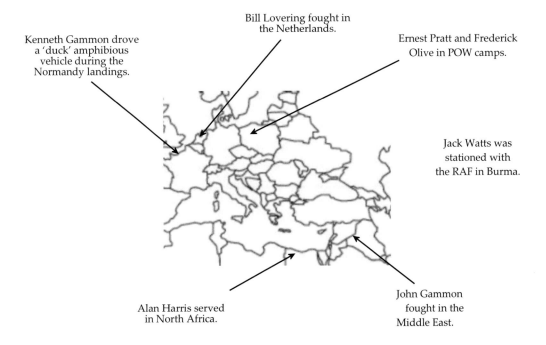

Bill Lovering fought in the Netherlands.

Kenneth Gammon drove a 'duck' amphibious vehicle during the Normandy landings.

Ernest Pratt and Frederick Olive in POW camps.

Jack Watts was stationed with the RAF in Burma.

Alan Harris served in North Africa.

John Gammon fought in the Middle East.

Above: Marwood men at War in Europe, Middle East & Africa 1939-1945.

In the space of two decades, Britain had found herself at war with Germany on two occasions, entering into global conflicts that made the twentieth century one of the most brutal in history. Mercifully, since 1945, any British involvement in military operations has caused negligible impact on life at home. They have been fought by fully trained military career personnel, rather than young men from farms and factories, mines and shipyards, who were eager or conscripted to fight for their country.

Many Marwood men fought bravely for King, Queen and Country, between the years of 1899 and 1945. Thirty men made the ultimate sacrifice and it is hoped that recording their stories in this chapter, will help ensure that their great courage is never forgotten.

On Reflection ....

And so to reflect on the contrasts between life in previous centuries and the way we live today. I'll start in Chapter Two, where we gained a snapshot of Guineaford in the 1850s:

> Imagine the small hamlet of Guineaford in the 1850s, with John Geen, the blacksmith hammering at his forge by the bridge. The familiar smell of sawdust emerges from workshops just a few yards up the road towards Prixford; where his brother William is busy with the saw and the plane. Francis Fairchild stands outside his inn, surveying the busy scene as he puffs on his pipe. John Marshall has opened up the post office for business, and Mrs Slocombe, the grocer, is selling her wares from the comfort of her own home. Local children hurry by, on their way to the Church school, passing the women chatting as they fill their pails with water from the spring, ready for the day's chores.

Today there is still a farmer, a carpenter and a schoolmistress who live and work locally, but the vast majority of the inhabitants of Guineaford and indeed any other Marwood hamlet must now travel beyond the parish for their employment. The once bustling hamlets are now dormant during the day and the peace is only disturbed by the cars that pass through to the towns of Ilfracombe or Barnstaple - for this reason most children are no longer able to walk to school due to concerns over road safety. We no longer need to leave our houses to fetch water as we are supplied by the mains and the local supermarkets will deliver the weekly shop to our doorsteps. As a result, opportunities to maintain regular contact with our neighbours inevitably decrease especially in the winter months, yet the sense of community still remains strong in Marwood.

The other most striking revelation in the lives of our ancestors seen throughout this narrative has been the hardship and distress experienced by the poor. During the nineteenth century some Marwood families faced serious poverty and it is almost impossible to imagine how they coped on such meagre incomes, reliant upon the overseers of the poor to provide essentials such as the next pair of shoes or a blanket for the winter months. Many families had to provide for as many as ten children, and the harsh reality of having to release them for apprenticeships as soon as they reached the age of nine must have been heart-breaking for both parent and child. It is in fact uncomfortable to imagine what their lives were like, and certainly the thought of any nine year old being forced into service or labour to us, is quite disturbing.

By the time we reach the late nineteenth and early twentieth century, on the whole living conditions had begun to improve bringing us to a period that some still yearn for due to its apparent simplicity and slower pace. It brought the beginnings of formal school education, acceptance of the diversity in Christian faith and continuing progress in farming methods. It was still tough to make ends meet, but families were thrifty and managed to support themselves and each other through difficult times and the war years.

The Victorian era also brought about an increase in leisure time creating innocent pleasures such as the annual Sunday school trip to Woolacombe in the charabanc and the concerts where local characters would perform musical numbers. By the 1890s, these activities were becoming popular in Marwood, and were particularly well chronicled in the *Marwood Church Monthly* newsletters. People from every corner of the parish would unite to celebrate national events such as coronations and jubilees, and the fellowship that was nurtured within the churches and chapels, helped to extend the sense of community.

Many parishioners who grew up in Marwood between the 1920s and 1940s remember that families remained strong because future generations were able to settle in affordable homes in close proximity rather than seek pastures new. They have fond memories of life before the introduction of mains electricity and water, before televisions and telephones became 'must have' items in every home and before it was the norm for every household to own at least one car. Children made their own entertainment and spent as much time as possible in the great outdoors. Harold Hopkins, Peter Gammon, David Fairchild, Norman Brooks and Lou Spear have all described how they spent their halcyon days playing in the open fields, hedges, woods and streams.

Having now written thousands of words and added hundreds of images, it would be nice to think this book gives a comprehensive record of life in Marwood parish between 1840 and 1950. The truth is - there is so much more to tell, much more than can be captured within a single volume.

We are yet to explore the great Marwood tradition of ploughing matches, the sports events, celebrations of coronations and jubilees of former monarchs and the hamlets which are yet to give up their secrets such as Whitehall, Patsford and Blakewell, not to mention the many families who have lived in the parish for generations that have yet to share their stories. There are the amusing tales of petty crimes and misdemeanours which were part of life in the parish, the beginnings of the Marwood Women's Institute, the legends, the concerts performed by locals ... the list goes on. It is often said that an author has to draw the line somewhere, but the yearning to continue the journey remains. There are always clues and reminders of days gone by that stir up the imagination and entice us to open the door to the past.

Over the last year as I have researched and written this book, I have learnt so much about this parish and been privileged to meet so many people who have welcomed me and my family, and made us feel we belong, like never before. Now I can only hope that you have enjoyed reading it as much as I have enjoyed researching it!

A.L.B

Agreement for the enclosure and division of Whiddon Common between John Nicholetts, Frances Drake, Anne, Harriet and Emma Cutcliffe, Thomas Carder and John Gould - 30 August 1850. Transcribed from digital images of the original in North Devon Record Office (ref. B142-1/209) by Desmond Painter, July 2007.

Articles of Agreement indented made and concluded upon this Thirtieth day of August in the year of our Lord one thousand eight hundred and Fifty

Between John Nicholetts of South Petherton in the County of Somerset Esquire of the First part Frances Drake of Springfield within the Parish of Heanton Punchardon in the County of Devon Widow and Anne Cutcliffe and Harriet Elizabeth Cutcliffe both of Hudscott in the Parish of Chittlehampton in the said County of Devon Spinsters and Emma Cutcliffe of Ilfracombe in the said County of Devon Spinster of the second Part Thomas Carder of Marwood in the said County of Devon Yeoman of the third part and John Gould of Marwood aforesaid Cordwainer of the Fourth part

Whereas the said John Nicholetts is lawfully seised and interested to him and his Heirs of and in Thirty equal and undivided Sixty two parts or shares the whole into Sixty Two equal parts or shares to be considered as divided of and in All that undivided Common Field or Moor commonly called or known by the name of Whidden otherwise Whiddon otherwise Weeding Common or Moor situate lying and being in the Parish of Marwood aforesaid and the said Frances Drake Anne Cutcliffe Harriet Elizabeth Cutcliffe and Emma Cutcliffe are lawfully seised and Interested to them and their heirs of and in Twenty Two other equal undivided Sixty Two parts or shares the whole into Sixty Two equal parts or shares to be considered as divided of and in the said undivided Common Field or Moor commonly called or known by the name of Widden otherwise Whiddon or otherwise Weeding Common or Moor and the said Thomas Carder is lawfully seised and interested to him and his Heirs of and in eight other equal undivided Sixty Two parts or shares the whole into Sixty Two equal parts or shares to be considered as divided of and in the said undivided Common Field or Moor commonly called or known by the name of Widden otherwise Whiddon otherwise Weeding Common or Moor

And the said John Gould is lawfully seised and interested to him and his Heirs of and in the remaining Two parts or shares the whole into Sixty Two equal parts or shares to be considered as divided of and in the said undivided Common Field or Moor commonly called or known by the name of Widden otherwise Whiddon otherwise Weeding Common or Moor

And Whereas the Lands lying in the said Common Field or Moor aforesaid have for many years past yielded but little or no profit and the same are every year more and more worn out and impoverished for want of due tillage and manure for remedying which and for encouraging the improvement of the said lands for the general benefit and advantage of themselves and of the community at large all and every the said Parties hereto have agreed to make a division and allotment of the said Common Field or Moor amongst themselves in such manner as hereinafter is expressed

Now These Presents Witness that it is hereby concluded and agreed upon by and between all and every the said Parties hereto and each of them doth accordingly, for himself and herself for his and her Heirs Executors and administrators agree with and to each and every of the other of them and his her and their heirs Executors Administrators and assigns by these presents in the manner and form following (that is to say) that a division and separation by metes and bounds and an enclosure by hedges and Fences of the lands and Tenements lying in the said common Field or moor called Widden otherwise Whiddon otherwise Weeding Common or Moor shall be forthwith made by Thomas Parminter of Westdown in the said County of Devon Gentleman and by him allotted and assigned to and amongst the several parties hereto at their own expence costs and charges according to their respective interests in such manner as hereinafter is provided and which enclosures and divisions by boundary stones shall from time to time be renewed preserved and continued for ever

And all and every of the said parties shall hold and enjoy his her or their share or portion so to be allotted to him her or them respectively of the said Common Field or Moor in severalty and as several and distinct parcels thereof with full liberty to plough manure and cultivate the same at pleasure as a separate and distinct Farm and shall have and enjoy the same Estate and Interest in the part so to be allotted to them respectively as they now have or at or immediately before the time of such division or allotment had in the parts or parcels of the said common Lands in lieu whereof such allotments were made and that after such allotments shall be made and hedges and Fences erected and divisions by boundary stones set out every of them the said parties hereto shall at their own respective costs and charges at all times thereafter keep the said hedges and Fences in good and proper repair and divisions by boundary stones properly set out **And** for the more just and impartial execution and performance of the said division and allotment it is hereby agreed that the said Thomas Parminter shall make the same by admeasurement survey and otherwise as he shall think fit in making which allotments and divisions due regard shall be had by the said Thomas Parminter to the quality and situation as well as the quantity of Land to be assigned or allotted and also to the assigning and allotting the same so as that every of the allotments to each of the said parties may be as nearly contiguous to each other as may be and who shall also assign allot and make proper convenient and sufficient roads and ways for every of the said parties to their respective allotments and also proper convenient and sufficient Highroads or Highways in such place and places and in such directions as shall appear to him the said Thomas Parminter to be most fit or convenient for the same which Roads and ways Highroads or Highways shall be allowed out of the whole of the said common Field or Moor according to the proportion thereof belonging belonging to each of the said Parties hereto the expences of making such Highroads or Highways it is hereby agreed shall be borne by the said parties hereto in proportion to their respective allotments

And for the preventing disputes and differences regarding the said several divisions or allotments each and every of the said parties hereto doth hereby further agree in the manner aforesaid from time to time and at all times hereafter to abide by observe and perform all and every the orders directions determinations and judgments which shall from time to time be had made or given by the said Thomas Parminter touching and concerning the same and other the matters and things hereinbefore mentioned or referred to

And it is hereby further agreed that after the said allotments and division shall be made and perfected the same and the situation and number of acres or other quantities thereof and the parties to whom the same shall be made and the number of acres or quantities of Land in lieu of which the same were made shall be put into writing at the expence of the said parties hereto and which said writing shall be enrolled at the next general Quarter Sessions or some subsequent General Quarter Sessions to be holden for the said County of Devon there to be preserved for the inspection and benefit of all parties to be at any time interested therein **And** it is hereby Further declared and agreed that after the said allotments and divisions shall be made and perfected each and every of the said parties hereto shall if required convey and assure to the other and others of them at their own costs and charges in all things his her and their respective Estates rights and Interests preparing this agreement and of carrying the same into execution and all other costs charges and expences incidental thereto shall be paid borne and discharged by all the said Parties hereto in proportion to their respective shares or Interests in the said Common Field or Moor

And it is hereby Further declared and agreed that this agreement shall be deposited in the Hands of John Henry Toller Solicitor Barnstaple for the benefit of all and every the said Parties hereto but that attested or other copies or extracts from the same may be at any time or times hereafter obtained by all or any of the said Parties hereto at the expence of the person or persons requiring the same and for the due and punctual performance of all and singular the covenants and agreements hereinbefore contained by the said Parties hereto each of them doth bind himself and herself and his and her Heirs Executors and Administrators in the sum of Five hundred Pounds to be paid unto such of them respectively his her or their Heirs Executors or Administrators as the said Thomas Parminter shall direct or appoint in that behalf and it is hereby further declared and agreed by and between the said Parties to these Presents that all that part of the said common Field or Moor lying on the Eastern or lower side of a line drawn from the south Western Corner of an Enclosure called or commonly known by the name of Robbins's Garden to the north Eastern Corner of an Enclosure called or known by the name of Grubbs Garden shall be excluded from these presents and left as an undivided Common in Consequence of a certain Quarry of Stone called or commonly known by the name of Milltown Quarry being situated therein And it is hereby lastly declared and agreed by and between the said Parties to these Presents that the Enclosures set forth in the Schedule hereunder written shall be treated and dealt with by the said Thomas Parminter as unenclosed Lands and divided separated enclosed and allotted and Assigned accordingly

In Witness whereof the said Parties to these Presents have hereunto set their hands and seals the day and year first before written

The Schedule above referred to

Names of Enclosures	Quantities (be the same more or less)			Tenants	To Whom
	A	R	P		
Potato Garden			2	George Summerwill	The above named Parties of the 1st and 2nd parts
Three Corner Kot		2	40	John Mitchell	Do. 3rd and 4th parts
Carders Potato Garden		2		Thomas Carder	The above named Parties of the 1st 2nd 3rd 4th parts
Drakes 40 acres		1	20	Samuel Boone	The above named Parties of the 2nd Part
Gubbs Garden		2		Thomas Bament	The above named Parties of the 1st 2nd 3rd 4th parts
Nicholetts's Forty Acres		40		William Robbins	The above named John Nicholetts
Johns Harvey Park	1			Thomas Isaac	The above named John Nicholetts

John L.S. Nicholetts　　　　　*Anne L.S. Cutcliffe*　　　　　*Thomas L.S. Carder*
Frances L.S. Drake　　　　　*Harriett Eliz. L.S. Cutcliffe*　　　　　*John L.S. Gould*
　　　　　　　　　　　　Emma L.S. Cutcliffe

Signed sealed and delivered by the within named　　　Signed Sealed and Delivered by the within named
John Nicholetts in the presence of　　　　　　　Thomas Carder and John Gould in the presence of

　　　John T Nicholetts　　　　　　　　　　*Jno Henry Toller, Solr.*
　　　of South Petherton Gentleman　　　　　Barnstaple

Signed Sealed and Delivered by the within named
Frances Drake, Anne Cutcliffe, Harriett
Elizabeth Cutcliffe and Emma Cutcliffe
in the presence of

　　　C. Cutcliffe Drake
　　　of Springfield Devon Gentleman

Dated 30th August 1850
Agreement
Between the Parties within named to a Division and
Enclosure of All that Common called Whiddon
Common situate in the Parish of Marwood Devon

- *Appendix B* -
Former Patrons of Marwood

Patrons	Details	Clergy
Henry de Tracy Patronage 1263 - 1274	Baron of Barnstaple in 1213 and Governor of Lundy. His ancestors were in possession of Barnstaple Castle. On his death, his heir was granddaughter Maud, who at the time was married to Geoffrey de Camville.	**Thomas Payn**
Maud (Matilda) & Geoffrey de Camville Patronage 1274 - 1308	Maud inherited the Manor of Tawstock and the patronage, a title that passed down generations along with Marwood, Holne and several other estates. Maud first married Sir Nicholas Martin, and their first-born son was named William. After the death of Sir Nicholas, she married Geoffrey de Camville, but she died soon after in 1279. Maud's son William Martin succeeded her grandfather as Baron of Barnstaple, and Maud's own inheritance.	**Thomas de Dynham** **Roger de Dynham**
William Martin **Eleanor Martin & Philip de Columbars** Patronage 1308 – 1346	First Baron of Combe Martin, married to Eleanor Fitz Piers. William was frequently summoned to do military service in Wales and Scotland, and in return in 1293 the King gave him a charter for a fair at Marwood and 'free warren' at Dartington and Combe Martin (the privilege to kill game in a certain area, usually a small forest.) After the death of his stepfather, Geoffrey de Camville in 1308, he succeeded the inheritance of his mother. In 1321, he was ordered to attack anyone who might rise against the King in Devon and Cornwall, though shortly afterwards he died in 1326. William's eldest daughter Eleanor was married to Philip de Columbars, First Baron of Nether Stowey, Somerset, and his youngest daughter Joane, married Sir Nicholas de Audley, naming their first born son, Sir James de Audley. After William Martin's death, his only son and heir died shortly afterwards, leaving the Barony of Martin in abeyance between his eldest daughter Eleanor and her nephew, Sir James de Audley.	**William Bloyou**, former Canon of Exeter, who later exchanged benefices with **William de Benetfeld**, of Camborne **Baldwin Aillemer**
James, Lord de Audley Patronage 1346 -1392	Upon the death of his uncle William Martin, James, aged just three years, became co-heir with his aunt, Eleanor. On Eleanor's death, he became sole heir. In 1348, he was arrested for failing to attend the King and Council when summoned. His eldest son and heir Nicholas, died without issue, therefore the inheritance was eventually succeeded by James' grandson, Fulk Fitzwarren.	**John Lycoryz**, exchanged benefices with **William Warthecope**

Patron	Details	Clergy
Elizabeth & Fulk Fitzwarren Patronage 1392 - 1403	Fulk Fitzwarren, of Whittington, Bere Charterie, Holne, Marwood, Nymet Tracey, Tawstock and Upexe, Devon married Elizabeth Cogan, but died age 29 in 1391. In 1392, Elizabeth remarried Sir Hugh Courtenay. They had no surviving issue. She died in 1397 and after the death of Sir Hugh; the estates went to the crown.	**Hamund de Brereton**
King Henry IV Patronage 1403 - 1406	The Episcopal Registers of Bishop Stafford – Exeter Diocese (1395-1419) record that between 1403 and 1406, **King Henry IV** possessed the patronage of Marwood and two-thirds of the manor of Tawstock, near Barnstaple (Pipe Roll, Devon, 7 H. IV.), lately belonging to Sir Fulk Fitzwarren. The King presented his personal chaplains, John Kyngton and Thomas Chauntrell.	**John de Kyngton** (clerk to the King), exchanged benefices with **Thomas Chauntrell**, Canon of St Martins Church, London
Fitzwarren Family **Elizabeth Fitzwarren & Richard Hankford** **Thomasine Hankford** Patronage 1420 - 1455	Fulk Fitzwarren's sister Elizabeth became the rightful heir, and married Sir Richard Hankford of Annery. Their daughter Thomasine gained the title of 8th Baroness Fitzwarren, through courtesy of her late mother, and later married William Bourchier, who was given the title of Baron Fitzwarren, Their first-born son and heir, Fulk Bourchier, became 9th Lord Fitzwarren.	**John Plommer** **William Hammond**
The Fitzwarrens **The Bourchiers, Earls of Bath** (from 1536) **The Bourchier Wreys** Patronage 1455 - 1715	Reverend Collison noted that the Earls of Bath were patrons from 1536, when John Bourchier, son of Fulk the 9th Lord, as awarded the title by Henry VIII. The family presented Simon Canham, Oliver Naylor and Richard Downe as clergy for St Michael & All Angels, both also being chaplains to the Earls, and Rectors of Tawstock and Marwood, both the Earls' seats	**Robert Frannces** **Richard Bryte** **John Pykeryng** **John Beaupul** **Robert Bulpayne** **John Shilston** **Simon Canham** **Oliver Naylor** **Richard Downe** **William Bourchier** **William Stuckey** **John Sommers** **Richard Harding**

Bibliography - Texts

Barratt, Nick *Who Do You Think You Are - Encyclopaedia of Genealogy* (2008)

Bartlett, Tom *Postcard Views of North Devon Volume II (1988)*

Beckett, John David *A Village Childhood - Bratton Fleming 1939-1945* (2006)

Blome, Bertil *Place names of North Devon* (1929)

Bridges, Emma Augusta *Not Many Years Ago, Memories of My Life* (1881)

Brock, Bob and Ann *From Cradle to Grave 1900-1919* (2002)

Christie, Peter *Even more North Devon History* (1998)

Copper, Frank Raymond *The Braunton Boys Who Went to War* (1998)

Coulter, James *Tawstock & The Lords of Barnstaple* (1996)

Cresswell, Beatrix F. *Devon Churches in the Deanery of Barnstaple - Marwood* (1924)

Fowler, Simon *Researching Brewery and Publican Ancestors* (2009, 2nd edn)

Friar, Stephen *The Local History Companion* (2001)

Gale, John et al *Watermills in North Devon* (1995)

Gatty, Margaret Scott *The Book of Sundials* (1900, 4th edn)

Gill, Anton & Barratt, Dr Nick *Trace your family history back to the Tudors* (2006)

Gover, JEB, Mawer, A and Stenton, FM *The Place Names of Devon* (1931)

Harris, Helen *Devon's Century of Change* (1998)

Hey, David *How Our Ancestors Lived* (2002)

Horn, Pamela *The Victorian & Edwardian Schoolchild* (1989)

Hoskins, WG *Devon* (1954)

Kentisbury Catalogue Steering Group *The Kentisbury Catalogue* (2000)

Larrea, Ruth *Memories of Barnstaple Cattle Market* (2003)

Lauder, Rosemary *Devon families* (2002)

Parracombe Archaelogy and History Society *Parracombe and the Heddon Valley* (2004)

Pearse, Colin *Mill to Mill and Stook to Flour* (2008)

Porter, Valerie *Yesterday's Countryside* (2006)

Reader's Digest *Explore your family's past* (2001)

Reed, Paul *The complete guide to Military Records* (2010)

Rubens, Godfrey *Lethaby* (1986)

Salter, Mike *The Old Parish Churches of Devon* (1999)

Sellman, R.R *Marwood Board School in the Nineteenth Century - report* (1964)

Shakespeare, Liz *The Memory be green - An oral history of a Devon village* (1990)

Stanes, Robin *Old Farming Days - Life on the land in Devon and Cornwall* (2005)

Stone, Avril *The Book of High Bickington - A Devon Ridgeway Village* (2000)

The ArchBishop of York et al *The Church Monthly 1894-1905 An Illustrated Magazine*

Toyne, Shan *Devon Privies - A nostalgic trip down the garden path* (1998)

Trubshaw, Bob *How to Write and Publish Local History* (1999)

Bibliography - Websites

http://.www.history.wisc.edu/sommerville/123/123%20week12.htm

http://en.wikipedia.org/wiki/Battle_of_Delville_Wood

http://en.wikipedia.org/wiki/British_Agricultural_Revolution

http://en.wikipedia.org/wiki/Charters_Towers,_Queensland#Town_layout

http://en.wikipedia.org/wiki/Chlorodyne

http://en.wikipedia.org/wiki/HMS_Highflyer_(1898)

http://en.wikipedia.org/wiki/Nunc_dimittis

http://en.wikipedia.org/wiki/William_Lethaby

http://www.1914-1918.net/recruitment.htm

http://www.bbc.co.uk/history/british/britain_wwtwo/evacuees_01.shtml

http://www.bradshawfoundation.com

http://www.british-history.ac.uk/report.aspx?compid=50550

http://www.british-history.ac.uk/report.aspx?compid=66654

http://www.britishlistedbuildings.co.uk/en-98208-the-chapel-marwood

http://www.buildinghistory.org/buildings/parsonages.shtml

http://www.celtic-casimir.com/webtree/14/36160.htm

http://www.charitycommission.gov.uk/Showcharity/RegisterOfCharities

http://www.charterstowers.qld.gov.au/web/guest/visitors/world_history.shtml

http://www.churchsociety.org/issues_new/churchlocal/iss_churchlocal_jargon.asp

http://www.cwgc.org/debt_of_honour.asp?menuid=14

http://www.educationengland.org.uk/history/timeline

http://www.explorenorthdevon.org/media/wink/Yeoman%20F%20W%20Davey.pdf

http://www.foda.org.uk/visitations/1779/Chanter232A/Marwood.htm

http://www.geneajourney.com/audley.html

http://www.gwydir.demon.co.uk/jo/units/length.htm

http://www.history.ac.uk/cmh/gaz/devon.html#Mar

http://www.historylearningsite.co.uk/rationing_and_world_war_one.htm

http://www.historyonthenet.com/Medieval_Life/feudalism.htm

http://www.lerwill-life.org.uk/history/ndevmap.htm

http://www.london-gazette.co.uk

http://www.lostbombers.co.uk/

http://www.medieval-life-and-times.info/medieval-life/medieval-fairs.htm

http://www.methodist.org.uk/index.cfm?fuseaction=opentogod.content&cmid=1525

http://www.muddifordinn.com/history.php

http://www.naval-history.net

http://www.northdevon-aonb.org.uk/pdf/lac002.pdf

http://www.pdavis.nl/ShowShip.php?id=56

http://www.thepeerage.com/p4728.htm#i47272

http://www.traditionalmusic.co.uk/folksw/001853

http://www.visionofbritain.org.uk

http://www.ww2f.com/air-war-western-europe-1939-1945

Bibliography - North Devon Record Office & Athenaeum

North Devon Athenaeum

Muddiford Congregational Church, J Ticehurst *726.5/MUD/TicP & 900 MAR TIC DP*

Colonel Harding's Manuscripts *H95A.62*

Memories of my part of North Devon, William Lynch *MSS-B08-92 D*

Sketch books by William Richard Lethaby, 1896 *B70c-05-11*

North Devon Record Office

North Devon Journal Archives

Commercial Directory and Gazetteer of Devonshire 1872

Kelly's Devonshire Directory 1893

Kelly's Devonshire Directory 1902

Kelly's Devonshire Directory 1906

Kelly's Devonshire Directory 1935

Kelly's Devonshire Directory 1951

Kelly's Directory of Barnstaple and Neighbourhood 1941

North Devon Journal archive: 1823 - 2000

Post Office Devonshire Directory 1856

White's Devonshire Directory 1878

White's Directory 1850

Account book, list of church wardens 1801-1870 *3398A/PW1*

Church Wardens minutes *3398A/PO1-4*

Annual Vestry Minutes *3398-4/102*

Blue Ball Inn, Marwood 1796 - sale of land *1142B/EN2*

Charities Commission 1853-1989 *3398-4/108-141*

Charities Commission 1853-1989 *3398-4/179-200*

Churchwardens Account book 1825 - 1871 3398A/PW 1

Covenant for merging of tithes - Rev Riley 1839 *1142B/SS1/16*

Daphne Drake - Marwood Parish Notes c.1940. *Marwood parish file.*

Devon Extracts 1665-1850 Vol.1 Part 2 L - Z *070 B LON*

Dobbs photographs *B900/4*

Emily Alford's account books 1940-1949, sales of stock & milk, wages *NRA 34402*

Glebe Terrier at Marwood *3398-4./12 & 3398/114/266*

Historical Notes of Devon Schools, Devon County Council - Robert Bovett

Letter from Rev FW Collison re: school in Marwood *B6Z/19/1-3 & B6Z/11/2/3*

Marwood Baptisms 1881-1985 *3398-A/PR/1/13*

Marwood Burials 1881 - 1986 *3398-2/PR2*

Marwood Collecting and deposit book 1888-1895 *B8A/6/1-5*

Marwood County Primary School Log books & administration *2315C EFL 1-10*

Marwood Domesday Book 1910 *3201/1/122*

Marwood Marriages 1837 - 1983 *33981-1*

Marwood Parish Apprenticeships 1773-1842 *3398/PO1 & PO2*

Marwood Parish Council meeting minutes 1894 - 1985 *B8A/1/1-5*
Marwood Poor Rate Book 3398A/PO 1 *1800 - 1823*
Marwood Tithe Map *B8A/9 & B8A/10*
Methodist Chapel minutes 1873-1874 *2347-16/23*
Methodist Chapel minutes 1882 *2347/125*
Methodism in Marwood *B513/103*
National School plans *BZ6/19/1*
North Devon Inn Deeds *B5222/1-11*
Plan of Church Chancel 1938 *3398-4./18*
Poem - 'Farewell to Marwood' by E.W.B., May 1900 *3398-4/270*
Queen's Jubilee at Marwood *3398-4./266*
Removal order for Wilkeys 1830 *3255 - 2/29*
Richard Wilkey Apprenticeship agreement *3398-4/100*
Schedule of fixtures in Rectory July 1900 *3398-4./17*
The Episcopal Registers of the Diocese of Exeter - vol.8 1395-1419
Vestry Journal *3398-4/266*
Vestry minutes 1827-1855 *to be donated to NDRO*
Vestry minutes 1870-1913 *3398A/PV1*
Vestry minutes 1916-1948 *3398-4/102*

Other Resources
Lecture notes of James Ambler Smart (1999)
Eulogy - Dr Smart, by John Snowdon (2002)
Victorian Medal of Honour Presentation Speech (1994)
Muddiford Congregation Church Anniversary Service Hymn Sheet (1882)
Muddiford & Milltown verse (1943)
The ledgers of Fred J Kelly (1903-1940s)
The minutes of the Marwood Women's Institute (1932-1968)
The Official Census Returns of England & Wales (1841-1911)

Index

L

M

Research into Marwood's history continues and if this book has evoked memories or information that you would like to share, please do send an email to **merewodebooks@live.co.uk** to arrange an opportunity to discuss further.

A rich archive of facts, fables and photographs of the parish is beginning to grow - a resource that will be treasured by present and future generations.